macromedia®
FLASH|MX
2004

certified developer
study guide

What every Flash developer needs
to know to pass the Certified Flash MX
2004 Developer Exam

Matt Voerman

macromedia®
CERTIFIED
PROFESSIONAL PROGRAM

Macromedia Flash MX 2004 Certified Developer Study Guide
Matt Voerman

Published by Macromedia Press, in association with Peachpit Press, a division of Pearson Education.

Macromedia Press
1249 Eighth Street
Berkeley, CA 94710
510/524-2178
510/524-2221 (fax)
Find us on the World Wide Web at:
www.peachpit.com   www.macromedia.com

To report errors, please send a note to errata@peachpit.com

Macromedia Press Editor: Angela C. Kozlowski
Editor: Robyn G. Thomas
Technical Editor: Kenneth J. Toley
Production Coordinator: Myrna Vladic
Copy Editor: Carol Henry
Index: Julie Bess
Interior Design: Happenstance Type-O-Rama
Cover Design: Happenstance Type-O-Rama
Page Layout: David Van Ness

ISBN 0-321-25602-6

9 8 7 6 5 4 3 2 1

Printed and bound in the United States of America

DEDICATION

This book is dedicated to my Mum—Jann Barry.
Her strength, wisdom, kindness and creativity
have been an inspiration to me throughout my life.
Her ability to raise two fantastic boys almost single
handedly is a testimony to her indomitable spirit.

—Matt

ABOUT THE AUTHOR

Matt Voerman is one of a small handful of Macromedia Certified Flash Instructors in the Asia-Pacific region. He is a regular speaker at industry events, Team Macromedia Member, founder and manager of the Perth Macromedia User Group, and long-time contributor to the Flash community. Through his Perth, Australia-based web development company, Schematic Design (www.schematic.com.au), Matt spends most of his time consulting, developing, and conducting Flash training courses for corporate clients and the public. A Flash user since its inception as Future Splash, he was one of five global subject matter experts invited to work with Macromedia in developing the official Macromedia Flash MX 2004 Developer certification exam.

ACKNOWLEDGEMENTS

I would like to thank my wonderful partner Karen Nasskau for her support, encouragement, and understanding throughout this whole process, and for being such a incredible part of my life.

Additionally, I'd like to thank my editors Angela Kozlowski, Robyn Thomas, Carol Henry, and Kenneth Toley for their patience, guidance, expertise, and professionalism throughout this foreign, new process of authoring.

CONTENTS AT A GLANCE

CONTENTS

Introduction

With such widespread knowledge and use of the Macromedia Web tools, it makes sense to offer a certification exam to ensure that Web developers are confident and competent with these tools. This method will also help the many people who now style themselves as multimedia development experts. Macromedia Flash MX 2004, one of the most widely used tools for creating dynamic content and custom applications, is a good candidate for a certification test. The development of the Flash certification exam naturally led to a companion Study Guide. Even Flash experts don't use every feature of the product or tackle every development problem every day, and thus will want to spend some time reviewing before the exam. The content of this Study Guide will not only help you assure yourself that you're well versed in Flash and related technologies for product development, but also that you're ready to move on to the certification process.

The approach of the Flash MX 2004 Study Guide is first to examine the overall Flash product and the tasks that developers carry out with it, and then to delve into the details. In this book you will not find an exhaustive study of every Flash feature or every method and argument available. You also won't find lots of tutorials and lengthy code examples. What you will find is a concise summary of Flash's salient features that a professional Flash developer should understand. You can learn how to use Macromedia ActionScript from this book (short code samples are provided), but the idea is to reinforce and complement your knowledge with a summary of ActionScript's features and capabilities.

As you read through the book, you may be tempted to skip certain chapters. But while you may feel confident that you know all about a particular subject, you will find many tips and notes, as well as helpful information on Flash's limitations, of which you may not be aware. These could crop up in the certification test, so we recommend that you start from the beginning and take the time to study the pages in order. Of course, you can jump about all you want, but you should skim each chapter for important points (tips, cautions, and notes) before taking the test.

We hope you find this book useful, encapsulating as it does a wide variety of information in a succinct format. Good luck on the certification test!

What Is the Certified Flash MX 2004 Developer Exam?

The popularity of Macromedia's products continues to grow and, along with it, so has the demand for experienced developers. Once upon a time (in Internet time, that is), claiming to be a Flash developer was easy; the product was simple enough that, with a minimal investment of time and energy, developers could realistically consider themselves experts.

This is not the case anymore. The product line has grown in both breadth and complexity, and the levels of expertise and experience among developers are diverse. Claiming to be an expert isn't that easy, and recognizing legitimate expertise is even harder.

The Macromedia Certified Professional Program

This is where certification comes into play. Formal, official certification by Macromedia helps to mark a threshold that explicitly sets apart developers by their knowledge and experience, making it possible to identify the true experts.

The *Certified Flash MX 2004 Developer* certification is one in a series of certification tracks from Macromedia, this one aimed at developers using Macromedia's Flash MX 2004. Other exams and certification programs being developed concentrate on other products and areas of expertise.

Reasons to Get Certified

There's really only one important reason for a Flash developer to become certified: being officially acknowledged by Macromedia as a *Certified Flash MX 2004 Developer* means you command the industry respect and recognition that's associated with being one of the best at what you do Macromedia Certification clearly demonstrates to your customers and colleagues that you have the specialized knowledge and skills required to effectively develop and deploy high-quality Flash based applications and solutions with Macromedia Flash technology.

Additionally, more employers these days are using official certification as a barometer by which to measure the potential and professionalism of candidates, applicants and employees.

Whether being certified helps you find a new or better job, helps persuade your boss that the pay raise you want is justified, helps you find new clients, or gets you listed on Macromedia's website so that you can attract new prospects—whatever the reason—it will help you stand out from the crowd.

About the Exam

Becoming a *Certified Flash MX 2004 Developer* requires being tested on your knowledge of Flash MX 2004 and related technologies. As far as exams go, this one isn't easy—nor should it be. In fact, more than a third of all test takers fail their first exam. This is not a bad thing; on the contrary, it means you really have to know your stuff to pass. You don't merely receive a paper certificate; the exam and subsequent certification have real value and real significance. "Very challenging but fair" is how many people describe the exam itself.

How You'll Take the Exam

The exam is a set of multiple-choice and true/false questions that you answer electronically. A computer application issues the test to you, and you'll know whether you passed immediately upon test completion.

In the test you're presented with each question and the possible answers. Some questions have a single correct answer, while others have two or more (you'll be told how many answers to provide). If a question stumps you, you can skip it and come back to it later.

After you have answered all the questions, you can review them to check your answers. After you're done, or the 70-minute time limit is up, you get your results. You need at least 70 percent correct to pass and achieve certification. If you don't pass, you need to wait at least 30 days before you can try taking the test again. You may take the test no more than three times in a single year, starting from the date of your first test.

Each time you take the test, you will be required to pay the full exam fee again.

What You'll Be Tested On

Being a Flash MX 2004 expert requires knowing more than just how to use all the menu items. As such, the exam includes questions on different aspects of Flash MX 2004 development. You'll be tested on the following subjects:

- Flash MX 2004 concepts
- Design and coding practices
- Object oriented programming concepts with ActionScript
- Dynamic data integration
- Solution implementation, testing, and deployment

Every question counts, and you can't assume that one particular topic is more or less significant than the others. You need to know it all, and you need to know it all well.

Preparing for the Exam

The most important way to prepare for the exam is by using Flash MX 2004 itself. If you don't use it regularly or haven't done so for an extended period, you probably won't pass the exam.

Having said that, we can tell you that many experienced Flash MX 2004 developers still find the exam challenging. Usually, they say this is because they don't use some features, or because they learned the product but never paid attention to changing language and feature details (and thus are not using the product as effectively as they could be).

This is where this book fits in. It's not a cheat sheet. It won't teach you Flash MX 2004 from scratch, nor will it give you a list of things to remember to pass the test. What it will do is help you systematically review every feature and technology in the product—everything you need to know to pass the test.

Where to Take the Exam

To offer the exams worldwide in as many locations as possible, Macromedia has partnered with a company called VUE, which offers exams and certification programs for a wide range of companies and products, and has more than 2,500 regional testing facilities in more than 100 countries.

You can take the Macromedia Flash MX 2004 Developer exam at any VUE testing center. For a current list of locations, visit the website:

```
www.vue.com/macromedia/
```

How Much It Costs

The fee to take the exam in North America is $150 (U.S.). Pricing in other countries varies. The fee must be paid at the time you register for the exam. If you need to cancel, you must do so at least 24 hours before the exam, or the fee will not be refunded.

How to Use This Book

This book is designed to be used in two ways:

- To prepare for your exam, you should start at the beginning of the book and systematically work your way through it. The book flow, layout, and form factor have all been designed to make reviewing content as pleasant an experience as possible. The content has been designed to be highly readable and digestible in small, bite-size chunks, so that it will feel more like reading than studying.

- After you have reviewed all the content, reread the topics that you feel you need extra help brushing up on. Topics are all covered in highly focused and very manageable chapters so that you can easily drill down to the exact content you need.

After the exam, you'll find that the style and design of this study guide make it an invaluable desktop reference tool as well.

Contents

The book is divided into seven parts, each containing a set of highly focused chapters. Each chapter concludes with sample questions (the answers are in Appendix A).

Part 1: Foundations of Flash

This part covers the basics of Flash MX 2004 development. It includes chapters on the following topics:

- Fundamentals of Flash
- Targeting objects and variables

Part 2: Discovery, Definition, and Planning

All web-based projects require a solid foundation upon which they should be built, and Flash is no exception. This part covers aspects from analyzing and appraising the target environment to ensuring your product is accessible to the widest possible audience. It includes chapters on the following topics:

- Target Environment
- Accessibility and Usability

Part 3: Design and Coding

This part covers the most common aspects of ActionScript development and conventions, working with multimedia assets, and the new v2 components. It includes chapters on the following topics:

- Variables
- Naming Conventions
- Control Structures
- Functions
- Events
- v2 Components
- Text
- Browsers
- Rich Media

Part 4: Object Oriented Programming with ActionScript

This part covers aspects associated with object oriented programming within ActionScript (1 & 2). It includes chapters on the following topics:

- OOP Basics
- XML and the Classes and Objects
- Classes
- Methods

Part 5: Dynamic Data Integration

Building web applications requires an understanding of how to work with various forms of dynamic data. This part covers topics such as XML, Web Services and web browser interaction, which are all instrumental in how dynamic data can be integrated into Flash. This section includes chapters on the following topics:

- Client/Server Communication
- XML
- Flash Remoting
- Web Services

- Data Classes
- Components

Part 6: Testing, Implementation, and Deployment

Often underestimated, testing is an integral element in the success of any project. This part outlines techniques for effective functional and usability testing, as well as some strategies for printing from Flash. This section includes chapters on the following topics:

- Functional Testing Methodologies
- Usability Testing Methodologies
- Printing

Part 7: Appendix

This part rounds out the book by providing the answers to the questions in each chapter:

- Sample Question and Answers

Conventions Used in This Book

The people at Peachpit Press have spent many years developing and publishing computer books designed for ease of use and containing the most up-to-date information available. With that experience, we've learned what features help you the most. Look for these features throughout the book to help you enhance your learning experience and get the most out of Flash MX:

- Code listings and command samples appear in `monospace type`.
- Terms that are defined in the text appear in *italics*. Italics are sometimes used for emphasis too.

TIP

Tips give you advice on quick or overlooked procedures, including shortcuts.

NOTE

Notes present useful or interesting information that isn't necessarily essential to the current discussion, but which might augment your understanding with background material or advice relating to the topic.

> **CAUTION**
> Cautions warn you about potential problems that a procedure might cause, unexpected results, or mistakes that could prove costly.

The Website

To further assist you in preparing for the exam, this book has an accompanying website. The site contains the following:

- Any updated exam information

- Any book corrections or errata (if any)

- A sample interactive test that you can use to help gauge your own exam readiness

The website can be found at `www.forta.com/books/032125602-6`

Where to Go From Here

Now you're ready to get started. If you think you're ready for the exam, start with the sample questions in the book or online to verify your skills. If you're not ready—or if the same questions indicate that you might not be as ready as you thought—make sure you pay attention to the topics that you need to review by reading the documentation and actually writing appropriate applications.

When you're ready, work through this book to review the content and prepare for the exam itself, as described here.

And with that, we wish you good luck!

PART 1

Foundations of Flash

CHAPTER 1

Fundamentals of Flash

Back in early 1993, John Gay and Robert Tatsumi, two software engineers who had become fed up with the complexity of existing computer-illustration software, set out to build an application that would make drawing on the computer easier than drawing on paper. The end result of their labors was a piece of software aptly named SmartSketch.

They spent a brief time in the market competing against the offerings of software powerhouses Aldus (Freehand) and Adobe (Illustrator). After that, John and Robert realized that if their up-and-coming software company, FutureWave, were to succeed, they needed to gain a higher profile for their product. So in the summer of 1995, with the with assistance of Michelle Welsh, they headed to the SIGGRAPH computer graphics trade show.

The general consensus from SIGGRAPH was that SmartSketch was a good product but could be made better with animation functionality added. It was also at this time that Robert and John were hearing murmurings about a new technology called the Internet. This got the guys wondering if the Internet would ever become popular enough that people would want to send graphics and animation over it. They decided to incorporate the new technology of the Internet with the animation functionality recommendations of their peers at SIGGRAPH.

In May 1996, the team finished their enhancements on SmartSketch and were ready to ship. In line with keeping the focus on the program's animation capabilities, they decided to change its name from SmartSketch to FutureSplash Animator.

Six months later in November 1996, a relatively new company, Macromedia, approached FutureWave with an offer to buy it and its FutureSplash product. This offer was consummated in December of that year, and FutureSplash Animator went on to become Macromedia Flash 1.0. The rest (as they say) is history. Today Macromedia Flash MX 2004 is arguably the most feature-packed platform for developing rich client applications for the Web.

This and the following chapter will assist you in recognizing the basic concepts of Macromedia Flash 2004 and structure of Macromedia Flash 2004 applications in order to successfully pass Domain 1 of the Macromedia Certified Flash Developer exam.

Content within this domain includes:

- Identifying the basic interface and structure of Macromedia Flash 2004 applications
  - Libraries
  - Timelines
  - Buttons
  - MovieClips
  - Text Symbols and instances
  - Keyframes
  - Sound
  - Components
  - Screens
  - Projects
  - Behaviors
- Identifying effective hierarchical and functional structure of Macromedia Flash 2004 applications
  - Targeting
  - Loading movies into both targets and levels
  - Using dot syntax notation
  - Where to place ActionScript

Timeline

When Walt Disney first started out animating the "Alice Comedies" back in 1923, he would paint images onto clear sheets of plastic known as cels. These cels were then photographed and subsequently cut and edited together. The collection of edited images was then played back through a hand-wound projector, and the once "still" images sprang to life in an animated form. Thus was born the first primitive form of a *Timeline*.

Flash, along with its cousin Director, was born from the animation stable of multimedia applications, in which objects, text, and colors are moved (or *cycled*) around the screen in a sequenced fashion. Within these types of applications, the standard mechanism for measuring motion graphics and animations is the frame rate (the number of frames that play per second). So in order to gain better control over the time and movement of onscreen elements, some form of visual representation of the frames was required. The Timeline seemed like the most logical method.

The Timeline is one of the key features that separates Flash from many traditional programming IDEs (integrated development environments). Animators and cartoonists, along with those that work with audio, film, or video, are very familiar with the concept of Timelines. But to programmers transitioning from more traditional development environments, the Timeline can be a novelty that is often a source of frustration and confusion.

Fundamentally, the Timeline can be thought of as a source of events, one based not on user input but on the passage of time. The major elements of the Timeline are layers, frames, and the playhead. As the playhead moves through the frames of the Timeline, the actions, events, and animations associated with each frame are displayed on the Stage.

The Timeline uses layers to separate and organize movie assets into an easily manageable, visually represented "stacking order." Layers can also be grouped into folders to further assist with movie asset management.

Each Flash movie clip instance has its own base (or _root) Timeline, which is located at level 0. If you load new movie clips into the levels above the base level 0, they are effectively layered on top of one another like the layers of a flaky pastry. Each new document loaded into a level of the Flash Player has its own unique Timeline, which can act independently of the main base Timeline.

When you are working with screens and forms within Flash MX 2004 Professional, the Timeline is minimized by default.

> **NOTE**
>
> Because Flash originated as an animation tool, much of its terminology has been borrowed from traditional cartooning vocabulary (Timelines, onion skinning, frames, keyframes, and frame rates, for example).

Frames

Frames are the base units by which we measure time within our Flash movies. They are also containers within which we can store our frame-based ActionScript code. Frames determine the order (or sequence) in which elements are displayed on Stage. Frames can be modified into *keyframes* to symbolize a change in Stage-based assets.

Flash offers two different methods for selecting frames in the Timeline. In *frame-based selection* (the default), you select individual frames in the Timeline. In *span-based selection*, the entire frame sequence, from one keyframe to the next, is selected when you click any frame in the sequence. You can specify span-based selection in Flash preferences.

Keyframes

When Walt Disney wanted to create the illusion of animation within still images, he would simply create two main images (a start point and an endpoint). Then, using a process of "onion skin" tracing, he would create new "in-between" images to represent the differences between the start and end cels. These two starting and ending cels (or frames) are known as *keyframes*.

Keyframes define a major change of state in the Timeline, such as the appearance of a new symbol instance or a change in direction of a moving asset.

Keyframes containing content are represented in the Timeline by a solid circle, and empty keyframes are represented by an empty circle within the frame.

Keyframes can also be used as repositories for your ActionScript. Placing your ActionScript code within a keyframe, on its own separate layer, facilitates good code management as well as assisting collaboration with other developers. It also helps alleviate instances of "spaghetti" code—code that has little or no organizational structure and is nearly impossible for anyone besides the original developer to interpret.

Frame Rate

The rate at which we view motion graphics is measured in *frames per second (FPS)*, also referred to as the *frame rate*. Thirty frames per second is the standard frame rate for video, and 24 fps is standard for film. Anywhere from 1 to 30 fps works for Web animation, although 10 fps is about the minimum rate for convincing motion.

The default frame rate in Flash is 12 frames per second (fps), but this can be set to anything between .01 and 120 fps.

When we set the frame rate, we are effectively setting the maximum number of frames that movie can play per second. Heavy scripts and complex animations using mathematical algorithms require more processing power and can cause the frame rate to drop below this maximum setting. While higher frame rates can give the appearance of smoother animation, they come at the cost of higher CPU usage, and may often play back in a jerky, stop/start manner if the frames can't be rendered fast enough. Lowering the frame rate can result in better playback on hardware-limited devices such as hand-held computers and older desktops. Consequently, it's a good practice to test your animations on a variety of machines to determine optimum frame rates.

> **NOTE**
>
> Within Flash, we often use loops as control structures within ActionScript. These loops only execute once per frame, so the speed at which they execute is tied directly to the frame rate of the movie. Faster frame rates mean faster loop execution.

In the case of nested movie clips, the frame rate is always determined by the movie clip located at level 0. For example if Movie B has a frame rate of 60 fps and is loaded into Movie A (which has a frame rate of 20 fps), the playback of Movie B will drop to the frame rate of Movie A (in this case 20 fps).

If you want to create script-based animations that are independent of frame rates, you need to use the setInterval function. This function allows users to set their own time-based event based on a user-defined interval of time (as opposed to the Timeline's predefined interval of time—the frame rate).

Layers and Levels

Layers, *levels*, and their cousin *depths* are the guiltiest culprits for causing confusion to Flash newcomers. We'll look at depths later in Chapter 2, but in the meantime, lets take a look at layers and levels.

Layers

Layers exist only in the Flash authoring environment, and they allow you to separate Flash movie assets within the Timeline into logical stacking orders.

Layers in Flash work exactly like layers in most other graphic applications. You can move a layer's position up and down the stack to determine whether an asset appears above (in front of) or below (behind) other onscreen assets.

Layers can also be grouped into folders to further assist with asset management. When grouped into folders, a layer's Timeline remains hidden when the folder is closed.

Levels

Each Flash movie has a stacking order of levels, starting with the main movie Timeline at level 0. Just like layers, these levels cannot physically be seen in the authoring environment and only become apparent at runtime.

Using actions such as loadMovie and attachMovie, you can load other Flash documents (SWFs) into a Flash movie on levels above the base level (level 0). loadMovie and loadMovieNum can load SWFs or Jpegs into the MovieClip, attachMovie can only put (or "attach") a MovieClip that is located in the library onto the Stage.

Documents loaded in this manner will appear "stacked" above each other as each successive level is added (that is, items loaded on level 10 will appear above items loaded on level 5).

If you load a document into level 0, the main Timeline of the newly loaded movie replaces the Timeline of the existing level 0 movie.

> **NOTE**
> Just remember: Layers are used at author time; levels are used during runtime.

Symbols

A *symbol* constitutes the base visual element of any Flash movie. Symbols are reusable items that are usually created manually (with the exception of movie clips, which can also be created programmatically) and are stored in the Library.

The three most common flavors of symbols are *graphic*, *button*, and *movie clip*. (The infrequently used *font* and *video* symbols actually bring the total tally up to five, but we won't be discussing these two here.)

While the various types of symbols have a lot of similarities, they are different enough to have their own unique sets of characteristics (and uses). For instance, button symbols and movie clip symbols both have Timelines that act independently of their parent Timeline, but their own Timelines have differing characteristics—buttons have only four frames, whereas movie clips can have any number of frames.

The following table is a good guide to help you decide which type of symbol best suits your needs:

	GRAPHIC SYMBOL	BUTTON SYMBOL	MOVIE CLIP SYMBOL
Timeline	Same structure as the document Timeline and synchronized with it.	Unique structure and independent.	Same structure as the document Timeline but acts independently.
Actions	Not permitted	Allowed on button instances but not within the button Timeline.	Allowed on movie clip instances and within the movie clip Timeline.
Instance Names	Not permitted	Permitted	Permitted
Uses	When you require a reusable symbol but don't require a Timeline independent of the main Timeline.	Whenever you want the unique button Timeline.	When you need a symbol that is required to act independently of the main document Timeline.

Graphics

The most basic and primitive symbol type is the graphic symbol. The graphic symbol is traditionally used for simple on-screen graphics that don't require any functionality or interactivity. Because symbols cannot have instance names attached to them and don't have an independent Timeline like a movie clip, their use for anything other than "eye candy" is restricted.

There are two main arguments for using a graphic instead of a movie clip symbol. First, the graphic symbol's Timeline is tied to its parent's Timeline, which can be handy in some cartooning situations. Second, there is a slight advantage in file size and memory overhead when you use a graphic symbol.

Graphic symbols are best used for static images and to create reusable pieces of animation that are tied to the main Timeline.

Buttons

Button symbols provide a quick and easy way to get the standard functionality you would expect from a button, such as rollover states and click events.

All of a button's features can be re-created in a movie clip with a little additional scripting; but buttons have the advantage of being all set up and ready to go.

Buttons have three states: up (mouse off), over (mouse over), and down (mouse pressed). There is an additional frame in the button symbol that lets you define a hit area, which is the region that will accept mouse input. The hit area is invisible but acts as the hot spot for the button.

You use button symbols to create interactive buttons that respond to mouse clicks, rollovers, or other actions. You define the graphics associated with various button states, and then assign actions to button instances.

Movie Clips

Movie clips provide the most functionality of all of the symbol types. The majority of a movie clip's power comes from a plethora of methods, properties, and events that are available for its use.

Also, being the central class in the Flash class hierarchy, movie clips can serve almost any purpose. They can function like buttons or graphics. Although there is a slight additional overhead when you use a movie clip instead of a graphic symbol, movie clips are the most flexible of the symbol types.

Movie clips have their own multiframe Timeline that is independent from the main Timeline—think of them as nested inside a main Timeline. The movie clip Timeline can contain interactive controls, sounds, and even other movie clip instances. You can also place movie clip instances inside the Timeline of a button symbol to create an animated button.

Projects

Similar to the Files Panel in Dreamweaver, Flash Projects allow you to manage multiple project-related files (from a variety of directory locations) into a single project interface contained within the Project Panel.

Once created, a Flash Project file (FLP) is an XML file that references all the document files contained within the Flash Project. The project documents don't even have to be of a Flash-compatible format. A Flash Project can contain any Flash or other file type, including previous versions of FLA and SWF files. If you try to open a project file that Flash doesn't normally handle, the file is simply opened by its default application.

Flash Projects are a great mechanism for team project collaboration. They contain *version control* functionality that allows you to check in and out files located on development servers, to ensure that the correct file versions are used during editing. Version control also helps prevent accidental overwriting by team members working on the same files.

In order to use version control, you first need to define a site for the project (similar to how it is done in Dreamweaver). Once the site is defined, you can specify a local, network, or FTP connection for your project directory. Alternatively, you can specify custom plug-ins, such as Microsoft Source Safe, for version control systems.

You can create a Flash Project in the Flash MX Professional 2004 authoring environment, or you can create the XML file for a Flash Project in an external application.

Flash Projects use UTF-8 text encoding, so all file and folder names in a Flash Project must be UTF-8 compatible.

Behaviors

Those of you who have worked with Macromedia Director before will no doubt be familiar with the concept of *behaviors*, which have been part of the mainstay functionality in that application for many years. Behaviors are new in Flash MX 2004. They are prebuilt "snippets" of ActionScript code that you can quickly and easily add to objects such as buttons, to control target objects such as a sound, a playhead location, or even the action of jumping to a URL.

Behaviors, which are located within the Behaviors panel, can be applied to movie clips, text fields, and video and sound files.

Although they are of great value for beginners and developers looking for an effortless way to add functionality to Flash movies, behaviors should be avoided for large or complex projects. Because behaviors are placed on symbol instances (and not in a common central location such as a keyframe), overuse of these elements can cause difficult to maintain ActionScript.

Sample Questions

1. What is the default frame rate of the Timeline in frames per second?

    A. 1

    B. 12

    C. 24

    D. 30

2. What are the three most common types of symbols in Flash?

    A. Graphic, button, and font

    B. Button, movie clip, and video

    C. Video, font, and graphic

    D. Graphic, button, and movie clip

3. Which of the following CANNOT have a behavior applied to it?

   A. Movie clip

   B. Text field

   C. Graphic symbol

   D. Sound file

4. What file formats can be included in a Flash Project?

   A. Only .FLAs

   B. .FLA, .SWF, and .FLP

   C. .XML and .FLA

   D. Any file format

CHAPTER 2

Targeting and Syntax

Those of you who have used Flash for any period of time will know that Timelines are the framework upon which we build the foundations of our Flash movies. Just as ironworkers can move with the greatest of ease between the steel girder frameworks of buildings under construction, so too must the successful Flash developer acquire the ability to navigate multiple Timelines in order to build robust Flash applications.

The concept of *targeting* is crucial for Flash developers to successfully navigate Timeline, function, and method structures. Without targeting, our Flash documents would be simply one-dimensional basic structures.

Take variables, for example. Each one of them has the scope to be referenced on a local, Timeline, or global level. And now with the introduction of ActionScript 2.0, classes that are created also support public, private, and static variable scopes. The availability of all of these various variable, function, and class scopes adds greater importance to the whole concept of targeting.

In this chapter, we will discuss:

- Targeting objects, such as movie clips and their Timelines
- Targeting rules (syntax)

ActionScript Placement

When you first start working with ActionScript, in order to grasp the fundamentals of assigning actions to objects, you usually start by placing your actions directly onto object instances. I mean, this makes sense, doesn't it? This is the object I want to control, so this is where I should place my code. The introduction of behaviors in Flash MX 2004 further reinforces the placement of ActionScript code onto object instances. It's a quick, easy, and (now) acceptable coding practice.

But as your Flash projects become larger and more complex, it's imperative that the code remain easy to locate and manage. Unfortunately, this code-on-objects method of organization does not lend itself to efficient code management or team collaboration.

Don't get me wrong—instance-based code placement has an appropriate role: that being mainly in small, single Timeline-based movies. But using this method with anything more complex—for example, in movies with nested or externally loaded scripts and/or movies—has the potential to generate spaghetti code and to become rapidly too difficult to manage.

So where should you place your ActionScript code? The most logical place is somewhere obvious and easily accessible, like a keyframe. Keyframes are great repositories for code, especially if they're located on their own separate layer within the Timeline. This makes them far easier to locate and manage than when you have to wade through multiple object instances (or even files). But eventually, even frame-based code placement can become a bit tedious (especially if you have over 100 lines of code to scroll through).

This is where the #include directive steps in. The #include directive allows you to write ActionScript in an external (.AS) file in your favorite text editor, and then include it within your Flash movie at runtime. This form of externalizing ActionScript code was extended in Flash MX 2004 with the ActionScript 2.0 import keyword. The import keyword was introduced to implement the functionality of external classes and packages.

When you define custom classes or interfaces using ActionScript 2.0, their associated code may only be stored externally in a designated *classpath* directory. Classpaths are exactly that: paths to the location of a class file, just like files on a hard drive. For example:

```
import mx.styles.StyleManager;
```

If you attempt to place custom class definitions anywhere but in an external directory, say on a frame or object instance, a compile error will occur.

You can further organize your external class-definition files by placing them into *packages*. A package is simply a directory that contains one or more class files that reside in a designated classpath directory. A package can, in turn, contain other *subpackages*, each with its own class files.

Syntax

Often when you're learning a new language such as Japanese or German, you first learn individual words; then, with the use of syntax, you learn to combine these words into meaningful sentences. Luckily for us, ActionScript is easier to learn than Japanese. To create scripts that compile and run correctly, we still have to follow rules, but they aren't nearly as strict as those for writing Japanese.

Case Sensitivity √

Case sensitivity refers to the capitalization of a programming language's tokens (constants, identifiers, operators, keywords, and so forth). Most common object-oriented (OO) scripting languages adhere to strict capitalization standards. Capitalization refers to the case (either upper or lower) of the letters contained within a name or variable.

Due to Macromedia's desire to maintain a degree of backward compatibility with older versions of the Flash Player, the only form of case sensitivity you may have previously encountered in your day-to-day ActionScript coding was with keywords. This is despite the fact that the ECMA-262 standard upon which ActionScript was based is completely case sensitive. In an effort to right the wrongs of the past and produce a more robust object-oriented scripting language that more closely adheres to the ECMA-262 standards, Macromedia has released ActionScript 2.0 with Flash MX 2004.

Unlike its predecessor, ActionScript 2.0 is a fully case-sensitive programming language. For example, variable names that differ only in case (country and Country) are considered different from each other. If you're using ActionScript 2.0, you should get in the habit of making use of the Check Syntax button. On the upside, consistent capitalization within your coding makes it easy to identify names of functions and variables within your ActionScript code.

When you publish your files for Flash Player 7 or above, Flash will automatically implement case sensitivity regardless of which version of ActionScript you're using. This includes external scripts such as ActionScript 2.0 class files or scripts that you import using the #include directive. This means that keywords, class names, variables, method names, and so on are all now case sensitive. For example:

```
// The following will set the properties of two different objects
dog.breed = Labrador;
DOG.breed = Labrador;

// The following creates three different variables
var highestScore=100000;
var highestscore=100000;
var hIgHeStScOre=100000;
```

Dot Versus Slash

Back in the days of Flash 3 and 4, slash syntax was the only means by which you could indicate the target path of a movie clip or variable you wished to control, like this:

```
myParentMovieClip/childMovieClip:myBabyVariable
```

Fast forward to today, and while slash syntax is still supported within the Flash Player 7, it was officially laid to rest and deprecated in Flash 5. It is not supported in ActionScript 2.0.

Slash syntax was most commonly used with the `tellTarget` action, whose use has also been deprecated and is no longer recommended. The with action is now preferred over `tellTarget` because it is more compatible with *dot syntax*.

After slash syntax was deprecated, dot syntax stepped up to the plate to take its place. In ActionScript, a dot (.) is used to indicate the properties or methods related to a class, object, or movie clip. Dot syntax is also used to identify the target path to a movie clip, variable, function, or object.

Dot syntax expressions begin with the name of the class, object, or movie clip and are followed by a dot, and end with the element you want to specify. For example, the `alpha` movie clip property represents a movie clip's alpha (or transparency) value. The expression `window_mc._alpha` refers to the `alpha` property of the movie clip instance `window_mc`.

To express a method of an object or movie clip, you simply follow the same pattern. For example in `window_mc.play()`, the `play()` method of the `window_mc` movie clip moves the playhead in the Timeline of `window_mc`.

Data Typing

When we set out to initialize data within Flash, we often do so via variables. Variables are simply containers that hold data that we can modify and discard as we see fit.

To make our variables more user friendly, we usually start out by giving them meaningful names, such as homeAddress or phoneNumber, to assist in their identification. To further extend the identity of our variables, we can also assign them a *data type*.

Data types provide a range of categories for identifying variables. For example, our homeAddress variable may have a String data type, and our phoneNumber variable may be a Number data type.

Automatic Data Typing

Because ActionScript 1.0 is a relatively forgiving scripting language, it has the ability to automatically assign data types to several different kinds of language elements, including

- Variables
- Parameters passed to a function, method, or class
- Values returned from a function or method
- Objects created as subclasses of existing classes

Because you don't need to explicitly define these items as holding either a number, a string, or other data type, Flash automatically determines the data type of an item when it is assigned. In the following expression:

```
var highestScore = 9999;
```

Flash evaluates the element on the right side of the equals sign operator and determines that it is of the Number data type.

At a later point in time, we may want to change the data type assignment of highestScore; for example, the statement highestScore = "Matt" changes the data type of highestScore to String (as opposed to its initial type of Number). Any variable that hasn't been assigned a value has a type of undefined.

ActionScript also converts data types automatically when an expression requires it. For example, when you pass a value to the trace() action, trace() automatically converts the value to a string and sends it to the Output window.

In expressions with operators, ActionScript converts data types as needed. For example, when used with a string, the + operator expects the other operand to be a string. In this expression:

```
"Highest Score " + 9999
```

ActionScript converts the number 9999 to the string "9999" and adds it to the end of the first string, resulting in the following string: "Highest Score 9999".

At the end of the day, though, if you want to explicitly assign data types to your items, there's nothing stopping you. In fact, it is actually a good practice to get into. Explicitly setting your data types helps prevent (and diagnose) errors in your code and makes the data types of your variables instantly apparent. It is especially useful in situations where the compiler is not sure of the data type of your expression items and may therefore display undesired results.

Strict Data Typing

In the preceding section, we discussed ActionScript 1.0's forgiving nature when it comes to enforcing data types. ActionScript 2.0, on the other hand, is not as laid back as its predecessor. While it does not strictly enforce the data typing of syntax, a warning will be displayed if the compiler encounters a data type mismatch.

So what are the primary benefits of strict data typing? First, it makes it easier to identify the data types of your variables. In our previous example, we saw how highestScore could have been either a numeric value (9999) or the name of the player with the highest score (Matt).

Strict data typing also helps ensure that you don't inadvertently assign an incorrect type of value to an object and cause a compile error. For example, suppose you type the following code:

```
// Score.as class definition file
class Score{
  var myScore:Number; // property
}

// in our game script
var playerScore:Score = new Score();
mattsScore.myScore = "highest";
```

When Flash compiles this script, a "Type mismatch" error is generated because the compiler is expecting myScore to be of the Number type, when it's presented with a string.

Another advantage of strict data typing is that Flash MX 2004 automatically displays method code hints for built-in objects when they are strictly typed.

If you wish to implement strict typing, you must specify ActionScript 2.0 in your publish settings. Then when you declare your variables, you must include its data type. For example, when we declared our highestScore variable in ActionScript 1.0, it looked like this:

```
var highestScore = 9999;
```

Now in ActionScript 2.0, with strict data typing, this statement can be written as follows:

```
var highestScore:Number = 9999;
```

> **NOTE**
>
> Developers coming from true OOP backgrounds (such as Java and C++) might find the declaration of the `<datatype>` before the `<variable>` slightly back-to-front. The logic behind this decision results from the ECMA-262 specification, on which ActionScript is based.

Timelines and Paths

Every new Flash file contains a single Timeline, the base or root Timeline, upon which you add all the content for your movie. However, when you add an instance of a movie clip (a bouncing ball, for example) to your movie, you are also adding to its Timeline. Now you have two Timelines acting independently. In order to communicate with (target) this movie clip's Timeline, we need to learn about using paths in Flash MX.

Simply put, a path is just a dot-delimited directory starting from the item closest to the root and working down to the specific asset to be targeted. In our previous game script example, we could target the bouncing ball instance (let's call it ball) from the root Timeline with the following line of ActionScript:

```
_root.ball;
```

In this statement, _root refers to the root Timeline, and ball refers to the ball movie clip instance sitting on the root Timeline. If ball itself had an instance of a movie clip inside it called paddle, it could be targeted with the following line of ActionScript:

```
_root.ball.paddle;
```

So if we want to change the transparency of the ball's paddle, we can simply write the following:

```
_root.ball.paddle._alpha = 50;
```

Absolute and Relative Paths

Up to this point, we've been using paths that start at the root Timeline. These are called "absolute paths." The key advantage of using absolute paths is that there is never any question as to what you're referencing. If any ActionScript in any Timeline of the original movie contains the absolute target path root.ball.paddle, the result will be the same. This is especially useful when you are communicating between movie clips.

There are two disadvantages to using absolute paths:

- They will only work if your movie clip is in the exact position dictated by the path. Putting the `root.ball.paddle` absolute target path inside the ball movie clip would work in that example, but not if it is moved to another Timeline or if the name of the `ball` movie clip instance is changed.

- They're somewhat tedious. Why should the `paddle` movie clip have to reference the root Timeline just to change its own transparency? The answer is that it doesn't, which is why "relative paths" exist.

> **TIP**
>
> One way to achieve the benefit of an absolute path without the tedium of typing it over and over again is to define it as a *global* variable. This is particularly useful if you plan to reference the path frequently. To assign the `_root.ball.paddle` path to a global variable, `myPaddle`, use the following ActionScript:
>
> `_global.myPaddle = _root.ball.paddle;`
>
> Now `myPaddle` will be synonymous with `_root.ball.paddle`.
>
> Another advantage of defining an absolute path as a global variable (though it certainly is no magic bullet) is that even if the absolute path changes at some point, you only have to modify the original global variable declaration rather than tracking down and changing all references to it.

Relative paths start at the current Timeline and work inward from there. For example, to change the transparency of the `paddle` movie clip from its own Timeline (not the root Timeline), we just write this:

```
_alpha = 50;
```

Now, wherever the `paddle` movie clip goes, it will always be able to easily reference itself.

> **NOTE**
>
> Whenever you create a movie clip symbol, you are creating a new Timeline, whether you take advantage of it or not. Therefore, a movie clip sitting on the same Timeline as another object cannot target it without referencing the Timeline in common. Buttons and text, on the other hand, have no Timeline, so they share the Timeline upon which they reside and can target other objects without having to reference the Timeline in common.

_parent

Being able to reference objects on inner Timelines using relative paths is very useful. But if you have a movie clip that has multiple Timelines itself, how will the innermost objects be able to reference the upper Timelines if you're not sure upon which Timeline the movie clip instance will reside?

Fortunately, by using the _parent property you can easily step up the Timeline hierarchy as many levels as necessary. For instance, you might use the following absolute path as a reference:

```
_root.house.chimney.brick
```

If the brick movie clip wanted to access the house movie clip (two levels up) to increase its height by 20 pixels, brick could use the following line of ActionScript to target house:

```
_parent._parent._height = _parent._parent._height + 20;
```

Using this syntax, we can now put the house movie clip in any Timeline, and the line of code will always work. However, it should be noted that if the child objects of the house movie clip were put into another Timeline, they most likely would not work. If this were a possibility, using an absolute path would be a better way to go.

NOTE

Any changes to parent movie clips will affect child movie clips as well. For instance, if you change the _alpha of the chimney movie clip, the _alpha of the brick movie clip will be changed accordingly.

TIP

If you're ever curious about the exact path to the current object or movie clip you're using, you can use the following line of ActionScript:

```
trace(targetPath(this));
```

This will call a trace statement that outputs the current target path.

this

Another way of defining relative paths is using the `this` keyword, which refers to the object instance that contains the script or method that is being run.

In this next example, there is a button on the main Timeline named `myButton`. In the first keyframe of the main Timeline, add the following code:

```
myButton.onRollOver = function(){
    trace(this._name);
}
```

This defines a rollover event handler for the button `myButton`. Despite the fact that the script exists in the main Timeline, notice that because we have attached it to the button instance, the keyword `this` refers to the button instance within the body of the method. When the mouse rolls over the instance, it will trace the name of the button; in this case, `myButton`.

Dynamic Addressing

It is not always necessary to target variables or movie clips by a hard-coded path (absolute or relative) to their identifier. This is a common concern when your code dynamically creates many variables or movie clips.

The properties of objects in ActionScript are accessible by using a property or method name enclosed in square braces. For example, the two following lines are equivalent. Both access the _x property of the movie clip named `ballMC`.

```
this.ballMC._x
this["ballMC"]._x
```

These alternate methods of targeting provide the ability to dynamically specify the variable or object you are trying to target. In the following example, a series of movie clips will be created and named sequentially: `ball1`, `ball2`, `ball3`, and so on. Rather than target each of the 10 movie clips by hard-coding their paths, we can dynamically target all 10 in a small `for` loop.

```
for(var i=0;i<10;i++){
    this.attachMovie("Ball","ball"+i,i);
}
onEnterFrame = function(){
    for(var i=0;i<10;i++){
        this["ball"+i]._x += Math.random()*10;
        this["ball"+i]._y += Math.random()*10;
    }
}
```

This code assumes that a movie clip is exported from the Library with the symbol ID `ball`. The result is the creation of 10 ball instances and their random movement to the lower-right corner of the screen.

with

If you find yourself targeting many properties within an object in a single section of code, ActionScript provides a shorthand method to accomplish this. If we take a variation of the last code sample and add several more properties that we want to target and change, the code starts getting a little messy. We continue using the dynamic addressing to target our movie clip. Using the with statement cleans up the code and allows us to target the movie clip one time and change many properties at once. The result is a rather random kaleidoscopic effect.

```
for(var i=0;i<100;i++){
    this.attachMovie("Ball","ball"+i,i);
}
onEnterFrame = function(){
    for(var i=0;i<100;i++){
        with(this["ball"+i]){
            _x = Math.random()*1000;
            _y = Math.random()*1000;
            _alpha = Math.random()*100;
            _xscale = Math.random()*1000;
            _yscale = Math.random()*1000;
            _rotation = Math.random()*100;
        }
    }
}
```

Targeting Variables and Functions

Just like the Flash documents that hold them, variables and functions can also be targeted using the same path syntax. For instance, in this next example, one movie clip instance sitting on the root Timeline will increment the counter variable contained inside the lap movie clip instance, which is also sitting on the root Timeline:

```
_root.lap.counter = _root.lap.counter + 1;
```

Targeting functions is just as easy. If the lap movie clip had a function inside it, addOne(), which added 1 to itself, the same effect as before could be achieved by the previous movie clip instance with the following line of ActionScript:

```
_root.lap.addOne();
```

Movie Stacking Order

If I had to pick one thing that I've found confuses a large proportion of new Flash students, it would be the concepts of levels and depths.

Most people understand the notion of Timeline-based layers because they are a tangible element, which we can see and manually control within the Flash integrated development environment (IDE). It is when things swap across to the realm of the programmatically generated levels and depths that things start to get a bit hazy.

I've always found a good analogy for levels and depths is the Dagwood-style multi-layered sandwich. Think of the sandwich as the Flash Player. Within this sandwich we have several pieces of bread (levels) upon which you place your favorite ingredients such as lettuce, cheese, and tomato (depths). If you wanted to, you could even take this a step farther and say the butter you spread on each piece of bread is the equivalent of internal Timeline layers.

Levels   *(loadMovie ( )   load MovieNum ()*

Using our sandwich analogy, the stack of bread that we start with (before we add fillings) is the equivalent of the *level stacking order* within the Flash Player. Each piece of bread represents a new level within the sandwich (Flash Player).

Every Flash document we create has a main (or root) Timeline located at level 0 in the Flash Player. Using actions such as loadMovie and loadMovieNum, we can load (or stack) other Flash documents into the levels on top of our original file within the Flash Player.

This is a great way to conserve file size when you're creating large Flash projects. Rather than having all of your project wrapped up in one single document, you can chunk your project into smaller separate files, which you can then load into different levels of the main document as they are required.

When you load movies into levels above level 0, their Timelines are considered nested inside that of the main document. A movie clip nested inside another movie clip becomes the child of that movie clip. Relationships between nested movie clips are hierarchical, in that any modifications made to the parent will also affect the child.

Child documents nested within their parents still maintain the ability to act independently of their parent. For example, if movieB.swf contains 100 frames and is loaded into movieA.swf (which contains only one frame), movieB.swf will still continue to play all its frames despite the fact that movieA.swf has only one.

Only one movie can exist on any given level at any time. If you load a movie into an already occupied level, the new movie will unload the existing one and effectively take its place on that level.

Just like layers in the Timeline, movies loaded into levels above other movies will appear in front of the movies on the lower levels. The converse applies for movies loaded into levels below them; the movies on the lower levels will appear behind the ones on the higher levels.

The SWF file located at level 0 sets the frame rate, background color, and frame size for all other SWF files loaded into levels above it.

Depths

Each Flash movie has a its own unique *z-order stack* (otherwise known as *depth*) that can be programmatically populated with new movie clips. This can be done using the attachMovie(), duplicateMovieClip(), or createEmptyMovieClip() method.

Every movie clip has an associated depth value, just as it has associated layers and levels, which determines whether it will render in front of or behind other movie clips in the same movie clip Timeline.

When you create (or attach) a movie clip at runtime using one of the methods described in this chapter, you need to specify a depth on which the new clip will be placed. In the following example, we create a new movie clip with an instance name of perth_mc at a depth value of 10:

```
createEmptyMovieClip("perth_mc ", 10);
```

The following code attaches two new movie clips (perth and sydney) from the Library to australia_mc. The first parameter, linkageName, refers to the name entered in the Identifier field in the Linkage Properties dialog box (which is obtained by right-clicking the object instance within the library). The first clip, named perth, will render behind sydney because it was assigned a lower depth value.

```
australia _mc.attachMovie("linkageName", "perth", 10);
australia _mc.attachMovie("linkageName ", "sydney", 15);
```

Depth values within movie clips can range from –16384 to 1048575, so you have plenty of range to work with. But to ensure that you're always working with an unused depth, you can use the getNextHighestDepth to determine the next unused depth.

$$-2^{14} \sim (2^{20} - 1)$$

> **NOTE**
>
> With such a range of depths to work with, it is easy to lose track of your movies. As a result, Macromedia has included a new feature in Flash MX 2004: the DepthManager class. The DepthManager class has two main purposes: to manage the relative depth assignments within any document, and to manage reserved depths on the root Timeline for system-level services such as the cursor and tooltips.
>
> In addition to the depthManager class, Flash MX 2004 also contains several new methods such as getInstanceAtDepth and getNextHighestDepth. Both of these methods further assist you in managing depths within your Flash movies. getInstanceAtDepth returns a reference to a movie clip instance located at a specified depth. While getNextHighestDepth returns an integer representing the next available depth index.

Sample Questions

1. Which of the following is the recommended character to use for separating target path levels?

   A. / (slash)

   B. $ (dollar sign)

   C. _ (underscore)

   D. . (dot)

   E. % (percentage sign)

2. Which keyword is used to implement the functionality of external classes and packages?

   A. include

   B. import

   C. attach

   D. clamp

3. In which level does the original movie reside?

   A. 0

   B. 1

   C. 100

   D. 1000

4. What happens if a SWF is loaded into an already occupied level?

   A. An error is thrown.

   B. The new SWF is rejected and the old one stays.

   C. The old SWF is unloaded and the new one is loaded.

   D. They share the same level.

5. Which of the following is an objective of the DepthManager class?

   A. To manage the loading (and unloading) of movie clip instances into particular depths.

   B. To manage relative depth assignments within any document.

   C. To retrieve movie clip instances from a specified depth.

   D. To act as a traffic controller to ensure movie clips on certain depths are not overwritten.

PART 2

Discovery, Definition, and Planning

CHAPTER 3

Identifying the Target Environment

Before embarking on any web development project, it is critical that certain procedures be followed in order for the project to be a success. Goals and objectives need to be set. Target audiences need to be defined, and robust project plans put in place.

An integral part of this planning process is defining the target environment on which your application is required to run. What are the hardware specifications of the machine running your application? Will the Macromedia Flash Player 7 be required on your client to utilize specific functionality.

The ability to clearly establish who your end users are and their environmental requirements is paramount to creating a successful web application. The more detail and depth you can determine about your target audience and its setting, the clearer your mental picture of the end user will be. This ultimately assists the entire development team to think more like users than developers (something a lot of developers have difficulty grasping).

In this chapter, we will discuss operating environments including:

- Flash Player versions
- Host applications
- Hardware considerations

Target Environment

Where will your application be deployed? Will it run over the Internet or from a CD-ROM? Will users be on a T-1 network connection or a dial-up 56K modem? Will users be required to have a minimum configuration in order to use your application?

Many of these specific questions can be answered by first determining the general situation under which your application will be deployed.

Operating System

One of the greatest advantages of applications developed in Flash is platform independence. In the vast majority of cases, the users' operating system is not as important as the Macromedia Flash Player version they have installed. Still, there are slight variations in Flash Player's performance on different platforms. As with any application development, be sure to test on all target platforms.

As of this writing, Flash Player 7 is available on Macintosh and Windows, with a Linux version coming soon. Flash Player 6 is available for Linux, Sun Solaris, HP-UX and Pocket PC, and Flash Player 4 supports additional platforms.

Projectors

A Projector is an executable file (.exe) that includes the Flash Player along with your Small Web Format (SWF) file. The Projector provides a few simple fscommands that let you do things like go full-screen and close the projector.

Projectors are commonly used on CD-ROMs as a means of playing Flash content without requiring the end user to have Flash Player installed on their system. Projector files are platform specific, meaning a Macintosh projector cannot play on a PC, and vice versa.

If you wish your Flash Projector to start playing automatically when the user inserts the CD-ROM into their PC, you will need to include an *autorun* script.

Autorun is a system-level feature that launches a designated application on a CD when the CD is inserted. This feature is implemented when the CD is burned. On Windows platforms, the autorun feature is implemented by putting an INF file in the parent directory of the CD. You must create a text file (using a program such as Simple Text or Notepad) called "Autorun.inf" and include the following text, replacing whatever with the name of the application you wish to launch:

```
[Autorun]
open=whatever.exe
icon=whatever.ico
```

The third line (icon=whatever.ico) allows you to change the icon associated with the CD drive.

> **NOTE**
>
> With the introduction of Flash Player 6 standalone, security functionality was added to disable cross-directory accessibility. The primary purpose was to eliminate any potential hacking issues, which could arise from unauthorized directory access. As a result, any files that you want your projector to launch using `fsCommand` ("exec") along with the projector must reside in a folder, named "fscommand."

Stand-Alone Applications

Stand-alone applications don't allow us to make many inferences about the environment. Your end users can be on very diverse systems. Unlike a web-based application, for a stand-alone application you don't even have the benefit of assuming the existence of an Internet connection, although it's fairly simple to test for one.

If you're developing a stand-alone application, it's important to begin gathering as much information as possible about your likely users. For instance, will your application be distributed only to a particular group?

Macromedia Central

At the time of writing, Macromedia had just released the software development kit (SDK) for *Macromedia Central*. Central is a revolutionary new application, which can be simply described as a custom browser for Flash-based applications.

The beauty of Central is that it has been designed specifically for "occasionally" connected applications—that is, applications not requiring a full-time network connection in order to function properly. When the user connects to a network, the application downloads the required data in the background. The user can then take the application offline and still use it with all the freshly updated data.

Another benefit of Central is that you can use push technology to notify users when an update is available for them to download. Rather than users having to periodically check for new updates, Central simply notifies them when an update is available and gives them the option of downloading it right then and there.

Internet Connection

Probably the most common deployment situation is this: The client will load your application from a web server, and the application will run from a browser. In this situation, you can assume the client has an Internet connection. Due to the diverse nature of web visitors, however, there is little else you can take for granted. You know they're connected to the Web, but you can't predict at what speed.

Intranets

There's a large and growing demand for applications that will be run within the confines of a company's intranet. In many ways, this situation is similar to an Internet-based application, but from a developer's perspective it has some distinct advantages.

Intranets usually have a much faster connection between the client and the server. This makes issues of file size and preloading requirements much less important than they would be for an Internet-based application.

Company infrastructures tend to be more homogeneous than the Internet as a whole. It's not uncommon to have a reasonably consistent platform that you can develop for—midrange PCs running Microsoft Windows 98, NT, or 2000 being the most common at the moment.

Kiosks

Application development for kiosks raises a few unique issues. Although kiosk applications are often stand-alone, they can be Internet-based if the kiosk has an Internet connection. The main difference in kiosk development is that you will often have a very well defined platform, but one that may not behave in a typical way.

Kiosks often have touch screens. This lets users make their selections without using a mouse. As a consequence, your movie won't receive certain events, such as onMouseMove.

If possible, you should become familiar with the specific kiosk on which your application will run. Does it even have a keyboard?

Flash Player Version

 The Flash Player version installed by your users is the single most important factor in determining compatibility with your application. Your users must have at least Flash Player 6 installed in order to view applications produced by Flash MX. If you need to export for earlier versions, you will need to sacrifice some functionality. Consult your Flash MX 2004 Help documentation for full details.

The Flash Player is backward compatible with movies produced with older versions of Flash. The newest version of the Flash Player is capable of playing all previous versions of Flash movies.

Flash Player Version Detection

One of the new publishing features of Flash MX 2004 allows you to configure your document to detect the Flash Player version of your users.

If you've selected *Detect Flash Version* option in the Publish Settings dialog box, you are presented with a series of options allowing you to configure your Flash detection (and redirection) files. Users who access your Flash application will be transparently directed to an HTML file that contains a SWF file designed to detect their Flash Player version. If they have the specified version or later, the SWF file again redirects the user to your content HTML file, and your SWF file plays as designed. If users don't have the specified version, they're redirected to an alternate HTML file that Flash automatically creates (or alternatively one that you've previously created), requesting the user to update their version of the Flash Player.

Minor Versions

The second set of numbers in a version number refers to a minor release—for example, Shockwave Flash 6.0 r47 is release 47 of the Flash Player 6. When minor changes are made to a version of the Flash Player, Macromedia releases an update. This number following the *r* changes to reflect what release you have installed.

You can use the $version variable to access the Player platform and version from ActionScript. The value of $version is a string that looks something like WIN 6,0,47,0, depending on the version.

> **NOTE**
>
> In many cases, the release version isn't of any particular significance to your project. However, if you intend to use a specific feature addressed in an update release, that release version might be vital to ensuring your application works as expected. It's a good idea to acquaint yourself with the changes between Flash Player releases.

Clients

More often than not, the Flash Player running your application will be hosted in another application. You need to evaluate the limitations or added features that may be part of the host application. A few commonly used hosts include browsers, Macromedia Central, projectors, or third-party wrappers.

Browsers

A web browser—the most common host for the Flash Player—provides a number of features. JavaScript functions can be called, fscommands can be defined with JavaScript or VBScript, and Netscape LiveConnect may be available.

The Player is implemented as an ActiveX control in Internet Explorer and as a Netscape plug-in in other browsers that are compatible with the plug-in architecture.

The ActiveX version of the Player can also have a transparent background. This background has engendered the development of an interesting new type of dynamic hovering ad that has become familiar to anyone using Internet Explorer on Windows. Using a combination of the layers feature of dynamic HTML (DHTML), and Flash files published with a transparent background, these new types of rich-media advertisements appear to float (or hover) over a web page as though they are totally separate from the page.

Macromedia Central

As previously mentioned, Macromedia has released the SDK for Macromedia Central, best described as a custom browser for Flash-based applications. Central provides Macromedia Flash developers with a prebuilt infrastructure for creating, distributing, and selling applications. More information about Central and example applications can be found at: http://www.macromedia.com/software/central/

Projectors

As outlined earlier, a Projector is an executable file (.exe) that includes the Flash Player along with your Small Web Format (SWF) file. It is commonly used to distribute and display Flash content from CD-ROMs because it doesn't require the end user to have the Flash Player installed on their system.

Third-Party Wrappers

The standard Projector executable provides limited functionality. Several third-party vendors have developed alternatives that offer significant improvements. From file-system access to sending email directly from your movies, these third-party tools can provide a powerful addition for developing stand-alone applications.

A great example of these third-party tools is MDM's Flash Studio Pro (http://www.multidmedia.com/software/flashstudio/). Flash Studio Pro allows you to create fully customizable projectors (exe) or screensavers (scr) from your SWF files. It also extends ActionScript with over 400 new and extremely powerful fscommands, including advanced commands, which allow database connection, real time socket communication and true video, and HTML support for real multimedia capabilities.

Hardware

The hardware on which your application will run can impose limits on how you will develop your application. Certain features may not be available in the target environment, and application performance may be poor if you are not careful to develop within the limits of the target machine.

The `System.capabilities` object can be used to access information about the system that is running your Flash movie. This object contains a number of properties that provide information about features such as screen resolution, the operating system, and whether and which codecs are available.

Kiosks

As discussed earlier, kiosks are usually regular desktop computers but with unusual configurations, often lacking a mouse or even a keyboard. It's important to know the details of the system for which you're developing.

Kiosks were once primarily the domain of Macromedia Director developers. But with the increasing features of the Flash Player, many new kiosk installations are being developed with Flash.

Hardware-Limited Devices

Sometimes the style in which you choose to develop will be dictated by the processing power of the computer you're developing for. Some eye candy—like transparency and animation—that occupies a large portion of the screen can bring a slow processor to its knees.

Pocket PC Devices

Microsoft Pocket PC has added a new category of Flash development. The existence of limited memory and processor speed require efficiency when developing your application. Make an extra effort to minimize file size and develop code that is as efficient as possible. The recent release of Pocket PC devices with 400 MHz processors holds the promise of incredibly rich applications running on an otherwise tiny platform.

Resolution is the other limitation to keep in mind for these devices. When you are working with a vector-based application like Flash, resolution is not as large an issue as it is with raster-based applications. With Pocket PC devices, however, the small screen demands that you take this consideration seriously. Creative use of white space is just not an option when designing for a small screen.

Mobile Phones

The compact nature of Flash files makes them ideal for wireless carrier networks, where transfer rates range between 9.6 and 60 kilobytes per second (Kbps).

Mobile devices, unlike desktop computers, have limited storage capability, so the small footprint of Flash is ideal. Flash MX 2004 contains a series of new mobile-device templates, which allow you to create content for many of the mobile devices available on the market today, such as the Nokia 3650 or Motorola A920.

In addition to the new mobile device templates, Macromedia has also recently launched Flash Lite and iMode (the Content Development Kit (CDK) for the Japanese NTT DoCoMo mobile phone network). Both of these further facilitate the development of Flash content for mobile phones. More information on Flash Lite and iMode can be found on Macromedia's web site (`http://www.macromedia.com/devnet/devices/i-mode.html`).

Legacy Desktops

Despite the falling prices for powerful PCs, not everyone is inclined to upgrade on a regular basis. There are millions of substandard PCs still in use today. If you have ever seen a Flash movie with heavy use of animation and alpha channels running on a 66 MHz computer, you realize what a miserable experience it can be.

> **NOTE**
>
> Many older PCs have processors that are much slower than the new Pocket PC devices. To make matters worse, legacy desktops have larger screens (remember 640x480?) than Pocket PC devices, resulting in more CPU usage for running your application.

There's a point where it may not be worth downgrading your application to support an increasingly small portion of the population. It's up to developers and their clients to decide where that point is and how to handle the technological stragglers.

Sample Questions

1. Which of the following assumptions *cannot* be made when developing an application for intranet deployment?

   A. The connection speed between computers will be generally faster than on the Internet.

   B. Users will have the same version of the Flash Player.

   C. The computers accessing the application will have pretty similar capabilities.

   D. Users will have an Internet connection.

2. Which of the following is the most important factor in determining the compatibility of your application?

   A. The Flash Player version installed

   B. The operating system installed

   C. The screen resolution

   D. The use of external assets

3. Which of the following is *not* a typical host application for the Flash Player?

   A. A browser

   B. A Projector

   C. A Java executable

   D. A third-party wrapper

4. Which object allows you to access information about the user's system?

   A. `System.settings`

   B. `System.capabilities`

   C. `System.status`

   D. `System.requirements`

CHAPTER **4**

Accessibility and Usability Best Practices

As we discussed in the preceding chapter, planning for the target audience is critical to the success of any web project. When developing Flash content for any target audience, accessibility for the user is not something that should be considered as an afterthought.

For several years now, countries such as Australia, Canada, Japan, the United States, and those within the European Union have encouraged developers to adhere to the accessibility standards set down by the World Wide Web Consortium (W3C). To promote global accessibility standards, the W3C released the Web Content Accessibility Guidelines document in 1999. This document outlines the necessary actions web developers should take in order to make their web content accessible to users with sight, hearing, and learning disabilities. More information about the W3C's Web Accessibility Initiative can be found at their website at http://www.w3.org/TR/WCAG10/.

In addition to the W3C Web Content Accessibility Guidelines, developers should also endeavor to ensure that their code accommodates *assistive technology*. Assistive technology comprises hardware (or software) that is used to increase, maintain, or assist the functional capabilities of individuals with disabilities. Examples of assistive technologies include screen readers, closed captioning, magnifiers, and keyboard enhancements. Assistive technology uses the coding and content of your website and makes it accessible.

In the United States, the law that governs accessibility is commonly known as Section 508, which is an amendment to the U.S. Rehabilitation Act. Section 508 prohibits federal agencies from buying, developing, maintaining, or using electronic technology that is not accessible to those with disabilities. In addition to mandating standards, Section 508 allows government employees and the public to sue agencies in federal court for noncompliance.

Throughout this chapter, we'll discuss considerations for providing accessibility to special need users, including:

- Alternate Navigation
- Logical Layouts
- Tab Order
- Screen Readers

Accessibility Guidelines

When developing accessibility friendly content for Flash, there are four broad groups to be considered: users with visual, hearing, and mobility impairments, and users with learning disabilities.

Part of every web developer's role is to help minimize (or eliminate) any potential barriers that a person with a disability may encounter when navigating a site. The following guidelines serve as a good starting point for developing accessibility-friendly Flash content.

Animation Issues

One of the most popular uses for Flash today is for web-based animations, in the form of site introduction pages, loading sequences, screen transitions, or even navigation buttons. It is important to remember that when developing accessibility-friendly Flash content, onscreen animation and motion can be distracting and may even make some screen elements unreadable for people with learning disabilities.

> **NOTE**
>
> People who are blind or visually challenged will often use Screen Reader software to facilitate navigation around computer interfaces or web pages. Screen Reader software, such as Freedom Scientifics' JAWS, convert onscreen textual elements, such as content, navigation menus, or ALT tags, to computer generated speech.

A unique feature of Macromedia Flash content is that it can change over time. As the content changes, Flash Player 7 sends a signal to the screen reader notifying that there has been a change. When the screen reader receives this notification, it automatically returns to the top of the page and begins reading it again.

The following example illustrates the implications of Flash content created without consideration for users of screen readers: Imagine a poorly designed banner ad placed at the top of the page and looping constantly through a few frames. When Flash Player encounters this banner, it will send repeated notifications to the screen reader of changes in the content, and the screen reader will continually return to the top of the page. This problem can seriously erode the website experience for a user with a screen reader.

To address this specific issue, Macromedia worked with GW Micro to create a "*Halt Flash Events*" keystroke (Alt+Shift+M) for the Window-Eyes screen reader (described later in this chapter). This keystroke allows a screen reader user to suspend Flash notifications on the page. Pressing the keystroke again will resume the Flash notifications.

Generally speaking, try to avoid animating text, buttons, and input text fields in your document. If you keep these kinds of objects stable, you reduce the chance of causing a screen reader to emit extra "chatter" that might annoy users.

Keyboard Navigation Issues

Since members of your audience may be mobility impaired and have difficulty working with a mouse, providing them with a keyboard-based means of navigation will assist them in interacting with your Flash movie more easily.

The `tabIndex` property was first introduced in Flash MX. It allows developers to assign a tab index to objects such as buttons and text fields, so that users can use the Tab key (rather than the mouse) to navigate through these onscreen objects.

To facilitate keyboard access, try to keep scripts within frames as opposed to attaching them directly to objects. Also, avoid using empty movie clips as buttons. Screen readers do not recognize these hit areas. Finally, add keyboard shortcuts to commonly used buttons to facilitate access.

Including support for keyboard navigation greatly assists users who have special needs in terms of mobility and sight and might not normally use a mouse to navigate your onscreen items.

Use ALT Tag Equivalents

One of the principal mechanisms by which assistive technologies such as screen readers are able to identify graphical elements within HTML documents is via the ALT tag (the ALT attribute of the <IMG> tag).

Developers can select objects on the Stage and specify ALT tag–equivalent options such as the object's name, description, keyboard shortcut, and tab index order, within the Accessibility panel in Flash MX 2004.

> **TIP**
>
> All objects in Flash documents must have instance names in order for you to apply accessibility options to them.

Issues for Hearing Impaired Users

To assist users with hearing impairments, think about providing captions when delivering Flash content that contains narrative audio. Captions display spoken dialog as printed words on the screen. In addition to showing dialog onscreen, captions can be used to identify speakers, onscreen and off screen sound effects, music, and laughter.

An easy means of delivering captions is the Hi-Caption SE captioning creation product by HiSoftware, Inc. With the third-party Hi-Caption Viewer component for Macromedia Flash (http://www.macromedia.com/software/flash/extensions/hicaption/), designers and developers need only point to a caption file and customize the user interface to deliver captions.

Use a Logical Layout

If your users will need to fill out a form, make sure that the layout and flow of the form is logical and predictable. To help facilitate this, you can use the `tabIndex` property to assign a tab order to each object to be read. The screen reader can then read these objects in the order designated—regardless of their physical location on the stage.

Validate Your Content

As is the case with any form of development, testing is an integral part of the entire process. Flash is no different, and designers and developers should use a variety of methods to validate their content for accessibility. In terms of testing for accessibility, a good starting point is to try accessing your Flash content using assistive technologies such as screen readers and magnifiers. This will provide a good overview of the content's usability from the challenged user's point of view. Also, be sure to test your site using only the keyboard without a screen reader running. Keyboard access differs when a screen reader is not present.

Perhaps the most obvious method of validating your content is to test it with actual users. Accessibility issues aside, User Acceptance Testing (UAT) is critical in any web project. So before claiming that your content is accessible, it should be evaluated either formally or informally by people with special needs.

Developing for Accessibility

By default, Macromedia Flash MX 2004 is able to make text, input text fields, buttons, movie clips, and even entire movies accessible. Despite this, Flash developers should get into the habit of using the Accessibility panel to add text equivalents (such as description text or ALT tag equivalents) or even to hide elements from assistive technologies.

Using the Flash Accessibility Panel

The Accessibility panel, lets you assign names and descriptions to text, input text fields, buttons, movie clips, and entire movies. This is somewhat akin to using the ALT tag in HTML. These assigned names and descriptions are read by a screen reader when the appropriate objects appear on the Stage. In addition to adding names and descriptions, you can hide elements that you think might be distracting to the user if read by the screen reader.

> **NOTE**
> Although you can assign names and descriptions to both static and dynamic text, it's not necessary because the text will be read by the screen reader unless you intentionally hide it. It is more important to add names and descriptions to buttons and input text fields, as these aren't read by the screen reader in the same manner that static (and dynamic) text is.

Screen Reader Detection

Screen readers are assistive technology software designed to navigate through a website and convert its text to speech. Visually impaired users often rely on this technology to "listen" to the content on web pages.

Two of the most common screen readers are JAWS, from Freedom Scientific (www.hj.com/fs_products/software_jaws.asp), and Window-Eyes, from GW Micro (www.gwmicro.com).

The Flash Player automatically provides names (ALT tags) for static and dynamic text objects, which are simply the contents of the text. To enable a screen reader to read non-textual objects in your application, such as vector art and animations, you need to use the Accessibility panel to associate a name and description with the object, which the screen reader reads aloud.

To ascertain whether the Flash Player is running in an environment that supports assistive technologies, use the System.capabilities.hasAccessibilities method. If there are active Microsoft Active Accessibility (MSAA) clients, and the player is running in an environment that supports communication between Flash Player, and MSAA clients, the value of this method will return true. (You'll read more about MSAA clients later in the chapter.)

> **NOTE**
>
> If you call the System.capabilities.hasAccessibilities method within 1-2 seconds of the first appearance of the Flash window in which your document is playing, you might get a return value of false even if there is an active MSAA client. This is because of an asynchronous communication mechanism between Flash and MSAA clients. You can work around this limitation by ensuring a delay of 1-2 seconds after loading your document before calling this method.

To create Flash content designed for use with a screen reader, you must be running the Windows version of Flash MX 2004. Those viewing your Flash content must have Flash Player 6 or later, and Internet Explorer 4.0 on Windows 98 or later.

Accessibility and Components

Macromedia Flash MX 2004 UI components are an excellent way to help accelerate development of accessible applications, because each of the core Macromedia V2 components has been developed with an in-built accessibility object. Because of the manner in which components are constructed, there is no simple means of removing an object once it has been added to the component. Therefore, these accessibility options are turned off by default.

All the developer needs to do to enable accessibility for each component is use the enableAccessibility() command. This command includes the accessibility object with the respective component at compile time. This is done only once for each component, and it is not necessary to enable accessibility for each instance of a component.

Here is the sample code for adding the list component:

```
import mx.accessibility.ListAccImpl;
ListAccImpl.enableAccessibility();
```

Accessibility Parameters for the Entire Movie

When nothing on the Stage is selected, the Accessibility panel offers two options that apply to the entire movie: Make Movie Accessible and Auto Labeling.

- If you check Make Movie Accessible, the screen reader will by default attempt to read everything in your movie. If you uncheck this option, the screen reader will attempt to read only objects that have individually been made accessible.

- If you check Auto Labeling, the screen reader will look for input text fields and buttons with associated text (that is, labels). If one of these elements is found, the screen reader will use the label to identify the field or button.

TIP

If you check Make Child Objects Accessible, the contents within movie clips will also be read. So, enable this option when you want the individual elements of your movie clips to be read.

Accessibility Properties for Individual Objects

As mentioned earlier, when the Accessibility panel is open you can assign names, descriptions, and shortcuts to individual objects simply by selecting them. The Accessibility panel then displays the current properties for that object.

NOTE

Static text must be converted to dynamic text before applying accessibility options to it (including making it unaccessible). Similarly, graphics must first be converted to movie clips.

CAUTION

Make sure all accessible objects have instance names. They cannot be accessed without them. Static text is the only exception to this rule.

The parameters available for individual objects are similar to those available for the entire movie, although there are additional options.

- The option Make Object Accessible is pretty obvious. Check this box if you want your object to be read by the screen reader. You can also use this option to strategically group a series of objects with only one that is to be read (known as grouping). For instance, you can use this technique to identify a complex diagram with many objects. You make all but one of the objects inaccessible (by leaving their Make Object Accessible boxes unchecked) and then provide the one accessible object with a name or description that adequately describes the diagram or its purpose.

- Make Child Objects Accessible to allow you to specify whether child object information is passed to the screen reader for the entire movie. This option is selected by default when you make an object accessible.

- Use the Name field to enter a concise and useful label for the object.

- The Description field allows you more room to describe the object if necessary. This field is useful if you've grouped your objects and want to explain their relationship. You can also use it to provide users with instructions on how to interact with this object.

- The Shortcut field lets you assign a key-based shortcut to the selected object. This is particularly helpful for users who have difficulty using a mouse. For instance, you might have the Ctrl+K key-combination go to the object currently selected in the Accessibility panel. When applying shortcuts to input text fields and buttons, you also have to use the Key object to detect the key-combination. The following example code will detect whether Ctrl+K is being pressed:

```
function trapKeys() {
 var myListener = new Object();
 myListener.onKeyDown = function() {
  // trap CTRL + K - only one time...
  if(Key.isDown(17) && Key.isDown(75) && !this.caughtCombo) {
   trace("CTRL + K pressed");
   // add CTRL + K statement here
   // ensure this only gets called once...
   this.caughtCombo = true;
  }
 }
 myListener.onKeyUp = function() {
  this.caughtCombo = false;
 }
 Key.addListener(myListener);
}
this.trapKeys();
```

Setting the Tab Order

A Flash document's tab order determines the order in which objects receive input focus when users press the Tab key. You can specify a document's tab order either manually via the Accessibility panel (Flash Professional only), or programmatically through the use of ActionScript.

Keep in mind that the tab index you assign in the Accessibility panel does not necessarily control the reading order (see the upcoming section).

To assign a tab order using ActionScript, you simply assign an order number to the tabIndex property, as in the following example:

```
_this.myOption1.btn.tabIndex = 1
_this.myOption2.txt.tabIndex = 2
```

If you create a tab order for a frame and you don't specify a tab order for an accessible object in the frame, Flash Player ignores all the custom tab order assignments. You should therefore provide a complete tab order for all accessible objects. Additionally, all objects assigned to a tab order, except frames, must have instance names specified in the Instance Name text box of the Property inspector. Even items that are not tab stops, such as text, must be included in the tab order if they are to be read in order.

Because static text cannot be assigned an instance name, it cannot be included in the list of the tabIndex property values. As a result, a single instance of static text anywhere in the movie causes the reading order to revert to the default.

Controlling the Reading Order

In addition to controlling the tab order of onscreen elements, you can also set the order in which a screen reader will read information about the object (known as the reading order).

To create a reading order, you use ActionScript to assign a tab index to every instance on the Stage. Note that you must create a tab index for every accessible object, not just the focusable objects.

For example, dynamic text must have tab indexes, even though a user cannot tab to dynamic text. If you do not produce a tab index for every accessible object in a given frame, Flash Player will ignore all tab indexes for that frame whenever a screen reader is present and will use the default tab ordering instead.

Accessibility Support

Fortunately, if you plan to make your Flash movie available to the widest audience possible, there are several new resources to make the job much easier. Macromedia, Microsoft, and third-party vendors such as GW Micro have introduced new products and features to support the needs of those with visual disabilities.

Screen Readers

True to its name, a screen reader reads what's on the screen. Using text-to-speech technology, a screen reader reads aloud the text encountered in the active window in a generally top-to-bottom, left-to-right order. Screen readers also track keyboard and mouse actions so that the user is always aware of what is being typed, moused over, or clicked. Many other features beyond the scope of this book are also available.

As of this writing, the two screen readers with Flash support are GW Micro's Window-Eyes (for which a free trial demo is available on the company's web site, http://www.gwmicro.com/) and Freedom Scientifics' JAWS for Windows 4.5 (more information at http://www.freedomscientific.com/fs_products/ software_jaws.asp).

Traditionally, to determine the reading order, screen readers only had to deal with a static environment in which text didn't change without some user interaction. However, with Flash content so dynamic in nature, the screen reader's job becomes much more difficult. If the content of a page being read changes, the screen reader must begin again. With constantly changing content, it can quickly become impossible for the screen reader to do an adequate job of relaying to the user what's on the screen. It therefore becomes necessary for the Flash developer to assist the screen reader when creating content by using the tools and methods discussed in this chapter.

Accessibility Panel

Although Flash has supported assistive technology since the release of the Macromedia Flash Player 4, until Flash MX no accessibility tools have been available to the developer during authoring. With Flash MX, Macromedia added the Accessibility panel, which lets you add, modify, and remove textual elements read by the screen reader. Additionally, you can hide certain elements that you believe would be a distraction to the user if read by the screen reader.

Microsoft and MSAA

Microsoft has developed a Windows-based technology called Microsoft Active Accessibility (MSAA) that provides assistive technology with a common interface for communicating with operating systems and applications. Flash Player 6 uses MSAA to communicate with screen readers.

Microsoft Internet Explorer 5 was the first Microsoft browser to feature robust support for MSAA. In fact, Internet Explorer for Windows, versions 5.*x* and later, is the only browser with built-in support for assistive technology. As of this writing, Window-Eyes and JAWS for Windows 4.5 are compatible only with these Internet Explorer versions. Hence, true screen-reader–friendly Flash movies can be deployed only on Windows systems using these browsers.

> **CAUTION**
>
> MSAA is not currently supported in opaque windowless and transparent windowless modes. These modes should be avoided when designating your Publish settings if you want your content to be accessible. Also, MSAA is not supported in stand-alone players.

> **NOTE**
>
> The Mozilla browser supports MSAA, although Window-Eyes and JAWS for Windows are not currently compatible with it. More information about the Mozilla browser is available at `http://www.freedom scientific.com/fs_products/software_jaws45newfea.asp`

More information about MSAA can be found at Microsoft's Accessibility Home Page: `http://www.microsoft.com/enable/`.

Additional Resources

Macromedia provides numerous resources, including at least one tutorial, for developers writing for people with special needs. I suggest the following list for further reading:

Macromedia's Accessibility Center:
`http://www.macromedia.com/macromedia/accessibility/`

Macromedia's Flash Accessibility Center:
`http://www.macromedia.com/macromedia/accessibility/features/flash/`

The W3 Web Accessibility Initiative:
`http://www.w3.org/WAI/Resources/`

Sample Questions

1. When does the `System.capabilities.hasAccessibilities` method return true?

    A. When the current Flash movie is in an MSAA-compatible browser

    B. When a screen reader is detected

    C. When an input device for people with disabilities is detected

    D. When Flash content has been designated as Accessible

2. Which of the following items *cannot* be hidden from screen readers?

    A. Static text

    B. Dynamic text

    C. Buttons

    D. Movie clips

3. Which of the following properties can be used to control the order in which the user can tab through the elements in a Flash movie?

    A. tabOrder

    B. tabNumber

    C. tabValue

    D. tabIndex

4. To control the reading order of objects on the Stage, you use which of the following properties?

    A. readingOrder

    B. tabOrder

    C. tabIndex

    D. readingIndex

PART 3

Design and Coding

CHAPTER 5
Variables

A *variable* is a container into which we place a value. The value that a variable holds can be unchanging throughout the life of the variable or may change periodically in both value and type. A variable with an unchanging value is referred to as a *constant*.

Even if you have never done any programming before, you are probably familiar with variables. The ever-present x in algebra is an example of a variable. Rather than representing the letter x, it is a placeholder for something else. A glass is another good example of a variable. It's a container that can hold many different types of liquids, such as water, milk, or vodka. These different liquids can be thought of as variable values. We can increase, decrease, or even change the contents of our glass, just as we can the value of variables.

Throughout the rest of this chapter, we'll look at:

- Variable naming guidelines

- Variable scope

- Variable types

- And finally; the removal of variables

Variable Naming

For a variable name to be valid in ActionScript, it must adhere to a predefined set of criteria. First, it must be in valid identifier format: The first character must be a letter, underscore (_), or dollar sign ($); and each subsequent character must be a letter, number, underscore, or dollar sign.

A variable name cannot be one of the reserved ActionScript keywords. These include words such as new, return, if, while, and function. A complete list of reserved keywords can be found in the ActionScript dictionary that is included with Flash.

A variable name must be unique within its scope. If you declare a variable with the same name as another variable in the same scope, the second variable declaration will overwrite the first.

Variable Scope

Variable *scope* defines from where in your scripts a variable will be accessible. Some variables are only useful within a specific code block; others must be available from anywhere within your application. The three scopes (*local*, *Timeline*, and *global*) allow you to define what sections of code can see a given variable.

Local Scope

A variable with local scope is only accessible from within the code block where it was declared. This scope is useful for variables that are only needed during the execution of the code block.

A local variable is declared using the var keyword. An example is the often-used i, which is often used as a counter for the number of times a loop has been executed. Once the loop has completed, there is really no useful reason to keep i around.

When the following function has finished executing, the variable i goes out of scope and is cleared from memory. Using local scope prevents this i from colliding with another i in another function.

```
function traceItems(){
 for(var i=0;i<this.items.length;i++){
  trace(this.items[i]);
 }
}
```

Timeline Scope

Timeline-scoped variables belong to a particular object, such as a MovieClip, but are accessible from anywhere else using a target path. (See the "Varable Scope" section later in this chapter.) Timeline-scoped variables exist as long as the object to which they belong exists, or they are specifically removed using the delete keyword.

Any variable that is specific to an object and must persist should be a Timeline-scoped variable. A built-in example of a Timeline-scoped variable is the MovieClip property _x. Every MovieClip has an _x property that is specific to that MovieClip. MovieClips can access the _x property of other MovieClips simply by targeting them using valid target paths.

NOTE

A quick and useful definition of a property is "a variable that belongs to an object." Because MovieClips are objects, all Timeline-scoped variables in a MovieClip are effectively properties of a MovieClip instance.

A Timeline-scoped variable can be declared by using the set function or by assigning the variable a value with the assignment operators. Both of the following lines are functionally equivalent:

```
set(age,10);
age = 10;
```

Global Scope

Some variables must be accessible from anywhere in your movies. The _global identifier allows you to arrange this. We need not use the _global identifier when accessing the variable, only when declaring it. Once it is declared as global, we can just use its identifier to get or set its value. In the following example, we are declaring and assigning a global variable named accountNumber:

```
_global.accountNumber = 2394523023487;
```

We can now access accountNumber from anywhere.

CAUTION

Once we declare a variable to have global scope, there can only be one variable by that name in our movie. Once it is declared global, that variable is now shared by every object. This is a good reason to think carefully about what you are assigning to global scope.

Variable Type

The kind of information that a variable contains is referred to as the variable's *type*. You do not need to specifically declare the variable type. Variables take on the type of whatever value they are set to, and they can be changed at any time by resetting their values to something of a different type.

Not all information is the same. Numbers have a different use than strings and should behave differently. The type of a variable determines how a variable will respond when it interacts with the rest of your script. A simple example below illustrates a difference in how the simple addition operator (+) reacts with string as compared to number values.

```
word1 = "10";
word2 = "5";
trace(word1 + word2);
//concatenates the values, traces 105
number1 = 10;
number2 = 5;
trace(number1 + number2);
// adds the values, traces 15
```

Notice the difference between the two sets of variables. The numbers are the same, but the first part is in quotes. Any value in quotes is assumed to be a string value. Numbers not in quotes are assumed to be of the Number type. The keywords true and false, not in quotes, identify the variable as a Boolean value. Any other unquoted value is assumed to be an identifier that points to an object.

> **CAUTION**
>
> A common programming error arises when you try to evaluate a string as a number. The values "10" and 10 are not the same type and will respond differently. This error is especially common when loading variables from external data sources such as XML or LoadVars.

> **TIP**
>
> If a value needs to be operated upon as a number and there is any chance that it may be interpreted as a string, you can force it to be a number by using the `number()` function. For example, the string value "100" is converted to the number 100 like so: `Number("100")`.

Variables in ActionScript are very flexible and have the ability to hold any type of information that ActionScript supports. You can change a variable's type at any time by assigning it a different value.

> **CAUTION**
>
> In some cases, type flexibility can be very useful, but it often becomes confusing. Unless there is a compelling reason to have a variable change type, it is best to decide up front what type the variable will represent and stick with it.

Primitive Types

Flash has three *primitive data types*: String, Number, and Boolean. Primitive data types contain the actual value of the string, boolean, or number that they represent.

Because of this, when you assign one variable to the value of another, you are copying the value. Later, changing the value of the first variable will not affect the second. We have essentially cloned the value of the first, but the two variables are not connected in any way. Rather, they are independent of each other. This is illustrated in the following example:

```
var1 = 10;
var2 = var1;
var1 = 15;
trace("var1 = " + var1 + " var2 = " + var2);
// traces var1 = 15 var2 = 10
```

Reference Types

Reference data types, such as MovieClip and Object, are more complex than primitive data types. Rather than containing the actual value, reference types contain a reference, or *pointer*, to the value that they represent. Because of this, two or more variables can refer to the same value. Changing the value of one will affect all the others that refer to the same value. The following example illustrates this:

```
Person = function(name,age){
this.name = name;
this.age = age;
}
var1 = new Person("Bob",30);
var2 = var1;
var1.name = "Fred";
trace("var1.name = " + var1.name + " var2.name = " + var2.name);
// traces var1.name = Fred var2.name = Fred
```

In this case, when we assign the value of the first variable to the second variable, we are causing both variables to point to the same value.

> **TIP**
>
> Many times it is necessary to target a movie clip that is deeply nested, resulting in long and complicated target paths. Because reference data types do not make a copy of the object, but rather only point to it, you can create a variable in an easy-to-target location that points to the desired movie clip. You can then target the variable instead of the actual movie clip.

Other Types

There are two special data types that are neither primitive nor reference types. The null data type has only one value, null, and is used to indicate a variable that has no value. The undefined data type is used to indicate that a variable has not yet been assigned a value.

No value ≠ not assigned a value

Strict Data Typing (Strong Typing)

With the release of ActionScript 2.0 in Flash MX 2004, you now have the ability to explicitly declare the object type of a variable when you create it; this form of type declaration is known as *strict data typing*.

The main benefit of using strict data typing is that it helps you avoid data-type mismatches (assigning the wrong type of data to an existing variable), which trigger compiler errors when you're publishing for ActionScript 2.0.

Use the `var` keyword and post-colon syntax to assign a specific data type to an item:

```
// strict typing of variable or object
var name:String = Matt;
var carPrices:Array = new Array();
```

If during the course of your testing you encounter type mismatch errors, you can use the `typeof` operator to determine a variable's data type and ascertain where the problem may be occurring. Here's an example:

```
trace(typeof(variableName));
```

> **NOTE**
>
> In order to take full advantage of the V2 component class structure (discussed in more detail in Chapter 10, "UI Components"), you need to ensure that your classes are strictly typed. This ensures that you can use the new Getter and Setter methods (and improved error handling functionality) of ActionScript 2.0.

Variable Removal

A variable will continue to exist until it goes out of scope or is manually removed using the `delete` keyword. A local variable will go out of scope and be removed as soon as the block of code that contains it finishes executing. A Timeline variable will continue to exist as long as the movie clip that contains it exists. A global variable will persist throughout the life of your movie.

Sometimes a variable can outlive its usefulness even though it has not gone out of scope. In this case, it is a good idea to clean out such variables to prevent unneeded memory usage. Just setting a variable's value to null does not remove the variable itself. ActionScript provides a special keyword, delete, to completely remove a variable.

In the following example, we first create a variable and then delete it. This will remove any trace of its existence.

```
myVar = "String Value";
delete myVar;
```

> **CAUTION**
> Setting unneeded variables to `null`, rather than removing them using the `delete` keyword, can result in memory leaks in your scripts. This is especially true when large numbers of temporary variables are created dynamically. *use delete to avoid memory leaks*

Sample Questions

1. The value of a variable of Timeline scope will persist until:

   A. The code block in which it was declared finishes executing

   B. The variable is removed using the clear keyword

   C. The player moves to a new scene

   D. The object to which it belongs no longer exists

2. Which of the following statements creates a new global variable, `birthyear`, with an initial value of 1968?

   A. `new Global birthyear = 1968;`

   B. `global(birthyear) = 1968;`

   C. `_global.birthyear = 1968;`

   D. `global.birthyear = 1968;`

3. Which of the following statements should be used to manually dispose of the variable `myVar`, in order to prevent memory leaks?

   A. `delete myVar;`

   B. `remove myVar;`

   C. `myVar = null;`

   D. `myVar = 0;`

4. What is the main benefit of strict data typing?

   A. Assists other developers identifying variable data types

   B. Helps avoid data type mismatches

   C. Allows you to more clearly identify compiler errors

   D. Adheres more closely to other OOP-related languages

Identifiers, Case Sensitivity, and Naming Conventions

When we communicate in our day-to-day lives, we use names to address each other. Rather than yelling across the room, "Hey you! Can you come here for a sec?" and having several perplexed heads turn and say, "Who me?", it makes more sense to call out a name.

So, too, is the case when we're coding ActionScript. Obviously, we can't refer to the "thingy" within the "whatchamacallit" when we need to execute a block of code. We have to address our code elements accurately in order for them to function correctly. ActionScript uses *identifiers* to name its elements.

Identifiers are the names we give to variables, functions, objects, and classes, and any old Tom, Dick, or Harry name won't do. The identifiers we give our code elements must adhere to a few rules.

Throughout the rest of this chapter we'll discuss some of the rules surrounding the naming of identifiers, including:

- Cases Sensitivity
- Recommended Naming Conventions

Naming Rules

The first character of your identifier must be a letter, underscore (_), or dollar sign ($). Identifiers cannot start with a number.

Subsequent characters can be a letter, number, underscore, or dollar sign; you cannot use spaces, punctuation characters, or backslashes.

Identifiers are not allowed to match any of ActionScript's reserved words (for example, this, delete, or continue).

Case Sensitivity

As discussed in Chapter 2, case sensitivity in object-oriented programming languages refers to the capitalization of the language's tokens (that is, constants, identifiers, operators, keywords, and so forth).

In ActionScript 1, only reserved words (keywords) have the honor of adhering to case-sensitivity standards. Other tokens are not case sensitive, including internal identifiers such as function and property names. Following is a list of the reserved keywords within Flash.

> **NOTE**
> The keywords in **boldface** are new to Flash MX 2004.

break	case	**class**	continue
default	delete	**dynamic**	else
extends	for	function	**get**
if	**implements**	**import**	in
instanceof	**interface**	**intrinsic**	new
private	**public**	return	**set**
static	switch	this	typeof
var	void	while	with

ActionScript 2.0, on the other hand, is a fully case-sensitive programming language. For example, the following code in case-insensitive ActionScript 1:

```
var firstName="Matt";
trace(FirstName);
```

would result in "Matt" being traced to the output panel. But type the same block of code in ActionScript 2.0, and you'll get an undefined value returned in the output panel. In case it's not obvious, in a case-sensitive language such as ActionScript 2.0, firstName and FirstName are considered two different variables.

The trick to mastering case sensitivity is consistency. A lecturer once jokingly told me, "It's okay to be wrong as long as you're consistently wrong." Unfortunately, this doesn't work with ActionScript 2.0. Disregarding the case sensitivity rule can mean the difference between code that throws errors and code that compiles correctly.

It's important to remember that when you publish your files for the Flash Player 7 or later, Flash will automatically implement case sensitivity rules, regardless of whether you are using ActionScript 1 or ActionScript 2.0. As a result, you must adhere to case sensitivity standards if you want your Flash code to compile without errors.

Recommended Naming Conventions

When you start working on large Flash projects, you'll quickly realize the importance of naming your variables and identifiers intuitively and descriptively. For example, an object named ShoppingCartCheckOut is a lot more meaningful and easier to identify than an abbreviated version such as CO (short for Check Out).

Additionally, you may not always be the only person working with your code, and while CO may be instantly recognizable to you as the ShoppingCartCheckOut object, the next developer who has the misfortune to work with your code will no doubt waste valuable time trying to decipher your cryptic naming convention.

Essentially, an identifier should tell you what the element is used for and, in the case of a variable, what value type it contains.

There are three formats used in naming identifiers, depending on whether they identify a constant, an instance, or a class.

It should be noted that the naming conventions described throughout this section are not requirements and are not enforced by Flash in any way.

Constants

Constants are variables that contain the same value throughout their life. Multiple-word Constant names are written in all uppercase, with spaces between words replaced by an underscore. Using an identifier to refer to a constant value is often easier and makes for more readable code.

The Math object has a constant, Math.PI, that contains the value 3.14159265358979. Because the value of pi never changes, it makes sense to store this value in a constant rather than having to reenter the number every time you need to work with pi.

Instance Variables

Instance variables comprise most of the variables you will use. These are the variables that contain values that may change often throughout the variable's life. Instance variable names start with a lowercase letter; each subsequent word starts with a capital letter and is added to the preceding word with no spaces. Using this convention, a variable used to hold the value of someone's first name could be called firstName.

To facilitate speedy coding (as well as better comprehension for people first starting out with ActionScript), it helps to add the type of value contained in the variable (or instance) to the end of the variable/instance name. For example, by adding the suffix _txt to our firstName variable, we end up with firstName_txt. Now our variable quickly tells us what its value represents, as well as what variable type it contains—in this case, a text value. Flash recognizes this naming format and provides you with a list of all the text methods and properties in a code-hinting popup for quick selection.

Variable-type suffixes shouldn't be confused with data typing, which happens automatically in Flash with variables, parameters, values, and objects created as subclasses. In ActionScript 2.0, data typing can also be explicitly declared, as follows:

```
//strict data typing of an object or variable using ActionScript 2.0
var highestScore:Number = 9999
var anniversary:Date = new Date();
```

> **TIP**
>
> Using the object type suffix to gain access to the Flash code-hinting feature is an excellent way to become more familiar with the object methods and properties. Using code hinting can also help you make your variables more identifiable and, in turn, your code more readable and maintainable. Code hinting is also enabled when you explicitly declare data types in ActionScript 2.0.

Class Constructors

Essentially, a class consists of two parts: the *declaration* and the *body*. The declaration is made up of a class statement followed by an identifier (for the name) and a pair of curly braces. The class body is anything that sits neatly between the curly braces.

```
class ClassNameIdentifier{
    // class body
}
```

When you first set out to declare your class, it's important to begin by establishing whether you will work with ActionScript 1.0 or ActionScript 2.0, as they have different methods of defining classes.

- In ActionScript 1, classes can simply be defined within the Flash IDE on a single frame.

- ActionScript 2.0 is slightly different. When you construct your class, you can only do so in an external ActionScript (AS) file, and the name of your class must be the same as that of the AS file.

Like instance variables, class constructors are written without spaces. Unlike an instance variable, however, class constructors should begin with a capital letter; use a capital letter at the beginning of each new word.

```
// located within the external CapitalCity.as file
class CapitalCity{
        // CapitalCity class body
}
```

An Inclusive Example

The following code listing demonstrates all the naming styles discussed in this chapter:

class

```
TraceValueLoopObject = function(){
    this.MAXIMUM_LOOP_COUNT = 10;        constant
    this.traceValue = function(valueToTrace){   instance      variable
        for(var i=0;i<this.MAXIMUM_LOOP_COUNT;i++){
            trace(valueToTrace);
        }
    }
}
myLooper = new TraceValueLoopObject();
myLooper.traceValue("I am looping");
```

In this code, the variables i and myLooper are both instance variables. TraceValueLoopObject is a class and begins with a capital. The variable MAXIMUM_LOOP_COUNT is an example of a constant and is all capitals.

The naming conventions described in this example are not requirements and are not enforced by Flash in any way. There are several other standards used in other languages that could be applied to ActionScript. The conventions here have been adopted as the de facto standard for ActionScript and other ECMA based languages.

TIP

At the end of the day, even if you choose not to adopt these naming conventions, it is strongly recommended that you use some form of naming principle and stick to it consistently throughout your scripts.

Sample Questions

1. Which of the following characters can be added to the identifier `mylengthyvariable`, to make it more readable?

   A. A minus sign (for example, `my-lengthy-variable`)

   B. An underscore (for example, `my_lengthy_variable`)

   C. A period (for example, `my.lengthy.variable`)

   D. A plus sign (for example, `my+lengthy+variable`)

2. Which of the following conventions is/are recommended for the name of a constant?

   A. Spaces between each word in the name

   B. All capital letters

   C. A number before the characters

   D. A name followed by `()`

3. What should be inferred from a variable named `birthPlace_str`?

   A. It is a short-term variable and will be disposed of once its script is executed.

   B. It can store multiple values.

   C. It is a string.

   D. It can hold only 64 characters.

4. Which of the following is most likely a class constructor?

   A. `CLASS_CONSTRUCTOR`

   B. `ClassConstructor`

   C. `classConstructor`

   D. `class_constructor`

5. What value will displayed in the output panel when the following block of ActionScript 2.0 code is compiled?

```
function personalDetails
(firstName:String,lastName:String,age:Number){
    trace(firstName+" "+LastName+" "+age);
}
personalDetails("Simon","Reid",30);
```

A. Simon Reid 30

B. undefined

C. Simon undefined 30

D. type mismatch

CHAPTER 7

Control Structures

Control structures are scripts that allow code to respond to changing conditions. There are two basic types of control structures, *conditionals* and *loops*. The conditionals `if`, `else`, `else if`, and `switch` do or do not execute a block of code depending on the value of a test expression. The loops `while`, `do while`, `for`, and `for in` execute a block of code zero or more times, depending on the condition.

Throughout the rest of this chapter, we will discuss the following control structures in more depth:

- `if`

- `else`

- `else if`

- `switch`

- `while`

- `do while`

- `for`

- `for in`

- `break`

Conditionals

Imagine you're traveling down a road in a foreign country, and you come across an unmarked fork in the road. Taking one path will lead you to your destination, while taking the other will lead you to the wrong side of town. Facing more than one potential outcome is commonly referred to (in geek-speak) as a *conditional*.

A conditional statement is used to create (and control) situations that have more than one possible result. When you set up a conditional statement, you specify the condition that must be met for the subsequent block of code to be executed. If the condition is not met, the block of code is not executed.

```
if (a condition is met){
    // do something - like execute this block of code
} else {
    // the first condition didn't match so do something else
}
```

if, else, else if

These three conditional statements work together to provide a framework for controlling the flow of your scripts. The `if` statement is the foundation of the other two and will always be present. The other two, `else` and `else if`, are both optional and provide the means to handle more complicated situations than could be processed by a single `if` alone.

if

The first and most common conditional statement is the `if` statement.

The test for an `if` statement is contained in parentheses immediately following the `if` keyword. Almost any code can be used as a test, as long as it evaluates to a value of `true` or `false`.

The test can be composed of several tests joined with double ampersands (`&&`) or double pipes (`||`). The ampersands stand for AND; the pipes stand for OR.

Following are two examples of multiple tests being evaluated within an `if` statement. In the first `if` statement, both tests must evaluate to `true` for the `if` statement to execute. In the second example, the `if` statement will execute if either one or both conditions are `true`.

```
if(userName == "Shaun" && password == "sambakeo"){
  //this will only execute if both
  //userName and password match
}
if(userName == "Shaun" || password == "sambakeo"){
  //this will execute if either
  //userName or password match
}
```

> **TIP**
>
> Having many tests in a single `if` statement can quickly become difficult to read. If you find yourself writing four or five tests in a single `if` statement, consider rewriting it. Nesting several `if` statements is more readable, and a `switch` statement (discussed later) might be the best option of them all.

In the following example, the variable `userName` does equal "Simon," so this block of code will execute and the playhead will jump to the frame labeled "userScreen." If the variable `userName` is anything other than "Simon," then the code block will not execute and nothing will happen.

```
userName = "Simon";
if(userName == "Simon"){
  gotoAndStop("userScreen");
}
```

> **TIP**
>
> Sometimes the correct value for the condition you are trying to catch is `false`. If you put an exclamation mark in front of a `true` value, it becomes `false`. Remember, `(!true == false) == true`.

else

Often, you want one thing to happen when a condition is `true` and something else to happen in all other cases. The `else` keyword allows you to specify a block of code that will execute in all cases where the `if` test does not evaluate to `true`.

We can modify our previous example to include a second block of code that will execute when the `userName` variable equals anything other than "Simon."

```
if(userName == "Simon"){
  gotoAndStop("userScreen");
}else{
  gotoAndStop("loginScreen");
}
```

Now, if the `userName` variable equals "Simon," the movie will advance to the userScreen. In all other cases, the movie will return to the loginScreen.

By adding the `else` keyword, we have gained the ability to define a catchall block of code that will execute under all conditions that are not caught by the `if` statement.

else if

In many cases, it will be necessary to catch and react to several possible conditions. The `else if` statement allows us to specify additional tests and associated code blocks to an existing `if` statement.

We can modify the same example again to allow it to recognize three different usernames:

```
if(userName == "Simon"){
  gotoAndStop("simonUserScreen");
}else if(userName == "Shaun"){
  gotoAndStop("shaunUserScreen");
}else if(userName == "Matt"){
  gotoAndStop("mattUserScreen");
}else{
  gotoAndStop("loginScreen");
}
```

Now we can catch and respond to a total of four different conditions: userName equals "Simon," userName equals "Shaun," userName equals "Matt," and a fourth that will catch all other cases.

switch

The switch statement provides an alternative to the if, else, else if combinations in particular circumstances. When there are numerous possible conditions to catch and respond to, the if, else if, else syntax can become very cumbersome. Using switch, we can specify a sequence of simple tests and associated code blocks with a much less verbose syntax.

> **NOTE**
>
> The switch statement, which was added in MX, is a major improvement over a series of if else statements. If you are not already using it, you should be.

If we rewrite the last version of our code sample as a switch statement, it would look like this:

```
switch(userName){
  case "Shaun":
    gotoAndStop("shaunUserScreen");
    break;
  case "Simon":
    gotoAndStop("simonUserScreen");
    break;
  case "Matt":
    gotoAndStop("mattUserScreen");
    break;
  default:
    gotoAndStop("loginScreen");
    break;
}
```

You can see that for long lists of tests, the switch statement provides a cleaner, more legible alternative to a series of if else statements.

The switch statement evaluates the value of the statement that appears in the parentheses and then compares it to the value that appears after each successive case clause. The test that the switch statement performs is a simple "expression equals case" test. The first test in this sequence is equivalent to userName == "Shaun".

The default clause that appears at the end of the foregoing example is like the else in an if else statement. It catches anything that is not caught by the preceding statements.

A switch statement executes differently than an if statement in a very important way. When a case clause is true, the subsequent code is executed. But unlike the if statement, the switch statement will then continue executing all remaining code blocks until it encounters a break statement, at which time it will exit the loop.

In the preceding example, all clauses terminate with a break. As such, when any test is evaluated, code coming after it will not be executed. If we were to remove some of the breaks, as in the following example, the results would be very different.

```
switch(4){
  case 2:
  case 4:
  case 6:
  case 8:
  case 10:
    trace("even number");
    break;
  case 1:
  case 3:
  case 5:
  case 7:
  case 9:
    trace("odd number");
    break;
}
```

We have removed most of the breaks, so as soon as the test evaluates to true, the code will execute every code block until a break is encountered. For example, if the number being evaluated is 4, the second case clause will be true and that code block (if there was code in it) would be executed. Since there is no break, it will fall through to the next block and then the next. The code finally encounters a break within the case 10 clause and will trace "even number" and then stop executing.

> **TIP**
>
> This fall-through behavior can be very convenient when several cases all need to share a common code block. All you need to do is group the clauses and omit the breaks on all but the last one.

Loops

There are several structures in ActionScript that allow you to repeat an action. They vary in some details, such as the way you specify the number of times to repeat an action. Some loops are more appropriate to certain activities than others, but in most cases the loops are interchangeable. The looping structures supported in ActionScript are while, do while, for, and for in.

> **TIP**
>
> When writing a loop, it is important to make sure that at some point the loop will exit. When the Flash Player is executing a loop, all other activity stops until the loop is completed. If the loop never stops looping (an endless loop), your movie is effectively frozen and your user will get a script error.

while

The while loop uses a simple expression test very much like the if statement. As long as the test evaluates to true, the while loop will continue repeating.

The while loop is a convenient way to repeat an action a specified number of times. This is usually accomplished by creating a variable and incrementing its value within the body of the loop.

In this next example, we are duplicating a movie clip 20 times and laying the duplicates out horizontally:

```
var i = 0
while (i < 20) {
  myMC.duplicateMovieClip("myMC"+i,i);
  this["myMC"+i]._x = myMC._x+(myMC._width*(i+1));
  i++
}
```

If we were to fail to increment the variable i, this loop would never end, and the Flash Player would throw a script error.

do while

The do while loop is a variation of the while loop. The major difference is that the while loop only executes when the test expression evaluates to true. The do while loop, on the other hand, only tests after the first execution and will always execute at least once.

The following examples illustrate the results of a while versus a do while loop. The first test evaluates to false, so the loop never executes and nothing is traced.

```
var i = 10
while (i < 10) {
  trace("while loop " + i);
  i++;
}
```

The do while version will always execute once before testing, and so traces the first time.

```
var i = 10
do{
  trace("do while loop " + i);
  i++
}while(i < 10);
```

for

The for loop is a little more complicated in structure than the while loops. Instead of a single expression test, the for loop takes three expressions.

If you look at the while loop structure, we created a variable that will increment. We tested its value within the parentheses and then incremented it at the end of the loop. The for loop works in the same way, but it allows you to set the incrementing variable, test the incrementing variable, and increment the variable—all within the same parentheses.

The first part of the for loop's three expressions is the initial expression. This is where you can set the initial value of the variable to increment:

```
for(i=0 ; <test> ; <(in|de)crement>){
}
```

The second expression is where you test the current value of the incremented variable. This expression is equivalent to the expression of a while loop:

```
for(i=0 ; i<10 ; <(in|de)crement>){
}
```

The final expression is where you either increment or decrement the variable:

```
for(i=0 ; i<10 ; i++){
}
```

The for loop is the best choice for looping through the elements in an array. Because an array is zero based, we initialize the variable's value to zero and then repeat the loop for each item in the array, as in the following example:

```
myFruits = new Array("apple","orange","mango","guava");
for(var i=0;i<myFruits.length;i++){
  trace(myFruits[i]);
}
```

> **NOTE**
>
> Arrays are zero based; that is, the first item in an array has an index of 0. Because the array's length property returns the number of items in the array, the length is one number higher than the highest index in the array. If the length returns 4, the last item in the array has an index of 3. When you are writing your `for` loop, there is no need to loop until your incrementing value is equal to the length. It only needs to be 1 less than the array length: `i<myArray.length`, not `i<=myArray.length`.

for in

The `for in` loop is designed to loop through all the items in an object. Unlike arrays, the object's properties and methods are not indexed. The syntax for the `for in` loop is as follows:

```
for(<identifier variable> in <object>){
}
```

The identifier variable works a little like the incrementing variable in the other loops, except that instead of representing a numeric value, on each successive loop its value is set to the identifier name for the next property or method in the target object.

The following example first defines a `Person` class and then creates an instance of that class:

```
Person = function(name,age,sex,height,weight){
  this.name = name;
  this.age = age;
  this.sex = sex;
  this.height = height;
  this.weight = weight;
}
aWoman = new Person("Liz",23,"female",63,110);

for(var i in aWoman){
  trace(i + " = " + aWoman[i]);
}
```

The `for in` loop uses the identifier variable `i`. (Using `i` in this case is totally arbitrary. It could be called whatever you would like: element, item, etc.) We also specify what object instance we want to loop through, in this case aWoman.

Each time the loop is executed, `i` is set to a string value of the identifier name of the next property or method. The `for in` loop actually loops backward through the object. So, on the first loop, `i` is equal to "weight." On the second, it is equal to "height," and so on.

Because we now have the name of the identifiers for each of the methods and properties in an object, we can access their values by using the syntax

✓ `objectInstance[identifyerName]`

In the Person example, we are tracing the name of the identifier (weight, height, age, and so on) by tracing i and then tracing the value of that property (aWoman[i]). The result of running this script should look like this:

```
weight = 110
height = 63
sex = female
age = 23
name = Liz
```

You can quickly trace out all the available methods and properties of an object, as well as their types, with the following script. Just change XML to whatever object you are interested in.

```
myXML = new XML()
for(var i in myXML){
   trace("(" + typeof(myXML[i]) + ")" + " " + i);
}
```

break

As your loops become more complex, you may have a requirement to exit or terminate the loop before it has fully completed. To do this, we use the break statement.

The break statement, which can only be placed within the body of a loop, provides a means by which the loop execution can be terminated if the rest of the loop body is not required. In the following example, the break statement is used to exit an infinite loop:

```
i = 0;
while (true) {
   if (i >= 100) {
      break;
   }
   i++;
}
```

About Loops and the Frame Rate

The iteration rate for both Timeline and event loops is tied directly to the frame rate of the main movie. For example, in a programmatically generated animation using a loop, such as a missile flying across the stage, if we were to increase the frame rate of this movie, the speed of the missile animation would increase proportionately to the frame rate increase.

When considering increasing the frame rate of your Flash movies, keep in mind that the Flash Player doesn't necessarily play back movies at the rate you specified in the authoring environment. You may have noticed this in large Flash movies (especially those containing complex mathematical calculations). The Flash Player "chugs" or slows down the playback of your movies, based on the other processes running on your system (or even the processing power of your PC) at the time of playback.

Sample Questions

1. Which of the following if statements is correctly written?

   A. `if firstName = "George" then {};`

   B. `if {firstName = "George"} then ();`

   C. `if (firstName == "George") {};`

   D. `if (firstName = "George" & lastName = "Lucas") {};`

2. In which of the following situations would it be best to use a switch statement?

   A. You need to test for two possible values.

   B. You want to test for many possible values.

   C. You want a loop to run at least once.

   D. You only want one thing to happen if a condition is true.

3. Assuming myVar equals "fish," what will be traced by the following code block?

```
switch(myVar){
  case "cat": trace("cat");
  case "fish": trace("fish");
  case "bird": trace("bird");
  default: trace("default");
}
```

   A. `"fish"`

   B. `"fish bird"`

   C. `"fish default"`

   D. `"fish bird default"`

4. What is the key difference between while loops and do while loops?

   A. do while loops cannot get stuck in an endless loop.

   B. do while loops will always execute at least once.

   C. while loops are deprecated in Flash MX.

5. Which of the following statements uses proper for loop syntax?

   A. for(i=0 , i<10 , i++){}

   B. for(i=0 ; i<10 ; i++){}

   C. for((i=0),(i<10),(i++)){}

   D. for(i=0 i<10 i++){}

6. If it takes 2 seconds for an object to move across the Stage within an animation that is playing back at 12 fps, how long will the same animation take if the frame rate is increased to 24 fps?

   A. Half a second

   B. One second

   C. Two seconds

   D. Four seconds

CHAPTER **8**

Functions

Functions are blocks of ActionScript code that are defined once, and then "called" whenever they are required to be executed. They are a powerful and invaluable asset to every ActionScript coder's bag of tricks. Reusability is their primary benefit, drastically reducing the amount of code duplication required in your scripts. Additionally, by providing a single function that accomplishes a particular task, you greatly decrease your debugging time because the function's code exists—and needs to be debugged—in one location only.

Functions allow you to break complex processes and procedures into easy-to-manage bite-sized pieces. This lets you focus on defining and optimizing each particular step of your process, making the code more efficient and less error-prone.

As your Flash applications become more object oriented, it is not uncommon for most or all of your scripts to largely consist of functions and function calls. While this sort of construction is not a requirement, in larger projects it goes a long way to making your scripts more manageable.

Another advantage of functions is their scope. Once a function has been defined, it can be called from any Timeline—including the Timeline of a loaded SWF file, provided the correct target paths are used.

Throughout this chapter, we will discuss:

- Declaring and naming a function

- Passing paramaters to a function

- Returning values from a function

- Calling a function

- Using recursion

- Using internal functions

Creating Functions

There are several ways you can create a function. Although the specifics may vary, in all cases you will use the function keyword to identify the code block as being a function.

NOTE

A method is an instance of a function attached to an object.

Declaring a Function

When functions are declared, they are attached to the Timeline of the movie clip within which they are defined. As mentioned previously, part of a function's power lies in the fact that, once declared, they can be called (targeted) from any other Timeline. Alternatively, you can use the _global identifier to declare a function to all Timelines, without having to use a specific target path.

Following are three examples of declaring the same function. The first two are functionally equivalent. They define the function and assign it to the identifier helloWorld. The third example declares the same function, but because it hasn't been assigned to an identifier, it will go out of scope as soon as it is declared.

```
function helloWorld(){
   trace("Hello World");
}
helloWorld = function(){
   trace("Hello World");
}
function(){
   trace("Hello World");
}
```
} useless ?

Although the third example may seem rather obscure, it is important that you realize a function and its assigned identifier are not the same thing. It is possible to reassign the function associated with an identifier at runtime, as well as to remove a function from an identifier. The following example illustrates that a nameless (anonymous) function does indeed exist for a moment and functions as expected. The call method invokes the function directly, without the function being assigned to an identifier.

```
function(){
   trace("Hello World");
}.call();
```
. call

Naming Functions

A function's name is the identifier to which it is assigned. Most functions have a name, and you will use this name to identify the function you are calling. As you saw previously, it is possible to have an anonymous function, called a *function literal*, that is defined as an expression. You will see more examples of both named and anonymous functions later on in this chapter.

A function name must be a valid identifier. An identifier cannot contain spaces. If the name requires two or more words to accurately describe the function's purpose, the words must either be concatenated or separated by a character such as an underscore. An identifier must start with a letter, underscore, or dollar sign. Numbers are allowed in an identifier, too, as long as they're not the starting character.

Traditionally, the first letter of the first word in a function name is lowercase, and the first letter of each subsequent word is capitalized. The identifiers `getName`, `setName`, `onEnterFrame`, and `watchMouse` are all valid function names that follow this standard naming convention.

Passing Parameters

Parameters (arguments) allow us to pass information that you want to work with into your functions. To add parameters to a function declaration, simply include the list of comma-separated parameters within a set of parentheses after the function declaration. If you think of a function as a cake recipe, the parameters are simply the ingredients used to create the finished product.

```
//declare our function and its parameters
function
myChocolateCakeRecipe(eggs,flour,butter,cocoa,milk,cookingTime){
    trace("When we combine "+eggs+" eggs with "+flour+" of an ounce
of flour, and "+butter+" of an ounce of butter, and "+cocoa+" of an
ounce of cocoa, with "+milk+" of a cup of milk, and bake in a hot oven
for "+cookingTime+" minutes, we get a delicious, rich chocolate cake.")
}

//call our function and pass across the ingredient quantities
myChocolateCakeRecipe(2,.5,.25,.15,.5,25);
```

When we run this example, the ingredient quantity parameters passed across to the function are used within the function body to output the following statement in the Output panel:

```
"When we combine 2 eggs with 0.5 of an ounce of flour, and 0.25 of an
ounce of butter, and 0.15 of an ounce of cocoa, with 0.5 of a cup of
milk, and bake in a hot oven for 25 minutes we get a delicious, rich
chocolate cake."
```

As you can see, the ingredient quantity parameters we passed to our myChocolateCake() function became available for us to use within the body of the function, by means of the identifiers we defined.

The Arguments Object

In some cases, your function may need to accept an unknown number of parameters. Because you don't know how many parameters will be provided to the function, you can't define a list of parameters as in the chocolate cake recipe. For this reason, every function is also provided with an array-like object that contains all the parameters provided, whether you defined any arguments in your function declaration or not. This Arguments object is available in the body of your code via the identifier arguments. *Do I need to declare the object in AS2?*

In the following example, the function is not declared with a list of known parameters. It uses the Arguments object to access all the provided parameters, regardless of how many were supplied.

```
function concatenate(){
  var tmpString = "";
  for(var i=0;i<arguments.length;i++){
    tmpString += arguments[i];
  }
  return tmpString;
}
trace(concatenate("How ","now ","brown ","cow"));
```

This concatenate() function concatenates all the supplied parameters and then traces their value. The output result of this example will be How now brown cow.

> **TIP**
>
> When using the Arguments object, your function can support parameters of any value type. You can find out the type of each element in the parameters array by using the typeof() function. If you need to be more specific, you can use the instanceof operator to determine the class of which that particular element is an instance.

typeof()   *instanceof()*

Earlier, we referred to the `arguments` object as arraylike. Like an array, this object contains a list of elements accessible by an index number and has a length property as well as do all arrays. Unlike an array, the arguments object contains two additional properties, `caller` and `callee`.

The `arguments.caller` property is a reference to the function that called the function that contains this argument's object. If the function was called from outside a function, the `arguments.caller` property is undefined.

The `arguments.callee` property is a reference to the function that contains the arguments object—in other words, the function you are currently in.

Function Body

The body of a function is the "engine room" where all of the function's actual work is accomplished. This is the area defined by the function's curly braces: { . }

The function body can contain any number of statements. Although there is no limit to the size of a function, it is a good practice to keep functions only as long as necessary. Excessively long functions are often a sign that the function should be broken up into two or more functions. In the end, the size of a function is determined by the task it needs to accomplish.

CAUTION

When in the body of a function, the keyword `this` refers to the object that contains the function. A common example where this can be confusing is when a function is written in a frame of a movie clip but then assigned as a handler to an object such as the XML object. In this case, the function becomes a method of the XML object instance—`this` refers to the XML object instance and not the movie clip where the script was written.

The Return Action

When a function has finished doing its work, you often want to return a value to the location that called the function. ActionScript provides the Return action for this purpose. When the script arrives at a `return` statement, it immediately evaluates the subsequent expression, if one exists, and returns that value to the location that called the function.

In some cases, your function may need to return a particular value depending on the result of the statements in the function body. A function can contain multiple Return actions that can return different values or even value types, depending on the outcome of the function's execution.

As soon as a function reaches a return statement, the function returns the value of the expression to the right of the return and ceases to execute—even if there are multiple possible returns or if the return statement is in a loop.

```
function getClassNameFor(objInstance){
    if(objInstance instanceof MovieClip){
      return "MovieClip";
    }else if(objInstance instanceof Button){
      return "Button";
    }else if(objInstance instanceof XML){
      return "XML";
    }else if(objInstance instanceof XMLSocket){
      return "XMLSocket";
    }else if(objInstance instanceof Array){
      return "Array";
      trace("this will never trace");
    }else{
      return "Other";
    }
}
className = getClassNameFor(new Array());
```

In this example, the function will return only one value. As soon as one of the statements evaluates to true, the return below the test will execute, and the function will stop processing. In this case, the function will return the String value Array. The line containing the trace statement will never be executed, because it is unreachable due to its placement after a return.

Calling Functions

When the Flash Player reaches a frame that contains a function declaration, the function is created and assigned to an identifier, if one is specified. However, the statements within the function body will not execute until the function is called.

In our earlier example of the chocolate cake recipe, we discussed the function declaration that does nothing until we call it and pass any requested parameters.

Functions can be called in several ways. When a function is assigned to an event handler, the function will be called whenever the associated event occurs. In most cases, though, your scripts will call functions directly by specifying their name followed by the function call operator—the parentheses ().

The following example shows the syntax for calling a function that exists in the same Timeline as the script calling it:

```
function randomBetween(low,high){
  return Math.floor((Math.random()*(high-low))+low);
}
var ranNum = randomBetween(10,20);
```

To call a function, you must target the function in the same way that you would target a Movie Clip object. Remember—functions are targeted as methods of the object to which they were assigned. If the `randomBetween()`function existed in a movie clip instance named `tmpClip`, the line for calling the function would look like this:

```
var ranNum = tmpClip.randomBetween(10,20);
```

An alternate method for calling a function is to use the `call` method of the function object. Using the `call` method allows you to specify the value of the `this` parameter within the body of the function. For example;

```
function MyObject() {
}
function MyMethod(obj) {
  trace("this == obj? " + (this == obj));
}
var obj = new MyObject();
MyMethod.call(obj, obj);
```

Recursion

It is often necessary to have a function call itself. This is called *recursion* and enables your function to handle many situations that would be difficult to process by any other method. It is important to code recursive functions carefully, because they can easily result in an endless loop.

The following example is a recursive function that accepts an XML object as an argument. When called, the function will walk the entire depth of the XML object and trace the name of all nodes, with each level of depth indented more than the last.

```
function walkXML(xmlObj,indent){
  var kids = xmlObj.childNodes;
  for(var i=0;i<kids.length;i++){
    trace(indent + kids[i].nodeName);
    if(kids[i].hasChildNodes){
      walkXML(kids[i],indent + " — ");
    }
  }
}
```

Internal Functions

Throughout this chapter, we've seen how easy it is to create and use our own functions, but for newcomers to ActionScript, Flash comes with a set of pre-built functions. You have no doubt used some of these without even realizing it.

Actions such as `gotoAndStop` and `loadURL` are just built-in functions that you simply pass parameters to, such as the frame number (or URL).

A full list of the ActionScript internal functions can be found in the Help documentation of Flash MX 2004.

Sample Questions

1. Which of the following is *not* a valid function name?

   A. get_value

   B. _getvalue

   C. 4ever

   D. $23

2. Which of the following is a *true* statement about functions?

   A. Functions must specify exactly how many arguments they can accept.

   B. Function parameters should be comma-delimited.

   C. Functions can only exist within a pre-defined object instance.

   D. Functions names must begin with a capital letter.

3. Functions can be assigned to identifiers at runtime. Assuming sampleVar equals true, what will be returned by the following function?

   ```
   function sampleFunction (sampleVar) {
       if(sampleVar == true) {
           return "true";
           return "continue";
       }
   }
   ```

   A. Nothing

   B. true

   C. truecontinue

   D. continue

4. Which of the following is the correct syntax for passing parameters to a function?

   A. myFunction(param1,param2,param3);

   B. myFunction(param1;param2;param3);

   C. myFunction(param1:param2:param3);

   D. myFunction(param1.param2.param3);

5. *Recursion* within a function refers to what?

    A. An endless loop

    B. A function calling itself

    C. A function using parameters that have been passed to it

    D. The returning of a value once a loop has been completed

CHAPTER **9**

Events and Event Handlers

When working with any type of Web or multimedia software, it makes sense that during the life of an application events will occur that must be acted upon. These events may be user generated, such as a mouse click, or system generated, such as the loading of a series of classes from an external file. In order for the interpreter to act (or not act) upon any event, a set of instructions, in the form of a method, must be defined to outline clearly what should occur when an event is encountered. These instructions are known as *event handlers*. Generally, event handlers do nothing by default, and it is up to you to define the functionality of the event handlers required by your scripts.

The main difference between a typical method and an event handler is that most methods exist to allow your scripts to get or change the state of an object. An event handler, on the other hand, exists to allow an object to notify your scripts of a change of state. Event handlers are typically called by the object to which they belong; you will rarely call an event handler directly.

In this chapter, we will discuss what you need to know about events and event handlers including:

- How to name event handlers
- How to assign event handlers
- How to determine the scope of event handlers
- How to design custom event handlers
- How to listen for events

Event Types

Events generally occur on Buttons, MovieClips, or XML-related objects and can be broadly grouped into two categories:

- System events: These are events that aren't generated directly by the user. They are generated automatically by Flash Player as part of the internal playback of a movie, as in the initial appearance of a movie clip on the Stage.

- User events: These relate to any event that occurs as a result of direct user interaction such as a mouse click or a keypress.

Event Handler Names

Because an event handler is simply a regular method with a special purpose, it is bound by the same naming rules that all other functions and methods must follow. By convention, an event handler begins with the word on, followed by the type of event that occurred. For example, the MovieClip object contains an event handler, onEnterFrame, that occurs whenever the playhead enters a new frame.

Event Handler Assignments

Event handler methods are class methods that are invoked when an event occurs on an instance of that class. For example, the Movie class defines an onMouseDown event handler that is invoked whenever the mouse button is pressed on a Movie object. Unlike other class methods, event handler methods aren't invoked directly; the Flash Player invokes them automatically when the respective event occurs.

By default, event handler methods are undefined: When a particular event occurs, its corresponding event handler is invoked, but your application doesn't respond further to the event. To have your application respond to the event, you define a function using the function statement and then assign that function to the appropriate event handler. The function you assign to the event handler is then automatically invoked whenever the event occurs.

Event handlers are made up of three parts: the object to which the event applies, the name of the object's event handler method, and the function you assign to the event handler. Here is the basic structure of an event handler:

```
object.eventMethod = function () {
  // Event related code
}
```

In the following example, a button named home_btn has been placed on the Stage. This code assigns a function to the button's onPress event handler; the function moves and stops the playhead to the frame labeled home in the Timeline.

```
home_btn.onPress = function ()
   gotoAndStop("home");
}
```

Here, the gotoAndStop() function was assigned directly to the onPress event. If you like, you can also assign a function reference (name) to an event handler method and then define the function later, as shown here:

```
// Assign a function reference to button's onPress event handler
method
home_btn.onPress = goHomeFrame;

// Define the home() function
function goHomeFrame() {
   gotoAndStop("home");
}
```

> **NOTE**
>
> Remember, a method is just a function that belongs to an object. Any function with a name that matches one of the specified event handlers will override the default handler behavior.

on() and *onClipEvent()* Syntax

With the introduction of Behaviors in Flash MX 2004, the attaching of event handlers directly to Button or MovieClip instances has never been easier. Of course, since Flash 5 you've been able to do this manually by selecting the instance on Stage and adding the onClipEvent() and on() handlers directly to the instance via the Actions panel. Behaviors, on the other hand, are a great way for beginners to learn about event handling without getting their hands dirty with any code. They simply select the object instance on Stage and add the code via the Behaviors panel.

Generally speaking, onClipEvent()handles movie clip events, and on()handles button events. Having said that, though, you can also use on() with MovieClip objects to create movie clips that receive button events.

```
on (release) {
      this.gotoAndPlay("Start");
}
```

> **CAUTION**
>
> Any scripts that are placed on MovieClip or Button instances must be wrapped in the appropriate handler syntax (onClipEvent or on). If they are not enclosed in the handler syntax, your movie will not compile.

One of the good points about using the on() and onClipEvent()event handlers is that they don't conflict with other event-handling events, through event handler methods, that you have previously defined. For example, suppose you have a button placed on the Stage of your movie clip. That button can have an on(press) handler that tells the movie to play, and the same button can also have an onPress() method for which you define a function that tells an object on the Stage to rotate. When the button is clicked, the movie plays *and* the object rotates.

Depending on your preference, you can use either the on() or onClipEvent() event handler methods, or you can use both types of event handling. Keep in mind, however, that the scope of variables and objects in on() and onClipEvent() handlers is different from the scope of variables in regular event handlers and event listeners. (Listeners are explained later in this chapter.)

Another benefit of the on() handler is that you can specify two or more events for each handler. The only requirement is that the specified events be separated by commas. The function body within the handler executes on the occurrence of any of the events specified by the handler. For example, the following on() handler attached to a button executes whenever the user presses (or releases) the mouse button:

```
on(press, release) {
    trace("You pressed or released the button");
}
```

> **CAUTION**
>
> When using the onClipEvent or on techniques of defining an event handler, the argument is the name of the event, *not* the name of the event handler. The event handler for entering a new frame is onEnterFrame, but the name of the event is enterFrame.

Event Handler Scope

Event-handler scope is determined by the type of event handler you're using: event handlers and event listeners (described in more detail in the upcoming section), or on() and onClipEvent() handlers.

Functions assigned to event handler methods and event listeners (like all functions) contain a local variable scope, but the on() and onClipEvent() handlers don't. To understand this difference more clearly, let's look at the following two event handlers. The first is an onRelease() event handler associated with a movie clip named myMovieClip. The second is an on() handler attached to the same MovieClip instance.

```
// Attached to myMovieClip's parent clip Timeline
myMovieClip.onRelease = function () {
  var temperature; // local function variable
  temperature = "hot";
}
// on() handler attached to myMovieClip
on(release) {
  var temperature; // no local variable scope
  temperature = "hot";
}
```

Although both event handlers contain the same code, they have different results. In the first case, the temperature variable is only local to the function defined for onRelease(). In the second case, because the on() handler doesn't define a local variable scope, the variable scopes to the Timeline of the movie clip myMovieClip. In the case of on() event handlers attached to Button objects (as opposed to MovieClip objects), variables (as well as function and method calls) are scoped to the Timeline that contains the Button instance.

When overriding an event handler in an object, it is important to remember that the event handler is a method of the object, regardless of where the handler exists in your script. The keyword this within the body of the event handler refers to the object that contains the event handler method.

In the example following, the onLoad() event handler of the XML object is overridden by the myOnLoad() function:

```
function myOnLoad(){
    //this traces the text of the XML document
    trace(this);
}
storesXML = new XML();
storesXML.ignoreWhite = true;
storesXML.onLoad = myOnLoad;
storesXML.load("locations.xml");
```

When the XML document completes loading, the onLoad() handler, which is now defined as the myOnLoad() function, will be called. Within the body of myOnLoad(), the value of this is being traced. Because myOnLoad() is now a method of the XML object, and not a method of the MovieClip object where the script actually exists, the value of this is the XML object, not the MovieClip object. The example code would trace the text of the XML document that just loaded.

NOTE

Functions assigned to event handlers and event listeners define a local variable scope, with the only exception being onClipEvent() and on().

Custom Event Handlers

You are not limited by the handlers that are built into the native ActionScript objects. You can and should design your objects with custom handlers that are appropriate to their function.

> **NOTE**
>
> Many custom classes will inherit from one of the existing native ActionScript classes. Any event handlers that your parent class contains will also exist in your derived class. If your class inherits from the MovieClip class, your object will possess all of the MovieClip handlers, such as onEnterFrame() and onLoad().

The next example illustrates several concepts of using event handlers. It defines a class that inherits from the MovieClip class. As such, it will contain all of the MovieClip event handlers including onEnterFrame() and onPress(). We will use these existing event handlers to develop a new event handler, onMove(). This new event handler will be called whenever an instance of this Ball class is dragged around the Stage. Notice that the onMove() method does nothing by default. It will need to be overridden when we create an instance of the class.

Create a new movie clip symbol and export it from the Library as Ball. Copy the following code to the first keyframe of this new symbol. (The following code example uses ActionScript 1.0)

```
#initclip
Ball = function(){
  this.last_x = this._x;          ⎫  constructor
  this.last_y = this._y;          ⎬
}                                 ⎭
Ball.prototype = new MovieClip();
Object.registerClass("Ball",Ball);
/*
  This method will be called
  whenever the _x or _y of the
  ball changes while dragging
*/
Ball.prototype.onMove = function(){
}
/*
  This method is assigned as the
  onEnterFrame handler while the
  user is dragging the movieclip
*/
```

```
Ball.prototype.watchForMovement = function(){
  //if the _x or _y has changed, call the onMove handler
  if(this.last_x != this._x || this.last_y != this._y){
    this.onMove();
  }
  this.last_x = this._x;
  this.last_y = this._y;
}
Ball.prototype.onPress = function(){
  this.startDrag();
  this.onEnterFrame = this.watchForMovement;
}
Ball.prototype.onRelease = function(){
  this.stopDrag();
  this.onEnterFrame = undefined;
}
Ball.prototype.onReleaseOutside = Ball.onRelease;
#endinitclip
```

prototype

Now if we drag an instance of this new class to the Stage and name it myBall, we can override the onMove() event handler so that it will trace the current _x and _y values.

```
myBall.onMove = function(){
  trace(this._x + ":" + this._y);
}
```

The result of dragging this instance around the Stage will look something like the following trace sample:

```
60.75:52.25
62.75:58.25
84.75:91.25
108.75:99.25
157.75:92.25
```

Because our onMove() event handler relies on the onPress(), onRelease(), onReleaseOutside(), and onEnterFrame() handlers, these handlers are now unavailable to us. If we override them, our onMove() handler will cease to function properly.

Event Execution Order

Events within Flash are executed in either a *Synchronous* or *Asynchronous* manner. Synchronous event execution relates to the execution of frame-based code that the playback head encounters as it moves through a movie (regardless of whether it is in a non-lineal fashion—i.e. out of order). On the other hand, because events can occur in an arbitrary manner (i.e. when randomly interacted with) the code associated with them is said to be asynchronous—that is, its execution occurs in a non-predictable manner.

Event Listeners

Up to this point, we have been defining event handlers for objects that handle events from the same object. *Listeners* are objects that listen for events within other objects.

We can construct a simple example of a listener using the Stage object. The Stage object receives a Resize event when the user resizes the Stage. The Stage itself cannot process this event. Rather, the Stage needs access to the movie objects in order to reposition them appropriately.

Create a new movie and place an instance of a MovieClip object on the Stage; name it ball. Then add the following ActionScript 1.0 code to the first keyframe of the main Timeline:

```
ball.onResize = function(){
    var radius = (this._width/2);
    this._x = Stage.width-radius;
    this._y = Stage.height-radius;
}
Stage.scaleMode = "noScale";
Stage.align = "TL";
Stage.addListener(ball);
```

The first step in this code defines an onResize() method for the ball movie clip. After we register the ball movie clip as a listener to the Stage object, the ball movie clip will begin to receive the resize event. The result of the subsequent code is that the ball remains attached to the lower-right corner of the Stage as the Stage is resized, without scaling. This makes traditional application layouts possible, where the buttons stay fixed to the right or left sides as the application is resized.

Sample Questions

1. Which of the following statements best describes an event handler?

    A. A single, central script that handles all the events that take place and determines the appropriate action to take

    B. A security function, in the root of the Timeline, that controls access to events

    C. A means of allowing an object to notify your scripts of a change of state

2. Which of the following methods is most likely an event handler?

   A. `MouseDown()`

   B. `_mouseDown`

   C. `MouseDown`

   D. `onMouseDown`

3. Which of the following is a true statement about custom event handlers?

   A. Their use should be avoided.

   B. They can cause handler conflicts with native ActionScript handlers.

   C. They can inherit from existing ActionScript classes.

   D. They are not supported by the Flash Player 5.

4. True or false? `on()` event handlers can contain locally scoped variables if implicitly defined.

   A. `True`

   B. `False`

5. If the following event handler is attached to a three MovieClip instances named `myMovieOne`, `myMovieTwo`, and `myMovieThree`, which are each located on a separate layer. Which movie will play when `myMovieTwo` is pressed?

```
onClipEvent(mouseUp) {
        play();
}
```

   A. `myMovieTwo`

   B. The movie located on the highest layer

   C. None of them

   D. All of them

- How to create components by self ?

- check swc file in Flash

- familiar with all kinds of components

CHAPTER 10

v2 Components

Components were originally introduced in Flash 5 under the moniker of *smart clips*. Their primary purpose was to encapsulate a complex piece of functionality for simple, efficient, and frequent reuse. Smart clips were fundamentally movie clips with a series of predefined parameters that could be quickly and easily updated via the Property inspectors, without the need for any knowledge of ActionScript.

Smart clips, like other aspects of Flash, have evolved with time and are now called components. In fact, with the release of Flash MX 2004, they're actually known as *v2 components* because they're built on version 2 (v2) of the Macromedia Component Architecture (v1 was introduced with Flash MX in 2002). The v2 architecture is based on a series of new classes; styles and skins that allow you to customize the appearance of a component; a depth and focus manager; enhanced accessibility implementation; and a new broadcaster/listener event model.

WARNING

For those of you familiar with v1 components from Flash MX, it's important to realize that the v2 component architecture represents a necessary shift to a more integrated framework for constructing rich media applications by building on the enhanced ActionScript 2.0 standards. Although v1 components can still be used within Flash MX 2004, it's not advisable to mix the two formats because it's likely to cause unpredictable behavior. Refer to your Flash MX 2004 reference documentation for details on upgrading your v1 components to the v2 architecture.

As mentioned previously, each of the v2 components has predefined parameters that you can set while authoring. In addition, each has a unique API of Action Script methods, properties, and events to help you set parameters and other options at runtime

All 31 v2 components can be grouped into five broad categories. Some are available only in Flash MX Professional 2004.

- **User interface (UI) components** give an application its visual look and feel. Examples of UI components include RadioButton, TextInput, and List.

- **Managers** are nonvisual components that allow you to manage specific features such as focus or depth within a Flash application. The StyleManager, FocusManager, DepthManager, and PopUpManager are all examples of manager components.

- **Media components** (Flash Professional only) include MediaController, MediaPlayback, and MediaDisplay; these components integrate sound and video streaming.

- **Data components** (Flash Professional only) facilitate the connection of UIs to back-end business logic. Examples include the WebServiceConnector and XMLConnector components.

- **Screen components** (Flash Professional only) include the ActionScript classes that help you control forms and slides.

Throughout this chapter, you will get familiar with the use of the Macromedia v2 UI components within the context of ActionScript-driven application development. The actual creation of custom components can be a complex and time-consuming task, or it can be extremely simple, depending on your requirements. Because of this range of complexity, the process of creating new custom components is beyond the scope of this book (and is not part of the certification exam). This chapter focuses solely on the usage of the v2 components, including:

- The benefits of using components

- Categories of v2 components

- Working with SWC files

- Component implementation

- Using handlers and listeners for component events

- Setting component parameters

- Customizing components using styles, skins, and themes

Exploring the Benefits of Components

There are a number of major benefits to using the Macromedia v2 UI components.

- It takes far less time to install and manipulate a component than it would to re-create it from scratch.

- All v2 UI components make extensive use of inheritance and encapsulation. While adding the first v2 component does increase the document's overall file size by approximately 25KB, each additional v2 component uses the same initial core functionality of the first component, thus reducing the total file size when incorporating multiple v2 UI components.

- Components provide an excellent and sophisticated introduction to object oriented programming concepts in Flash, including abstraction, inheritance, class declaration, methods, and properties.

- Macromedia has implemented many user-driven features that you may not even know exist (such as using the arrow keys to change items in a List component).

- All v2 UI components make use of the GlobalStyleFormat class to set their default color and font values used within a Flash movie, ensuring style consistency throughout a file.

- Styles, skins, and themes allow you to quickly and easily change the appearance of any instance of a v2 UI component.

- Many Macromedia v2 UI components share visual elements that make global look-and-feel manipulation much more efficient (once you know what to change).

- The majority of the v2 UI components implement a clearly defined ActionScript interface, which allows advanced developers to use them without manipulating symbols on the Stage.

- The v2 UI components developed by Macromedia have built-in accessibility functionality to allow seamless communication between the component and supported screen readers.

- In order for v2 UI components to share common behaviors, such as resizing, and receiving focus and keyboard input, they all extend the UIComponent class. To use the methods and properties of the UIComponent class, you simply call them from the component you are using. For example, to use the setFocus() method on a textArea component, your code would look like this: myTextArea.setFocus();.

Examining Component Categories

As mentioned earlier, Macromedia v2 components can be grouped into five broad categories: UI components, manager components, media components, data components and screen components. Let's take a closer look at the components in each group.

UI Components *(21 components)*

Following is a list of the updated v2 UI components available in Flash MX 2004. All of them have an entirely new set of ActionScript 2.0 methods, properties, and event handlers, described in detail in the upcoming "Implementation" section.

UI COMPONENT	DESCRIPTION
Accordian (Flash Professional only)	A navigation component comprising of a set of vertical main (and sub) section buttons. The main section buttons expand (like an accordion) to reveal sub-section buttons.
Alert (Flash Professional only) *mx.controls.Alert*	Similar to a pop-up window, the Alert can be used to present custom messages to users. It also contains buttons to allow users to respond to the messages displayed.
Button	A standard button that can be customized to include an icon.
Check-Box	A standard check box that permits a Boolean choice (true or false)
ComboBox	A drop-down list allowing users to select from one of the items contained within the list. There is also an input field at the top of the list that allows users to search the ComboBox list items.
DateChooser (Flash Professional only)	Not to be confused with a fully functional calendar. This component allows users to simply select dates from a calendar formatted list of days/months.
DateField (Flash Professional only)	A non-selectable text field with a calendar icon that displays a DateChooser when a user clicks anywhere inside the bounding box of the component.
DataGrid (Flash Professional only)	Similar to an HTML table, this component facilitates the displaying of data within a series of columns.
Label	A non-editable, single-line text field.
List	A multi-selectable scrolling list of options.
✓ Loader	A resizable container that can hold a loaded SWF or JPEG file.

UI Components   (CONTINUED)

UI COMPONENT	DESCRIPTION
Menu (Flash Professional only)	A simple drop-down menu, containing dynamically generated headings/items.
MenuBar (Flash Professional only)	Similar to the Menu component. The MenuBar displays a horizontal list of sub section menu headings/items.
NumericStepper	A set of arrow buttons and a text field, that increment or lower a numeric value based on the button selected.
ProgressBar	Used for displaying the progress of a process (usually file loading).
RadioButton	Small round Boolean choice (true or false) buttons that allow users to select among mutually exclusive options.
ScrollPane	A scrolling pane that displays movies, bitmaps, and SWF files.
TextArea	A text field that renders HTML text and inline images.
TextInput	A single-line text input field.
Tree (Flash Professional only)	Allows the displaying and manipulation of hierarchical data.
Window	A draggable window used to display content, The Window component contains a title bar, caption, border, and Close button.

Managers   (4 components)

The manager components are a series of nonvisual, class-based components that facilitate the management of various aspects of your v2 components.

MANAGER COMPONENT	DESCRIPTION
DepthManager class	Facilitates in the management of the relative depths of components and movie clips.
FocusManager class	Used to manage the order in which components receive focus when a user presses the Tab key to navigate through an application.
PopUpManager class	Allows the management and creation (and deletion) of popup windows.
StyleManager class	Used to manage and register styles and colors of components.

Media Components (3 components)

The media components (Flash Professional only) assist in the incorporation of streaming media into Flash documents. All of the media components require Flash Player 7 or later and do not support accessibility.

MEDIA COMPONENT	DESCRIPTION
MediaController (Flash Professional only)	A series of buttons (volume, pause/play, etc.) for controlling streaming media playback within an application.
MediaDisplay (Flash Professional only)	A window (or pane) that displays streaming media in an application
MediaPlayback (Flash Professional only)	A combination of the MediaDisplay and MediaController components.

Data Components (9 components)

The data components allow you to connect to (and capture) remote data, as well as store and work with that data locally. There's also the facility to save the data and update it remotely via the RDBMSResolver component. All the data components (with the exception of the DataProvider API) are only available in Flash MX 2004 Professional.

DATA COMPONENTS/CLASSES	DESCRIPTION
Data binding classes (Flash Professional only)	Facilitates the sharing of data between components, via data binding.
DataHolder (Flash Professional only)	Acts as a data warehouse for storing data and generating events when that data has changed. It also acts as a connector between other components, via data binding
DataProvider API	A series of methods and properties that a data source needs to have in order to have Array, RecordSet, and DataSet-based classes communicate with it.
DataSet (Flash Professional only)	Allows the modification, searching, sorting and indexing of data as collections of objects.
RDBMSResolver (Flash Professional only)	Creates an XML update packet that can be passed across to an external data source, such as an ASP/JSP page, servlet or Web Service, via a connector component, such as the XMLConnector or WebServiceConnector.
Web Service (Flash Professional only)	A package of classes for accessing Web Services that use Simple Object Access Protocol (SOAP).
WebServiceConnector (Flash Professional only)	Provides scriptless connection and access to Web Service method calls.

Data Components/Classes (CONTINUED)

DATA COMPONENTS/CLASSES	DESCRIPTION
XMLConnector (Flash Professional only)	An adapter that facilitates the connection of components to external XML sources, and has the ability to read or write XML, via HTTP post or get operations.
XUpdateResolver (Flash Professional only)	The XUpdateResolver component is used to convert changes made to a DataSet component into XUpdate statements.

Screen Components

The Screen class is the base class for screens that you create in the Screen Outline pane in Flash MX Professional 2004. Screens are top-level containers for creating applications and presentations that were developed to assist traditional OOP developers with the transition to Flash application development. The Screen class has two primary subclasses: Slide and Form.

SCREEN COMPONENT	DESCRIPTION
Form class (Flash Professional only)	Permits the manipulation of form application screens at runtime.
Screen class overview (Flash Professional only)	The base class for Slides and Forms.
Slide class (Flash Professional only)	Permits the manipulation of Slide presentation screens at runtime.

Working with SWC Files

A SWC (Small Web Component) is a Flash component movie clip that has been exported for distribution and installation. Unlike v1 components, v2 components included with Flash MX 2004 are not FLA files—they are SWC files. Essentially, a SWC file is a Zip-like file (packaged and expanded by means of the PKZip archive format) that is generated by the Flash authoring tool, to facilitate easier component distribution and installation. In order for a SWC to be valid, it must contain the following when exported:

- An iterator interface

- A collection interface

- A collection implementation class

- A collection item class

First Run\ Components → Component Panel → Library

When you're ready to install the newly created component, the associated SWC needs to be placed in the `First Run\Components` folder. Once in this folder, the new component will appear in the Component panel. Then, when you add the component to the Stage, from the Components panel, a compiled clip symbol will be added to the Library.

The following table describes the contents of a SWC file.

SWC FILE CONTENTS	DESCRIPTION
`catalog.xml`	(Required) The primary purpose of this file is to serve as a directory reference for the other files within the SWC. This XML file outlines the contents of the component package (i.e. its classes).
Source code	The source code is one or more ActionScript files that contain class declarations for the component, such as; the iterator and collection interfaces, and the collection item and implementation classes. The source code is used only for type checking when sub-classing components and is not compiled by the authoring tool, since the compiled bytecode is already in the implementing SWF file.
Implementing SWF files	(Required) These are the SWF files that implement the components. One or more components can be defined in a single SWF file. If the component is created with Flash MX 2004, only one component is exported per SWF file.
Live Preview SWF files	(Optional) The Live Preview SWFs are used for previewing the component on the stage within the authoring environment.
Debug info	(Optional) The inclusion of a debug SWD file, that relates to the implementing SWF file, allows the component to be debugged at a later stage.
Icon	(Optional) This 18 x 18, 8 bit PNG file is used to display a custom component icon within the component library. If no icon is included, a default icon is displayed
Property inspector	(Optional) The Property inspector is an SWF file that is displayed in the Property inspector within the authoring environment. It serves as a custom GUI for modifying the components properties.

Deploying Flash Components

Despite the fact that the range of components differs between Flash MX 2004 and Flash MX Professional 2004, the technique for adding components and creating instances is exactly the same.

Adding a New Component

The process involved in adding a component into Flash is rather simple: You open the Components panel (Window > Components), choose the required component, and finally, either drag the desired component to your Stage or double-click it. Once this step is complete, a single compiled component instance will exist in your Library (and on the Stage/Timeline).

> **NOTE**
>
> If you wish to add a component programmatically at runtime, it's important to remember that an instance of the component must first exist in the Library before that component can be called.

Creating a Component Instance

Once your component has been added to the Library, there are two ways to add it to the Stage/Timeline:

- **With drag and drop.** Drag the component symbol from the Library into a keyframe on the Stage (or select a keyframe on Stage and double-click the desired component). After it's on Stage, the component's parameters can be set directly in the Component Parameters panel or by using ActionScript.

> **TIP**
>
> If you plan to use ActionScript to target the component at some time in the future, make sure you give the component an instance name in the Property inspector.

- **With ActionScript.** Either use the `attachMovie()` method (with the component linkage property), or use the `UIObject.createClassObject()` method. Examples of both these ActionScript techniques follow.

Here's an example of the `attachMovie()` method:

```
// attach component
var comp_mc = mcTarget.attachMovie("FCheckBoxSymbol",
 "myCheckBox", 5);
// use component methods to set parameters
comp_mc.setLabel("Click Me");
```

Symbol Identifier

And here is the `createClassObject()` method

depth

```
createClassObject(mx.controls.CheckBox,"myCheckBox",5,
 {label:"Click Me"});
```

> **NOTE**
>
> If ActionScript is used to attach the component, all parameters must also be set using ActionScript.

Handling Component Events with Handlers and Listeners

The simplest way to handle user-component interaction (events) is to use the `on()` event handler. The `on()` event handler code is placed directly within the component instance on the Stage and automatically generates an event object, `eventObj`, whenever an event is triggered and passed to the handler. The event object contains a series of properties that hold information about the event that has occurred.

In the following example, the `on(click)` event handler code has been attached to a `Button` component instance. When the user clicks the button, the message "Hello New York!" is sent to the Output panel:

```
on(click){
   trace "Hello New York!";
}
```

If you're an intermediate-to-advanced ActionScript user, a more powerful way to handle component events is via listeners—objects or functions that "listen or watch out" for an event to occur; for example, when a user interacts with a component. Within Flash MX 2004, all v2 components (with the exception of the `Alert` component) broadcast events that can be listened for.

Any object that is registered as a listener (via the `addEventListener()` method) with an event broadcaster (a component instance) can be notified of an event. The listener is assigned a function that handles the event when it's received. You can register multiple listeners to one component instance, or register one listener to multiple component instances. If the listener is an object, it must have a callback function defined that will be invoked when the event is triggered. Usually, that callback function has the same name as the event with which the listener is registered. If the listener is a function, the function is invoked when the event is triggered.

In the following example, our event object, eventObject, is passed to the listener object, myListenerObject, as a parameter. The listener object has a property, click, which contains information about the event that occurred (in this case, a function). You can use the event object inside the listener callback function to access information about the type of event that occurred and identifying the instance that broadcasted it. In addition, it represents a better approach to coding because it allows you to keep your code centralized and easy to read should you have to debug errors.

```
//define a new listener object
myListenerObject = new Object();
//define the click property and associated callback function
myListenerObject.click = function(eventObject){       } callback function
  if (eventObject.target == myButton){
    trace("You clicked the button!");
  }
}
//register the listener to the event broadcaster (myButton)
myButton.addEventListener("click", myListenerObject);
```

Setting Parameters

Every component has a series of parameters that can be updated to change its appearance or behavior. A parameter is simply a manually configurable property or method that is displayed in the Property inspector and Component inspector panels. These parameters have been predefined by the component author.

All parameters that can be set while authoring can also be set at runtime with ActionScript. It's important to remember that like all objects within Flash, components can only be targeted once they have completely loaded. Trying to set the property of a component (or an object) before it's loaded will produce unexpected results. In the following example, a blank checkBox component, myCheckBox, has been placed on the Stage and has its label and selected properties set via ActionScript at runtime.

```
myCheckBox.label = "Unclick Me!";
myCheckBox.selected = true;
```

> **NOTE**
> Setting a component parameter with ActionScript overrides any value set while authoring.

All v2 components inherit, or *extend*, the properties and methods of the UIObject and the UIComponent *superclasses*. They also contain a set of properties and methods that are unique to each component. For example, the ScrollPane component has a scrollDrag property, and the Tree component has a nodeOpen property.

Customizing Components

The default theme (collection of styles and skins) that accompanies all v2 components is called Halo. The Halo theme was designed and developed by Macromedia to provide a consistent overall look and feel for all components used within Flash documents.

As attractive as Halo is, it goes without saying that there will come a time when you will want to branch out. You will need to customize your components in order for them to fit within the style of a particular project. The following sections discuss the options available to you for customizing components. You can

- Modify or replace a component's skins

- Apply a custom theme

- Use the Styles API

Skins

Skins are the graphic or movie clip symbols that give components their user interface appearance. Most skins contain shapes that are representative of the item's functionality. For example, the down arrow of the ScrollBar subcomponent is made up of three skins: ScrollDownArrowDisabled, ScrollDownArrowUp, and ScrollDownArrowDown.

Unlike their v1 counterparts, v2 components are compiled clips (SWCs); so you can't open and modify their assets in the Library as you could with the v1 components. Instead, a series of FLA files (called *themes*) that contain the default component skins, are installed into the Macromedia\First Run\ComponentFLA directory when Flash is first installed. The individual skins for each component are located within the Themes folder in the Library panel of each theme FLA.

Themes

As mentioned previously, a theme is a collection of styles and skins stored in a separate FLA file, located in the Macromedia\First Run\ComponentFLA directory. Flash MX 2004 comes with two themes: the default Halo theme (HaloTheme.fla) and a Sample theme (SampleTheme.fla). The Sample theme makes use of the complete set of available styles.

Because the built-in components with Flash MX 2004 are now compiled (as SWC files), you are no longer able to edit these components' assets directly in your Flash project. In order to make changes, you'll need to modify and apply a theme to the component. At first, having to modify component assets outside your Flash project may seem a bit of a hassle, but it's actually a much cleaner and more reusable method of skinning components. While the styles allow you to tweak color, font, and other component properties, themes give you the ability to go in and edit the actual movie clip assets that a component uses.

Styles

Styles in Flash MX 2004 can best be described as properties that determine the way a particular component will be displayed. All components that install with Flash MX 2004 use the Halo theme by default.

The Halo theme uses a subset of available styles. For example, the Button component supports the following styles: themeColor, color, disabledColor, fontFamily, fontStyle, fontSize, and fontWeight.

Every component instance has a set of style properties and methods, as well as, the setStyle() and getStyle() methods. These are used to access and modify a component's style properties.

Style properties can be stored in one of several places:

- Directly on the component instance
- Within the component class
- Within the _global class

Traditionally, component styles are set using the style property of the _global object (i.e. _global.style). If you change a property's value on the *global* style declaration (as opposed to an *instance* style declaration), the change will be propagated to all component instances within your Flash file (provided no other styles have previously been declared). The following example demonstrates, modifying the text styles of an instance style declaration, and a global style declaration:

```
//Modify the text style only on myTextComponent
myTextComponent.setStyle("fontSize",12);
myTextComponent setStyle("fontFamily" , "_sans");

//Modify the text style on ALL components within my Flash file
global.style.setStyle("fontSize",12);
global.style.setStyle("fontFamily" , "_sans");
```

Now you might be wondering, which of the style declarations takes precedence within the Flash "chain of command." As is the case with most things in Flash, there's a structured hierarchy to the way Flash resolves issues (i.e. data, variables, styles, etc.). When working with component styles, Flash will always start in the center and work its way out. That is, Flash will first look on the actual component instance for a style declaration. If it can't find one, it will then move to the styleName property (of the instance), then to the class style declaration, (i.e. the

instance → component class → global → undefined

CSSStyleDeclaration), and then finally to the global style declaration. If no styles are returned for the full declaration hierarchy, an undefined value will be returned. So, in answering the question as to what takes precedence, the instance style declaration will always take precedence over the global style declaration.

The following table represents the complete list of the available component styles in Flash MX 2004. (2.)

STYLE	DESCRIPTION
backgroundColor	The background color of a component. This is the only color style that doesn't inherit its value. The default value is transparent.
borderColor	The black border section of a three-dimensional border or the color section of a two-dimensional border. The default value is 0x000000 (black).
borderStyle	The border of the component: "none", "inset", "outset", or "solid". This style does not inherit its value. The default value is "solid".
buttonColor	The face of a button and a section of the three-dimensional border. The default value is 0xEFEEEF (light gray).
color	The component label text. The default value is 0x000000 (black).
disabledColor	The disabled color for text. The default color is 0x848384 (dark gray).
fontFamily	The font name for text. The default value is _sans.
fontSize	The point size for the font. The default value is 10.
fontStyle	The font style: either "normal" or "italic". The default value is "normal".
fontWeight	The font weight: "normal" or "bold". The default value is "normal".
highlightColor	A section of the three-dimensional border. The default value is 0xFFFFFF (white).
marginLeft	A number indicating the left margin for text. The default value is 0.
marginRight	A number indicating the right margin for text. The default value is 0.
scrollTrackColor	The scroll track for a scroll bar. The default value is 0xEFEEEF (light gray).

Component Styles   (CONTINUED)

STYLE	DESCRIPTION
shadowColor	A section of the three-dimensional border. The default value is 0x848384 (dark gray).
symbolBackgroundColor	The background color of check boxes and radio buttons. The default value is 0xFFFFFF (white).
symbolBackgroundDisabledColor	The background color of check boxes and radio buttons when disabled. The default value is 0xEFEEEF (light gray).
symbolBackgroundPressedColor	The background color of check boxes and radio buttons when pressed. The default value is 0xFFFFFF (white).
symbolColor	The check mark of a check box or the dot of a radio button. The default value is 0x000000 (black).
symbolDisabledColor	The disabled check mark or radio button dot color. The default value is 0x848384 (dark gray).
textAlign	The text alignment: "left", "right", or "center". The default value is "left".
textDecoration	The text decoration: "none" or "underline". The default value is "none".
textIndent	A number indicating the text indent. The default value is 0.

Sample Questions

1. Which of the following is *not* a benefit of using Macromedias prebuilt v2 components?

   A. Possible time savings by using prewritten code.

   B. Good code examples to learn from.

   C. Macromedia components stream into the Flash Player over the duration of the main movie Timeline.

   D. Simple color and font changes are easier to make.

2. What is the downside of Macromedia components making extensive use of inheritance and encapsulation?

   A. Global variables cannot be used.

   B. Increased file size for first component added.

   C. Components cannot be modified.

   D. SWF files cannot be loaded at runtime.

3. Which ActionScript method should be used to bring a component from the Library to the Stage?

   A. attachMovie()    create ClassObject ()

   B. addComponent()

   C. insertMovie()

   D. openComponent()

4. What is the name of the default theme for Macromedia v2 components?

   A. Star

   B. Halo

   C. Blur

   D. Heaven

5. What is a SWC?

   A. A SWF that has been converted into a component

   B. An exported component file format

   C. A component's skin file format

   D. A compiled theme format

Working with Text

Flash MX 2004 contains several new text features that enhance the displayed appearance of and interaction with text in Flash documents. Timeline Effects, Cascading Style Sheets (CSS), small text optimization, hyperlink improvements, and inline images are just a few of these features.

Flash documents display text via three types of text fields: *static, dynamic* and or *input*. Static text fields are exactly that, *static*. They are created once at author time, and their content stays the same until the author manually modifies them. Dynamic and input text fields are TextField objects that, once assigned an instance name, can be targeted via ActionScript to dynamically set, change, and format their contents. The TextFormat class allows you to set character and paragraph formatting for the TextField object, and Flash Player 7 now supports a subset of HTML tags that you can use for formatting.

New multilingual enhancements within Flash Player 7 provide added support for Unicode text encoding. You now have the ability to display multilingual content within a single text field, provided the appropriate Unicode fonts are installed on the user's machine. Additionally, using the new Strings panel, developers can author a document in their native language and then have the same document displayed in another language when viewed on a non-native-language system (provided the appropriate translation XML files have been created). Full details on the Strings panel can be found in the Flash MX 2004 Help documentation Using Flash > Creating Multilanguage Text > Authoring multilanguage text with the Strings panel.

> **WARNING**
> If the text in a SWF file contains non-English language glyphs (characters or symbols) that are not supported by the specified font, Flash Player 7 will attempt to locate a substitute font on the user's machine. Undesirable results may occur if the Player is unable to locate an appropriate substitute font. For this reason, you must embed unique font sets within your Flash document if you are unsure whether the end user will have the required font set installed. Although this adds to your document's overall file size, at least you'll be certain the end user will be able to view the content.

With Flash MX 2004's new Timeline effects (prebuilt animation effects), you can now easily and quickly add motion effects to text. For example, you can use Timeline effects to make text bounce, fade in or out, or even explode.

You can also assign HTML formatted text, which may optionally use CSS styles, directly to a text field. In Flash Player 7 and later, HTML text that you assign to a text field can contain embedded media (movie clips, SWF files, and JPEG files). The text will wrap around the embedded media, just as a web browser wraps text around media embedded in an HTML document.

This chapter looks at the usage of text within Flash, including:

- Formatting text using supported HTML tags
- Creating and loading text styles
- Formatting text dynamically
- Using style sheets to format text

Supported HTML Tags

The following table lists the HTML tags supported by Flash Player 7.

TAG	NAME	DESCRIPTION
`<a>`	Anchor	Creates a hyperlink.
`<b>`	Bold	Renders text, located within opening and closing anchor tags, in boldface, i.e. provided a bold typeface exists for the font used to display the text.
` `	Break	Creates a new line (or line break) within a text field.
`<font>`	Font	Specifies the display font(s) for a block of text wrapped within opening and closing font tags.
`<img>`	Image	Allows you to embed external JPEGs, SWFs, and movie clips within dynamic and input text fields. Provided the text fields are set to multi-line, and text wrap is on, the text will automatically wrap around images that are embedded within the text field.

Supported HTML Tags   (CONTINUED)

TAG	NAME	DESCRIPTION
`<i>`	Italic	Renders text, located between opening and closing italic tags, in an italic typeface (i.e. provided an italic typeface exists for the font used to display the text).
`<li>`	List Item	Creates a bullet list item of the text located within opening and closing list item tags.
`<p>`	Paragraph	Creates a new paragraph.
`<span>`	Span	Applies a text style (as defined by a CSS) to a block of text wrapped within opening and closing span tags.
`<tagformat>`	Tag Format	Used within HTML text fields, this tag allows you to use a subset of paragraph-formatting properties (such as indentation, leading and margins) of the `TextFormat` class.

Text Styles

A text *style* is a collection of formatting rules that together specify the format of textual elements contained within a document. Each rule associates a style name, or selector, with one or more style properties and their values. For example, the following style defines a selector named `headingText`:

```
headingText { text-align: left}
```

The beauty of using text styles within your documents, is that you can define a custom style class once, and then apply instances of this style throughout your text. Then, if you need to make a modification to a particular style (for example all the body text within your document) you simply make the change once (within the class definition), and the change will be propagated throughout all instances of that class.

In Flash Player 7 and later, you have the ability to apply Cascading Style Sheet styles to dynamic and input text fields using the `TextField.StyleSheet` class. Using this class you can load styles from an external CSS file and apply them to HTML or XML formatted text using the `TextField.styleSheet` property.

Creating Styles

As mentioned earlier, in order to create text styles within Flash MX 2004, you use the `TextField.StyleSheet` class. Once you've instantiated the class, you add new styles to you TextField.StyleSheet object using the `setStyle()` method. This method accepts two parameters: the name of the style, and an object that contains the definitions of that style's properties.

In the following example, we instantiate a new TextField.StyleSheet object, named myClassicTextStyleObject, and then add two new text styles (classicBodyText and classicHeading).

```
//create an object instance
var myClassicTextStyleObject = new TextField.StyleSheet();
//add our styles to our object
myClassicTextStyleObject.setStyle("classicBodyText",
  {fontFamily: 'Times,Roman,serif',
  fontSize: '12px',
  color:'#000000',
  fontWeight: 'normal'}
);
myClassicTextStyleObject.setStyle("classicHeading",
  {fontFamily: 'Times,Roman,serif',
  fontSize: '18px',
  color:'#CC0000',
  fontWeight: 'bold'}
);
//save memory by deleting our object when we've finished with it
delete myClassicTextStyleObject;
```

You also have the choice of creating style sheets in your favorite text editor, saved with a .css suffix. These external style sheets can be loaded at runtime, as described in the following section.

WARNING

If you create a new text style that has the same name as that of an existing style, the new one will overwrite the old one.

NOTE

The `TextField.StyleSheet` class is only available for SWF files that target Flash Player 7 or later.

Loading Styles

In the preceding section, we outlined how to create a new style within the Flash authoring environment using ActionScript. As discussed, you can define styles within Flash, or in an external CSS file, using a standard text editor and then load that file into a StyleSheet object at runtime.

Styles defined in the external CSS file are added to the StyleSheet object at the time the style sheet is loaded. To load an external CSS file, simply use the load() method of the TextField.StyleSheet class. Using the onLoad event handler, we can determine when the CSS file has finished loading. Here's an example:

```
var myStyleSheet = new TextField.StyleSheet();
//call the load method of the myStyleSheet object
myStyleSheet.load("styles.css");
//check to see if the CSS has finished loading
myStyleSheet.onLoad = function(ok) {
      if(ok) {
      // output the style names
      trace(this.getStyleNames());
      } else {
      //theres been a problem loading the CSS
      trace("Error loading the CSS file.");
      }
}
```

(handwritten margin notes):
new TextField. StyleSheet
load ("style. css");
onload = function (ok)

Dynamic Formatting

In addition to using styles to set text properties, you can use the built-in `TextFormat` class to set text field properties. The `TextFormat` class allows you to change format settings such as font, size, and color for a TextField object—just as you would by using the Property inspector. Once you have created a TextFormat object, you can apply it to any text field with an instance name. Like most other objects, the TextFormat object must be instantiated before it is used.

In the following example, we create an instance of the TextFormat object called `myModernTextFormat`:

```
myModernTextFormat = new TextFormat();
```

Then we need to designate the specific format properties of the new TextFormat object. This can be done when you create the object, or you can set properties later.

```
myModernTextFormat = new TextFormat;
myModernTextFormat.font = "Arial";
myModernTextFormat.size = 12;
myModernTextFormat.bold = true;
myModernTextFormat.align = left;
```

To apply the new text format to a text field, use the `setTextFormat()` method:

```
myTextField.setTextFormat(myModernTextFormat)
```

where `myTextField` is the text field instance name, and `myModernTextFormat` is the name of the TextFormat object.

TextField.StyleSheet class

Earlier, we saw how to create a StyleSheet object, using the `TextField.StyleSheet` class, which contains text-formatting rules that define text properties such as font size, color, and other formatting styles. You can then apply these styles to a TextField object (i.e. either a dynamic or input text field) that contains either HTML or XML-formatted text. The text contained within the TextField object will then be formatted according to the tag styles that are defined within the StyleSheet object.

To apply styles to a TextField object, assign the StyleSheet object to a TextField object's styleSheet property:

```
myTextFieldObject.styleSheet = new TextField.StyleSheet();
```

Sample Questions

1. Which of the following HTML tags is *not* supported within Flash MX 2004?

   (handwritten: `<a> <b> <i> <br> <p> <span>`)

   A. `<a>`

   (handwritten: `<img> <tag formats> <li> <font>`)

   B. `<img>`

   C. `<p>`

   D. `<table>`

2. How many parameters are accepted by the setStyle() method of the TextField.StyleSheet class?

   A. 1

   (handwritten: `setStyle ( styleName, style );`)

   B. 2

   C. 3

   D. None

3. What event is used to determine whether an external CSS has finished loading?

   (handwritten: `Load ()`)

   A. loadComplete

   (handwritten: `onLoad ()`)

   B. loadTrue

   C. onLoad

   D. onLoadComplete

4. Which method is used to apply the new TextFormat object to a text field?

   A. setTextFormat()

   B. setTextObject()

   C. setTextFormatStyle()

   D. setStyleFormat()

CHAPTER 12

Beyond The Browser

One of the greatest advantages of the Macromedia Flash format over its competition is its ubiquity and consistency across platforms. At the time this guide was written, Flash Player 6 was installed on over 90 percent of all Internet-enabled PCs (according to the NPD Online Research Worldwide Survey conducted September 2003). Flash players have been developed for everything from desktop PCs and Web-enabled TVs to handheld devices. Flash provides a transportable application-development platform that is unrivaled in its ability to provide a consistent user experience across devices.

It is important to remember that your Flash movies are not discrete islands in an ocean of media. Whether it is running in the stand-alone player, in Macromedia Central, in a projector, or as a plug-in to a web browser, your movie is being hosted within another application. The host application may provide additional functionality that your movie can access. Flash provides several methods that your movie can use to communicate with its host application and device.

In this chapter, we'll look at the various methods by which Flash can communicate with the web browser, including:

- Calling the host application using the `fscommand()` function

- Extending Flash by incorporating JavaScript API elements

- Setting up a pseudo-URL

- Using third-party applications

Using *fscommand*

The fscommand () function provides a way for Flash movies to make calls to the host application. This function has been around since before Flash was Flash. The fs in fscommand refers to FutureSplash, the original name for the Flash Player.

When you use fscommand, the features supported will of course vary from application to application. Since the actual functionality is provided by the host application and not the Flash Player, the feature set and consistency can vary dramatically. It is extremely important to test thoroughly on all target platforms.

> **CAUTION**
>
> When your application relies on the fscommand, your movie becomes tied to a particular host application. When doing this, you may lose some or all of the portability and compatibility features that make the Flash Player so valuable. Use the fscommand only if there is no other way to accomplish what you need to do.

The fscommand takes two arguments. Both arguments are String-type arguments and are passed to the host application. The host application must evaluate the two arguments and make the appropriate response.

The first string argument represents the name of a command. This is not a true function call, and so the command argument is not a function object. It is a string that the host application will use to determine what should be done.

The second argument comprises the parameters that will be passed to the host application. Like the command, the parameters are passed as a string, and the host application must know how to deal with it. By convention, multiple parameters can be in the form of a comma-delimited list of values, but they will still be passed as a single string value.

> **NOTE**
>
> Keep in mind that fscommand does not return anything. It is a one-way street: You can make calls to the host application and pass parameters, but the host application will not return anything to your fscommand call.

The following table illustrates the specifics for FSCommands:

COMMAND	PARAMETERS	PURPOSE
quit	None	Quits and closes the projector.
allowscale	true or false	When set to true, allows the SWF to scale to 100% of the player window. When set to false, causes the SWF to be rendered at its pre-defined, original size.
fullscreen	true or false	When set to true, forces the Flash Player to render SWFs in fullscreen mode with no menu items. When set to false, the Flash Player reverts to default display mode and menu items are visible.
showmenu	true or false	Allows the default context menu items to be dimmed (when set to false) or active (when set to true). The About Flash Player option will always be visible.
exec	Path to application	Allows the projector to execute an application that lies within a specially named fscommand sub directory.
trapallkeys	true or false	Sends all key events to the onClipEvent(keyDown/keyUp) handler in Flash Player when set to true.

Using *fscommand* in the Browser

The fscommand can be used when your movie is hosted in a web browser, with varying success. The most outstanding exceptions are Netscape 6 and Netscape 7 PR1, which currently do not support the fscommand.

When used in a browser, the fscommand can call user-defined JavaScript functions. All fscommand calls made while your movie is hosted in a browser are passed to a single function that evaluates the arguments passed to it. This "hook" function must be named in a particular way so that your movie can target it. The name begins with the name of your movie as specified in the <OBJECT> and <EMBED> tags and is followed by _DoFSCommand. If your movie is identified as fscommandTestMovie, then your hook function will be named fscommandTestMovie_DoFSCommand. This allows several movies on the same page to each have their own fscommand hook function.

Following is an example of the code needed to embed a movie in a web page (which will only work in Internet Explorer). Notice that in addition to the filename of your SWF, there is an additional ID parameter. It is this ID that is used in targeting the hook function.

```
<OBJECT classid="clsid:D27CDB6E-AE6D-11cf-96B8-444553540000"
  codebase="http://download.macromedia.com/pub/shockwave/
cabs/flash/swflash.cab#version=6,0,0,0"
  ID="fscommandTestMovie" WIDTH="550" HEIGHT="400" ALIGN="">
<PARAM NAME=movie VALUE="fscommandTestMovie.swf">
<PARAM NAME=quality VALUE=high>
<PARAM NAME=bgcolor VALUE=#CCCCCC>
<EMBED src="fscommandTestMovie.swf" quality=high bgcolor=#CCCCCC
  WIDTH="550" HEIGHT="400" swLiveConnect=true
  ID="fscommandTestMovie" NAME="fscommandTestMovie" ALIGN=""
  TYPE="application/x-shockwave-flash"
  PLUGINSPAGE="http://www.macromedia.com/go/getflashplayer">
</EMBED>
</OBJECT>
```

In the Publish Settings dialog box, under HTML, select the Flash with FSCommand template. Flash will create an HTML page that contains the <OBJECT> and <EMBED> tags, along with the JavaScript and VBScript functions. The default template does not do anything; it just provides a place to add your custom code to catch your movie's fscommand calls.

The code sample that follows takes the default fscommand template and adds a switch statement that allows your movie to have access to a couple of browser-native JavaScript functions.

```
<SCRIPT LANGUAGE=JavaScript>          hook  function
<!—
var InternetExplorer = navigator.appName.indexOf("Microsoft") != -1;
// Handle all the the FSCommand messages in a Flash movie
function fscommandTestMovie_DoFSCommand(command, args) {
  var fscommandTestMovieObj = InternetExplorer ? fscommandTestMovie :
document.fscommandTestMovie;
//The following switch statement has been added to the default
//fscommand template
  args = args.split(",");
  switch(command){
    case "resizeTo":
      window.resizeTo(Number(args[0]),Number(args[1]));
      break;
    case "moveTo":
      window.moveTo(Number(args[0]),Number(args[1]));
      break;
    case "moveBy":
      window.moveBy(Number(args[0]),Number(args[1]));
      break;
  }
}
// Hook for Internet Explorer
if (navigator.appName && navigator.appName.indexOf("Microsoft") != -1 &&
  navigator.userAgent.indexOf("Windows") != -1 &&
navigator.userAgent.indexOf("Windows 3.1") == -1) {
  document.write('<SCRIPT LANGUAGE=VBScript\> \n');
  document.write('on error resume next \n');
  document.write('Sub fscommandTestMovie_FSCommand(ByVal command,
```

```
ByVal args)\n');
   document.write(' call fscommandTestMovie_DoFSCommand(command,
args)\n');
   document.write('end sub\n');
   document.write('</SCRIPT\> \n');
}
// —>
</SCRIPT>
```

We now have access to three JavaScript methods from within our movie. We can call these methods by using the fscommand as illustrated in the following example:

```
//resizes the browser window to the dimensions provided
fscommand("resizeTo","700,500");
//moves the browser window to the locations provided
fscommand("moveTo","100,100");
//moves the browser window by the values provided
fscommand("moveBy","700,500");
```

flash

Using the JavaScript API

The Flash *JavaScript API (JSAPI)* is a new feature in Flash MX 2004, which is based on the Netscape JavaScript API and Flash Document Object Model (DOM). The JSAPI allows developers to write custom scripts that extend the Flash authoring environment by:

- Adding custom commands to menus ✓
- Controlling on-Stage objects
- Repeating (or automating) sequences of commands or events ✓
- Adding custom tools to the tool bar

JSAPI scripts can be written in any standard text editor, such as Note Pad, Text Pad or even Dreamweaver, and need to be saved with a .JSFL extension within the `C:\Documents and Settings\<user>\Local Settings\ Application Data\ Macromedia\Flash MX2004\<language>\Configuration\Commands` directory.

One of the easiest ways to create a JSFL file is by using the Save As Command button in the History panel. Use the following steps to try creating a JSFL using this technique:

1. Open a new Flash document.

2. Select the Square drawing tool and choose the red fill color.

3. Draw a square on the center of the Stage.

4. Open the History Panel.

5. Select the Rectangle history item.

6. Open the History Options Panel and select the "Save As Command" option.

7. Name the command "Create Red Square" and click OK. The new command (JSFL) file will be automatically saved to the Commands folder, which we can open and edit the same as any other script file. Now, if you look under the Commands menu heading, within Flash, you'll notice that our new "Create Red Square" command has been added. Each time we select this command a new red square will be created in the center of the Stage.

Another way to use JSAPI scripts is to embed them within ActionScript using the `MMExecute()` function. Unfortunately, this function only works with custom user-interface element, such as a component Property inspector, or a SWF panel within the authoring environment.

Guy Watson, at FlashGuru, has developed a series of custom JSAPI scripts that he's bundled as extensions for easy installation into Flash MX 2004. One extension, the AutoSave panel, can save a significant amount of work in many situations. This extension adds a new panel to the Flash MX 2004 Authoring Tools, which enables you to specify an interval for automatically saving the document you are working on. Intervals can be set in minutes or hours. These extensions, which are free to download, are available from `http://www.flashguru.co.uk/extensions.php`

To find out more information on the JSAPI, go to `www.macromedia.com/go/jsapi_info_en`.

> **NOTE**
>
> JSAPI commands have no effect outside the Flash authoring environment or within the Flash Player, even if called from within ActionScript.

Using a Pseudo-URL

It is possible to make calls to JavaScript functions without using the `fscommand`. The *pseudo-URL* takes advantage of the `getURL()` function to pass a function call to the browser. Rather than passing a standard URL as the argument to the `getURL()` function, a specially formed URL is used in the following format:

```
getURL("javascript:functionName();");
```

Most browsers understand this special URL format, and by using it you can achieve better compatibility with a larger number of browsers than with the `fscommand` function.

Like the fscommand, the pseudo-URL does not provide any means for a value to be returned to the location of your call.

To use a pseudo-URL, the following function is defined on the same page that contains your movie:

```
<script>
function popUpWindow(URLStr,width,height){
  popUpWin = open(URLStr, 'popUpWin', 'toolbar=no, location=no,
status=no, menubar=no, scrollbar=no, resizable=no, width='+width+',
height='+height);
}
</script>
```

You can now call this popUpWindow() function and pass its arguments using the getURL() function and a pseudo-URL. A button in your movie used to launch the popup window might contain the following code:

```
on(press){
  getURL("javascript:popUpWindow(\"somePage.html\", 500, 600);");
}
```

You are not limited to calling user-defined functions only. You can make a call to any native JavaScript function or object method. You can open an alert box straight from your movie, without any supporting JavaScript functions. All you need to add to your movie is the following:

```
getURL("javascript:alert('hello, I am an alert called from a
→ movie');");
```

Though it is usually better to define your JavaScript functions in the page and make calls to them from your movie, it is possible to do it all from ActionScript. Using the pseudo-URL, the following code creates an instance of an object and calls a method of that object. There is no JavaScript on the HTML page; it is all being passed to the page, from the movie, using ActionScript. When run, this code will create an alert box that says "30."

```
on(press){
  var command;
  command += "fred={"
  command +=   "name:'Fred',"
  command +=   "age:30,"
  command +=   "getAge:function(){"
  command +=     "alert(this.age);"
  command +=   "}"
  command += "};"
  command += "fred.getAge();"

  getURL("javascript:"+command);
}
```

Employing Third-Party Applications

Several third-party companies offer applications that allow you to embed Flash movies within a stand-alone application. These applications provide your Flash movies with features not found in the stand-alone player or projector. The product feature sets differ, but most provide access to the host file system, can launch applications, and allow your movie to act as a screen saver. These applications usually offer a series of supported `fscommand` calls that your movie uses to communicate with the application.

Flash Studio Pro, by Mulitidmedia Limited (`http://www.multidmedia.com/soft-ware/flashstudio/`) is an example of one of these third-party SWF2EXE applications. It allows you to take SWF files and compile a Win32 EXE (projector) file or an SCR (screensaver) file. Unlike the standard EXEs that are output with Flash MX 2004, Flash Studio Pro extends the SWF command set with over 400 new custom FSCommands. Unlike the limited `fscommand` set that comes default with Flash MX 2004, Flash Studio Pro's custom FSCommands allow database connection, real-time socket communication, as well as support for video and HTML capabilities.

Sample Questions

1. Which of the following is *not* a disadvantage of using the `fscommand()` function?

    A. Your movie becomes tied to a particular host application.

    B. You can have only one `fscommand` call in your movie.

    C. Use of `fscommand()` use is not supported by Netscape 6.

    D. The host application will not be able to return values to your `fscommand` call.

2. Which of the following is the best reason for using the `getURL()` function, instead of `fscommand()`, when communicating with the host application?

    A. `getURL()` can receive return values from the host application.

    B. You don't have to use JavaScript to interact with the host application.

    C. `getURL()` is supported by the Flash Player 6.

    D. `getURL()` is compatible with more browsers than `fscommand()`.

3. Which of the following is the correct way to create an alert box using getURL() and JavaScript?

   A. getURL = function ("javascript:alert("Hello World!"));

   B. getURL(alert,"Hello World!");

   C. getURL(javascript (alert,'Hello World!'););

   D. getURL("javascript:alert('Hello World!');");

4. Which command allows you to embed JSAPI commands into ActionScript?   *How to*

   A. MMExecute()

   B. ExecuteJSAPI()

   C. RunMMJSAPI()

   D. MMCommandExecute()

5. Which of the following is *not* an advantage of using third-party SWF2EXE applications?

   A. They expand Flash's default fscommand set.

   B. They allow you to create SCR (screensaver) files.

   C. They integrate seamlessly into the Flash authoring environment.

   D. They allow access to the host file system.

CHAPTER 13

Rich Media

Rich media is the term given to those forms of Web-based media such as audio and video, which provide a richer, more satisfying end-user experience. As opposed to standard text-based websites, those sites employing correctly implemented rich media are far more likely to retain their customers through engaging content delivery. In this chapter, we discuss two elements of Flash MX 2004 that particularly lend themselves to the delivery of rich media: sound and video components.

The Macromedia Flash Player 7 can display high-quality digital video that need not be played within the QuickTime player. Gone are the days of presenting Flash movies with a long series of JPEG images. Gone are the days of creating Flash 4–compliant SWF files for the QuickTime player. We can now deliver highly interactive video—on the Web.

Macromedia has also added to Flash player 7 the capability to load (and stream) native MP3 audio content at runtime. Flash applications can now present a user with a remarkably long list of songs or sounds to be played upon request—without requiring costly server-side applications or manual compilation of media into SWF files.

With the release of Flash Player 7, Macromedia has introduced real-time audio, video, and text communications. This can be implemented with no additional downloads on the client machines. (It does, however, require installation of the Macromedia Flash Communication Server, which is not discussed in this book.)

In this chapter, we look at the types of audio and files that are supported by Flash MX 2004, and then examine techniques for implementation of these files. We'll discuss:

- Working with rich media
- Importing sound files into Flash
- Handling MP3 ID3 tags
- Implementing internal and external sound files
- Working with video file formats
- Importing video files into Flash
- Importing and exporting FLV files
- Capturing camera and microphone data
- Working with the Microphone and Camera classes

> **NOTE**
>
> If you have never worked with digital audio or video before, we highly recommend that you spend some time familiarizing yourself with appropriate sections of the Flash MX 2004 Help Documentation for additional information.

flash player version

Rich Media Considerations

If you plan to stream large external audio or video files into your Flash movies, it is highly recommended that you perform player detection for Flash Player revision 6.0.47 or greater. Earlier revisions of the Player contained a fairly serious bug that essentially prevented cancellation of a download after it had begun. The only way to cancel a requested download of streaming content was to close all instances of the browser. Obviously, this problem was significant when downloading Flash movies with bandwidth-intensive content and was particularly hard on users with slower connections. It's important to remember that Flash is a lightweight Web-driven solution for Flash content first, and everything else second. Many factors can affect a Flash movie's ability to stream video and audio, (quality of the video capture, tools used to create the FLV, dimensions of the frames, playback rate, file size, resolution, etc.) Developers should test early and test often. They should also be aware that Director may be a more flexible platform to work with when delivering large video.

file compression

Working with Sound

The most important factor to remember about working with digital audio is *file compression*. In most cases, audio content should be imported to the Flash MX 2004 editing environment at the absolute highest quality possible (that is, with the least compression and largest file size that can be accommodated), and Flash should be used to compress the file. If you own some high-quality digital audio software, you can import MP3 files and choose to leave them at their current compression level. In addition, if you plan on loading MP3 files at runtime, they must be compressed to acceptable levels *outside of Flash*, because these files will not receive any additional treatment in the Flash Player.

There are plenty of very good resources that describe the process of getting sound files into the Flash MX 2004 editing environment (for example, see the information at Help > Using Flash > Adding Sound). After you've imported a sound symbol and have set up the appropriate compression-to-file-size compromise in the Library, you will need to choose one of the implementation approaches described later in this section. Before we examine these implementations, let's take a look at the sound file formats supported by Flash MX 2004.

CAUTION

The Flash editing environment was not intended to be a full-blown digital audio workstation. As such, it tends to perform erratically, to say the least, when forced to deal with extremely large files (anything that creates a SWF file larger than 4MB). Obviously, this depends greatly on the speed and capability of your development system and target platform. If you're working on a project that is at risk of consuming comparably massive system resources, the first and most important thing you can do is to separate your content into multiple SWF files and create a single parent movie that loads, unloads, and otherwise manages them as a collection.

Importing Sound Files

Importing audio files is no different from importing any other form of rich media. Simply select File > Import> Import To Library. The imported audio file will reside in the Library alongside all the other Flash movie assets.

As mentioned previously, all audio content should be imported to the Flash editing environment at its absolute highest quality (least compression and largest file size possible), and Flash should be used to compress the file.

Once in the Library, audio files can either be placed directly onto the Timeline, preferably on their own separate layer, or they can be shared among other documents. In order to share a sound with other Flash movies, you first need to assign the sound file an identifier string in the Symbol Linkage dialog box. The sound's identifier is then used to access the sound as an object via ActionScript, using the `loadSound()` method.

Implementing Sound Objects

There are at least six ways you can implement sound in Flash MX 2004: as an event, a stream, a linkage, an external movie, an MP3 load, or an MP3 stream. These implementations can be separated into two primary groups: internal to the main movie, and external to the main movie.

Implementing Internal Sounds

The following options all apply to sounds that exist in the current movie either as an instance sitting on a Timeline or as a Library symbol with appropriate linkage settings.

The major drawback to placing these files in your main working movie is that you have to wait for each sound file to be compressed each time you export during movie development. Additionally, if you set the export setting in the Symbol Linkage dialog box to be Export In First Frame, that sound item will be downloaded before your user even gets a chance to see a loading animation. The only scenario in which it makes sense to live with these compromises is when the sound symbols are so small and there are so few of them that the additional pauses (both in compilation and in consumption) are negligible.

The following three implementation options are most often performed in a FLA file that is loaded into your main movie at runtime:

- *Event* (as the instance's Sync property): In this implementation, you load the entire sound before beginning and then play it back independently of any Timeline. This setting is appropriate for very small, short sounds such as button clicks. Assuming there are not too many sounds, the symbols themselves would typically appear in your main movie Library.

- *Stream* (as the instance's Sync property): In this implementation, you play back the sound synchronously with the Timeline on which it resides, and drop frames if necessary to keep the audio track consistent. If the sound is on the main Timeline of a movie, it will stream into the player along with the movie itself. Alternatively, if the sound is inside a nested Timeline, the sound will not actually stream. Generally, if this selection is made, the SWF file that contains the sound file(s) should be separated from the rest of the application and loaded into a main movie at runtime.

> **TIP**
>
> When loading a large streaming SWF file, it's a good idea to build a "buffer" component that could employ analysis of the current user's download speed to determine exactly how much of the file to preload.

- *Linkage* (the symbol's linkage property): In this implementation, you make the sound symbol available so that it can be attached to a Sound object (which is attached to a movie clip) at runtime. If you make this selection, the entire sound symbol must be loaded before any ActionScript attempts to reference it. This selection will typically be used inside SWF files that are being entirely preloaded into a main movie and then accessed by ActionScript.

> **TIP**
>
> One very common approach for building robust, maintainable Flash applications is to construct them with a multitude of SWF files. This can lead to some problems with regard to sharing common assets and simultaneously maintaining a singular instance for version control. The act of loading an entire SWF file into another doesn't necessarily make its symbols accessible to the other SWF. To overcome this issue, for any symbols (and all their children) that will be shared, you set the linkage property to Export For Runtime Sharing; then declare the SWF file into which to insert the symbols. Finally, you drag the symbols and their children from the FLA file of origin to the one that will ultimately access them. This solution applies to sound and video symbols as well as movie clips, buttons, and graphics.

Export for Runtime sharing

Implementing External Sounds

Since Flash MX, you have been able to load an external MP3 file into the Flash Player at runtime, simply by using the built-in Sound object. When used in conjunction with the ID3 property tags of MP3 files, a developer can now quite easily create a Flash jukebox or radio. These relatively new forms of Flash audio applications have now become commonplace on websites of many bands and singers.

For the sake of clarity, external SWF files that contain one or more sound symbols are also treated as external sound elements.

Following are the implementation methods appropriate for external sound files:

- *As an external movie:* This is the most common approach for most applications that use sound and is the best choice for long, linear, presentation-style Flash movies. The approach is being presented here as *external* from the perspective of the main movie of an application. That main movie would actually load one or more movies that contain *internal audio* symbols. How you set up the symbol linkage will determine how the item is implemented. If you want to place the symbol on a Timeline and lock it down to the frames (with the instance's Sync set to Stream), then the symbol's linkage should be set to Runtime Sharing. If you want to have the sound symbols available for ActionScript (in the Sound object), they should additionally be set up as Export For ActionScript and have a unique linkage identifier.

- *As an MP3 load:* This functionality is accessed using the `loadSound()` method of the built-in Sound object. The first argument of that method requires a target to an external MP3 file. The second argument is an optional Boolean value that determines whether to load the entire MP3 prior to playback (`false`) or to stream it and play it immediately (`true`). This approach could be effective in situations where you want groups of smaller sounds to be preloaded; in cases where none of the sounds exceeds a specified file size; or where bandwidth is not an issue.

- *As an MP3 stream*: By streaming an external MP3 file, your end user will be able to hear it play almost immediately. The streamed file will exist only in memory and will not ever be cached. The most unfortunate disadvantage of using this implementation is that there is no way to "scrub" the stream—that is, you can't tell the stream to `gotoAndPlay` at a specified timestamp or location. It makes sense to use the MP3 stream in cases where there are a large number of external files of various length and size.

Using the ID3 Tags in MP3 Files

Most MP3 sound files can contain ID3 tags, which provide metadata about the file. You may have noticed these tags if you've ever used an MP3 player and seen the name of the artist and the song currently playing. If you use either the `Sound.attachSound()` or `Sound.loadSound()` method to load an MP3 file that contains ID3 tags, you can query these properties, which are loaded at the beginning of the sound data stream.

A common problem many developers encounter when dealing with ID3 tags is that they attempt to read the values of the ID3 tag before the MP3 file has completely loaded. When this occurs a `null` value (rather than the ID3 tag value) is returned. To overcome this, a file loading routine needs to be written to monitor when the ID3 properties have been fully loaded. Once that has occurred the ID3 data can be initialized and the `onID3` event will execute correctly.

NOTE

Flash Player 6 r40 and later support ID3 v1.0 and ID3 v1.1 tags embedded within MP3 files. While Flash Player 7 adds support for ID3 2.0 tags, up to ID3v2.4. Refer to your Flash MX 2004 Help documentation for a full list of the standard ID3 2.0 tags and the type of content represented by the tags.

Let's look at an example. To query the artist and song name properties of an MP3 file called mySong, you simply need to target the appropriate ID3 properties of the audio file as demonstrated in the following line of code:

```
trace("The Current Song = "+mySong.id3.TRCK+"
→ The Artist Is = "+mySong.id3. TPE1"
```

Implementation Example

The following example is constructed with the assumption that there is an MP3 file named testSound.mp3 residing in the same directory as the SWF file. This example makes use of the MP3 load approach described in the preceding section.

```
function setSound() {
  // create an empty movieclip container
  this.sound_mc = this.createEmptyMovieClip("soundClip", 2);
  // instantiate the built-in Sound object
  this.mySound = new Sound(this.sound_mc);
  // load external mp3 file - tell it not to stream
  this.mySound.loadSound("testSound.mp3", false);
  // begin a loop that will wait until the MP3
  // has completely loaded...
  this.intervalId = setInterval(this, "checkSoundLoad", 500,
→ this.mySound, "doSetSound");
}
function checkSoundLoad(subject, callback) {
  // subject == Instance to check (in this case a sound object)
  // callback == function to call when the subject is loaded...
  // get the number of bytes loaded.
  var bytesLoaded = subject.getBytesLoaded();
  // get the number of total bytes.
  var bytesTotal = subject.getBytesTotal();
  // determine the percentage loaded.
  var perc = bytesLoaded / bytesTotal;
  // at this point - additional code would be added
  // update a display component to notify the user
  // of the anticipated wait time.
  if(perc >= 1) {
    // load is complete execute the callback function
    this[callback]();
    clearInterval(this.intervalId);
  }
}
```

(continues on next page)

```
function doSetSound(percent) {
    // this function would first be called from the
    // previous loading loop, and could later be called
    // by a slider component that would transmit a value
    // between 0 and 100 which will represent the
    // percentage location within the sound media.
    var dur = this.mySound.duration; // in milliseconds
    var newLoc = Math.floor( dur * (percent * .01) );
    var sec = Math.floor(newLoc * .001); // get seconds

    trace("duration : " + dur);
    trace("newLocation : " + newLoc);
    trace("seconds : " + sec);

    // stop the current sound object -
    // to avoid overlapping sounds and
    // irregularities...
    this.mySound.stop();
    // start the sound at the seconds position specified...
    this.mySound.start(sec);
}
// This call would normally be made from a button
// or some other interaction
this.setSound();
```

Flash-Supported Sound File Formats

One of the beauties of Flash is that it allows you to work with a combination of rich media within a single environment. Over the years, the range of file formats supported by Flash has grown considerably, with audio being no exception. Flash MX 2004 now supports nine different audio formats:

- WAV (Windows only)
- AIFF (Macintosh only)
- MP3 (Windows or Macintosh)
- AIFF (Windows or Macintosh) *
- Sound Designer II (Macintosh only) *
- Sound Only QuickTime Movies (Windows or Macintosh) *
- Sun AU (Windows or Macintosh) *
- System 7 Sounds (Macintosh only) *
- WAV (Windows or Macintosh) *

Requires QuickTime 4 or later installed on your system

Working with Video

Although basic video (export) support has existed within Flash since edition 4, true video integration wasn't supported until Flash MX. Prior to that, you could only simulate video using sequential bitmap images. With the release of Flash MX, Macromedia included the industry standard Sorenson Spark video compression codec into the authoring environment. (A *codec* is a compression/decompression algorithm that controls how multimedia files are compressed and decompressed during import and export.)

The Sorenson Spark video codec is a high-quality, industry standard, video encoder and decoder that radically lowers the file size of video files. Previously, the delivery of video files, via the Web, was an extremely bandwidth intensive process. The release of the Sorenson Spark video codec has proved a huge coup in the delivery of online video based content, due to its superb compression/decompression capabilities.

The Spark video codec is made up of an encoder and a decoder. The encoder applies a compression algorithm to the video file that compresses the content and reduces its file size (and quality). While, the decoder (which is embedded within Flash Player) decompresses the compressed content with a separate algorithm in order for to be played back. Two versions of Sorenson Spark are available: Sorenson Spark Standard Edition is included in Flash MX 2004 and Flash Player 7. The Standard Edition codec produces good-quality video for low-motion content, such as a person speaking. The Professional edition offers more features such as filters and greater levels of compression.

In Flash, you can treat video just like a movie clip. Import a video clip and put it into a keyframe, give it an instance name, and voilà—you can scale it, skew it, mask it, drag it, rotate it, unload it, and replace it to your heart's content. Just about everything that can be done to a movie clip instance can be done to a video instance. This doesn't mean that you *should* do all these things, of course, since most of them will produce incredibly bad image quality, not to mention drag down the performance on most systems.

Flash MX Professional 2004 provides several new ways to creatively use and deploy video in your Flash projects, via its built-in video templates and media components. The video templates provided with Flash Professional 2004 can help you create video presentations and user interfaces for selecting from multiple bandwidth-tuned streams of video.

> **NOTE**
> The audio preferences that are set in the Publish Settings dialog box (File > Publish Settings) determine the audio compression for your video assets. Make sure to set this appropriately before exporting the file.

Flash-Supported Video File Formats

To gain the most from working with video in Flash, your PC system must be able to support one of the industry standard video formats. Make sure that you have either QuickTime 4 or later (Windows or Macintosh) or DirectX 7 or later (Windows only) installed on your system before you start. Provided you have one of these applications, you can then import a variety of embedded video formats into your Flash documents.

By default, Flash documents that contain embedded video can be published as SWF files. While users of Flash MX Professional 2004 have the capability to export their embedded video files as FLV (Flash Video). The following video file formats are supported for importing embedded video if QuickTime 4 is installed (Windows and Macintosh):

- Audio Video Interleaved (AVI)
- Digital Video (DV)
- Motion Picture Experts Group (MPG or MPEG)
- QuickTime movie (MOV)

Importing Video Files

When you first import a video as an embedded file into Flash, the included Sorenson Spark codec will present you with several file importing options via the Video Import Wizard (which automatically launches when you import a video file). Using the Wizard, you can edit the video, apply customized compression settings including bandwidth and quality settings, as well as advanced settings for color correction, cropping, and other factors.

> **NOTE**
> It's important to remember that you cannot edit a video file after you have imported it into Flash.

Another great feature of working with video in Flash is the ability to link to an external video file rather than embedding the file within the Flash document. Instead of Flash embedding the externally linked QuickTime file into a SWF, Flash publishes it as a QuickTime file with a pointer to the original file. This feature is enabled when the publish as QuickTime option is selected.

Flash MX Professional 2004 contains a set of streaming media components that you can use to easily incorporate streaming media (audio and video) into Flash documents.

Although the Macromedia Flash Video (FLV) file format is not strictly a true video format, Flash MX 2004 does allow you to import these files. The FLV format can be used with communications applications, such as videoconferencing through Flash Communication Server.

> **NOTE**
>
> When you import a FLV file, it's treated the same as any other imported video or audio file. The only difference is that the FLV file has already been partially compressed. Just remember that the FLV is not a traditional "linked file," and if the original changes, you will need to manually update it in the movie that imports it.

Incorporating FLV Files

Introduced in Flash MX, the Flash Video (FLV) file format allows you to import or export a static video stream with encoded audio. When you export video clips with streaming audio in FLV format, the audio is compressed using the Streaming Audio settings in the Publish Settings dialog box. Generally speaking, this format is intended for use with communications-based applications such as videoconferencing, screen sharing, and files that contain screen-share-encoded data exported from the Flash Communication Server.

Because Flash was never developed as a video editing application, its video editing capabilities are limited to those provided within the Video Import Wizard. If you're more familiar with using video editing tools such as Apple's Final Cut Pro or Adobe's Premiere, you can use the FLV Export plug-in (installed with Flash MX Professional 2004 and QuickTime 6.1.1) to export FLV files directly from these video editing applications. You can then import these FLV files directly into Flash for use in your Flash documents. In addition, you can dynamically play back external FLV files in Flash documents at runtime.

To play back an external FLV file, you need to post a FLV file to a URL (either an http site or a local folder). Then you add ActionScript code to the Flash document to access the file and control playback during runtime.

Using external FLV files has several advantages over using imported video:

- Due to external FLV files being played back using *cached memory* longer video clips can be used in your Flash documents without slowing playback performance. The main advantage of this is that large video files are fragmented and stored in smaller pieces, which allows them to be accessed dynamically (rather than sequentially). This process requires less memory than embedded files.

- Historically, external files that are imported into a Flash movie clip are bound to the frame rate of the host movie clip. FLV files are not bound by this requirement, and have the advantage of being able to be played back at any rate specified by the developer. This feature gives the developer more precise control over the imported video thus ensuring optimum playback.

- FLV files have the ability to perform functions independently from the host Flash file. This feature is integral to ensuring smooth playback, even when the host Flash file may be disrupted due to it loading data from an external source (such as a CD-ROM).

- Captioning of video content is easier with external FLV files, because you can use callback functions to access metadata for the video.

Accessing Microphone and Camera Data

The Flash Player 7 has built-in support for capturing data from a user's camera and microphone. When enabled, these features immediately prompt users and give them the option to allow or deny access to their microphone and camera hardware. As a Flash developer, you have access to the `System.capabilities` class, so you can automatically determine if these components are even available. You'll want to check the `hasVideoEncoder` and `hasAudioEncoder` properties of this class to determine whether a user is capable of transmitting video data and audio data, respectively.

Some very good tutorials on accessing the user microphone and camera can be found at `http://www.macromedia.com/devnet/mx/flash/video.html`.

The Microphone Class

The Microphone class lets you capture audio from a microphone attached to the computer that is running Flash Player. This class is primarily used with Flash Communication Server, but can be also used in a limited fashion without the server—for example, to transmit sound from your microphone through the speakers on your local system.

The Camera Class

The Camera class, which was introduced in Flash MX, allows you to capture video from a video camera attached to the computer that is running the Macromedia Flash Player—for example, to monitor a video feed from a Web camera (webcam) attached to your local system.

Using Camera class methods such as setMotionLevel(), you can specify how much motion is required to invoke Camera.onActivity(true), and how much time should elapse without motion before Camera.onActivity(false) is invoked. Flash home-security applications can use these methods and switch on and stream a video feed to a remote URL if an intruder is detected within.

Sample Questions

1. In general, non-MP3 digital audio that is destined to be imported into the Flash MX authoring environment should first be compressed how much?

    A. 0% (largest acceptable file size)

    B. 50% (medium file size)

    C. 75% (smaller file size)

    D. As much as possible (smallest acceptable file size)

2. Which of the following is *not* true about FLV files?

    A. They contain video with all the compression selections already applied.

    B. They can be imported into other movies without a significant delay.

    C. They are not compatible with Macintosh OS 9.

    D. When imported, they are treated the same as other imported video files.

3. Which of the following methods can be used to determine if a microphone or a camera is installed on the user's machine?

    A. System.richMedia()

    B. System.accessories()

    C. System.capabilities()

    D. System.peripherals()

4. Which of the following video file formats *cannot* be imported into Flash?

    A. .avi

    B. .mpg

    C. .mov

    D. DIVX

5. What is the name of Flash MX 2004's built-in video compression codec?

    A. Sorenson Spark

    B. Sorenson Video Wizard

    C. Sorenson Studio Pro

    D. Sorenson Squeeze

PART 4

Object Oriented Programming with ActionScript

Object Oriented Programming Basics

With the release of Flash MX 2004, Macromedia has implemented more-robust support for industry-standard object oriented programming (OOP) techniques through the inclusion of ActionScript 2.0. Based on the ECMAScript 4 proposal (http://www.mozilla.org/js/language/es4/), ActionScript 2.0 introduces several new OOP concepts and keywords, including `class, interface, extends, and implements`. This new syntax not only brings ActionScript more in line with other object oriented scripting languages such as Java and C++; it also makes ActionScript easier to learn for programmers with backgrounds in the other languages.

Those of you coming from previous versions of Flash may never before have encountered the term *class*. (You certainly won't find it in a previous version of the ActionScript dictionary.) That's because ActionScript 1 is what's called a *prototype-based* language. Prototype-based languages use unique objects (known as *prototype objects*) that act like a class. In contrast, languages such as Java, C++, and now ActionScript 2.0 are *class-based* languages—that is, they use the `class` keyword to define (or *instantiate*) a class and its members.

Unfortunately, the scope of this book does not lend itself to fully expand on the complexities associated with OOP. Consequently, to more clearly understand some of the advanced concepts inherent to this form of programming, you need to have a sound foundation of comprehension. If you are unfamiliar with the concepts addressed in this chapter, invest some time with additional resources, either online or in books, that focus entirely on object oriented programming techniques and design patterns.

Throughout this chapter, we'll be covering some of the fundamental OOP concepts, including:

- Classes and their interfaces
- Targeting and storing classes via their classpaths and packages
- Class and object creation via instantiation
- Class and object inheritance
- Class members – properties and methods
- Public and private class designations
- Encapsulation and abstraction
- Object scope
- Housekeeping via deletion

OOP Concepts

The following explanations relate to OOP terms occurring throughout ActionScript. Some of these concepts will be discussed in more detail within the upcoming chapters but are briefly defined here to provide an introduction. During the course of this book, we mix terms from both ActionScript 1 and 2.0. Where applicable, terms that apply to a specific version of ActionScript will be noted as such.

Classes

A *class* can be thought of as a blueprint or template that is used to declare (or *encapsulate*) a set of properties (data) and methods (code). These "characteristics" of a class are referred to as its *members*. One of the main benefits of using classes is that these members are isolated from outside code influences (other classes and functions). This helps maintain cleaner, more reusable code. When a class is first instantiated, the functions and variables declared within it become available from within any of the class's object instances. Classes are unique to ActionScript 2.0 and can only be defined within an external AS file.

Interfaces

Interfaces are similar to classes except that the interface can only contain declarations of methods, not their implementation. That is, every class that implements an interface must provide an implementation for each method declared in the interface. Interfaces are a simple means of allowing classes to work together. Passing data, or using each other for subtasks without a developer having to know how each method in a particular class is implemented. The interface generally just provides what parameters are required to use them and thus, allowing classes to be created by individual developers that do not have to work together. The interface element is available in ActionScript 2.0 only.

Classpath

As indicated just previously, a class must be defined outside of the Flash authoring environment, within an AS file. In order for Flash to use these class definitions, it needs to be able to locate them. The list of directories in which Flash searches for class (and interface) definitions is known as the classpath. Classpaths are available only in ActionScript 2.0.

Packages

From time to time, you may have a project for which you must create a number of different classes. Each of these classes will have its own unique purpose. To assist in the organization (or housekeeping) of these classes, you can group them together within a common directory. Any directory that contains one or more class files is a *package*. Packages are available only in ActionScript 2.0.

> **TIP**
>
> In order to keep packages as homogenous as possible, it's recommended that the classes contained within a package do not extend functions from one another, or do not use each other for subtasks of larger tasks.

Instantiation

To create an object, you must first declare (*instantiate*) it. This is done using a *constructor* function. A *constructor* is a special type of function that is contained within the body of a class and is called automatically when you create an instance of a class using the new operator. In the following example, we have already declared a class (and constructor) called Dog:

```
//instantiate (or create) a new dog object from the Dog class
myNewDogObject = new Dog();
```

> **NOTE**
>
> Some of Flash's static classes, such as the Math class, can be used without instantiation. Please refer to your Help Documentation for a full list of these static classes.

Class Inheritance

Class inheritance is the act of producing new classes from previously defined (and initialized) classes. This process can introduce some potential issues, and you'll want to keep in mind a number of things in the early stages of working with inheritance:

- The class that is being inherited is known as a *base class* or *superclass*.

- The class that is inheriting another class is known as the *subclass*.

- A subclass has immediate access to all methods of its base class, as if they were its own.

- The subclass typically defines additional methods and properties, or *extends* the superclass.

- Any base class method can be overridden in a subclass by simply assigning a new method to the same variable name. When this is done, the original, unaffected base class method can be accessed by using the super keyword from within the subclass.

- All built-in objects can be easily extended for any purpose, using inheritance.

- All Macromedia UI components make liberal use of inheritance and provide excellent working models of the principles and concepts of class inheritance.

Objects

An *object* is a discrete container of properties (variables) and the methods (functions) required to manipulate them. All objects are nothing more than instances of a pre-defined class or group of classes. In object oriented programming, these class instances are used and manipulated at runtime. In the Flash editing environment, when you drag a movie clip symbol (for example) out of the Library and onto the stage, you are instantiating an object instance of the built-in MovieClip class.

Object Inheritance

Object inheritance refers to the acquisition (by an object) of a class's properties or methods by virtue of the object's instantiation. That is, when an object is created, it takes on the complete set of properties and methods from the class from which it was created.

Properties

A *property* is just a variable that has been declared within a class, but outside a method. Properties are typically used to define the state and/or a specific characteristic of a class. A class's properties are passed down to (inherited by) each successive instance of that class (that is, each object). As stated previously, the properties and methods of a class make up its members.

Methods

A *method* is any function that has been defined within a class. The methods of a class describe its behavior (what the class—and its object instances—can do). The methods and properties of a class, as stated previously, are its members.

Public and Private Designations

By default, all variables and functions defined within a class are considered *public*. That is, they are available to any class that calls them. The public keyword is used for stylistic reasons only, i.e. all variables and functions are considered public by default.

In some cases, you may wish to restrict access to a particular variable or function, in which case you would specify that variable (or method) as being *private*. When a variable or method has been declared as private, it is only available to the class that declares or defines it, or to subclasses of that class. Both the public and private elements are available only in ActionScript 2.0. The private keyword is only used and enforced during compile time in the authoring environment. Private variables and methods are accessible during runtime and are not at all restricted by the player. You cannot use the private keyword as any means of securing data access as you can do in C++ or Java.

Encapsulation

Encapsulation describes the process of building a capsule, in this case a conceptual barrier, around a collection of properties and methods of a class, effectively hiding (or obscuring) the internal workings. No class should be able to directly modify another class's properties. Instead, an *accessor* method should be used to act as a "go-between" for the outside world and the internal properties of a class.

> **TIP**
> Using accessors allows an object to provide validation to the values and ensure that property values fall within acceptable ranges.

In the following example, we will create accessors for the two properties of the
Person object (using ActionScript 1). The setter methods ensure that the value of
the name property is in all uppercase and that the age is a whole number.

```
Person = function(){
  this.name;
  this.age;

  this.getName = function(){
    return this.name;
  }
  this.setName = function(name){
    this.name = name.toUpperCase();
  }
  this.getAge = function(){
    return this.age;
  }
  this.setAge = function(age){
    this.age = Math.round(age);
  }
}
myPerson = new Person();
myPerson.setName("Fred");
myPerson.setAge(27.5);
trace(myPerson.getName()); //traces FRED
trace(myPerson.getAge()); //traces 28
```

It is also possible in ActionScript to wrap a property in accessors invisibly by using
the addProperty method. This allows you to access the value of the property as if it
were a regular property, rather than as a method call. All access of the property is
invisibly routed through the assigned accessor methods.

```
Person = function(){
  this.getName = function(){
    return this.nameUpperCase;
  }
  this.setName = function(newVal){
    this.nameUpperCase = newVal.toUpperCase();
  }
  this.getAge = function(){
    return this.ageWholeNumber;
  }
  this.setAge = function(newVal){
    this.ageWholeNumber = Math.round(newVal);
  }

  this.addProperty("age",this.getAge,this.setAge);
  this.addProperty("name",this.getName,this.setName);
}
```

Using this variation of the `Person` object, we can access the name and age properties directly, but the getter and setter methods are still invoked.

```
myPerson = new Person();
myPerson.name = "Fred";
myPerson.age = 27.5;
trace(myPerson.name); //traces FRED
trace(myPerson.age); //traces 28~
```

Abstraction

Abstraction is the process that allows for the grouping of related characteristics into separate and distinct classes while identifying instance-specific properties. The term abstraction can be used as both a process and an entity. Abstraction, as a process, denotes the extracting of the essential details about an item, or a group of items, while ignoring the inessential details. Abstraction, as an entity, denotes a model, a view, or some other focused representation for an actual item. Abstraction is most often used as a complexity mastering technique. For example, we often hear people say such things as: "just give me the highlights" or "just the facts, please." What these people are asking for are abstractions. It is this process that allows us to generalize parameters and create class definitions that are more robust and more widely useful. This "distillation" process is perhaps one of the most important steps in the early phases of technical design.

> **TIP**
>
> An effective example of abstraction (and encapsulation) is found in the `FUIComponentClass` that exists deep within your Library after dragging any of the Macromedia UI components into a Flash movie. This class is implemented by each and every UI component (at least once).

Scope

All objects that are instantiated will exist as long as their variable reference exists, and within the scope of that variable. Scope may change as variables are used in object and class structures, or as methods call from within events. Think of the persistence of objects just as you do the persistence of the variable that references them.

> **NOTE**
>
> When working on methods within objects, it is extremely important to remember that the keyword `this` now refers to the object itself, as if the object were itself a movie clip Timeline. The keyword `this` no longer refers to the movie clip Timeline upon which the object resides. The only exception to this rule is when the object in question extends the MovieClip class and is instantiated using the `attachMovie()` method (or by dragging the object onstage).

Persistence and Deletion

Once an object has been created, it will persist (or exist) for as long as its variable reference remains in scope. Without careful object management, your Flash application can very quickly absorb system resources to an excessive degree. It is important to remember that objects that extend the MovieClip class and are instantiated using attachMovie() consume far more system resources than objects that do not "draw to the screen." In any case, you must constantly be aware of which objects are currently in existence, taking care to manually remove them as soon as they are no longer needed.

Removal is most effectively done using the object reference prefaced by the keyword delete:

```
delete myObject;
```

or, in the case of movie clip instances, call the removeMovieClip method:

```
instanceNameOrObjectReference.removeMovieClip();
```

Summary

Object oriented programming has been around for quite a few years longer than Flash. The software engineering community has focused intensely for a number of years on developing, documenting, and distributing detailed frameworks, processes, naming conventions, and best practices for application development using OOP. Part 4 of this study guide may help you to brush up on concepts that you already know, or make you aware of concepts you've never heard of. These chapters are not, however, intended to be the "end of the line" for someone trying to learn OOP concepts for the first time. There are many books and websites widely available that are devoted solely to presenting OOP concepts, principles, and design patterns. A good place to start researching OOP is http://www.omg.org.

> **NOTE**
> There are still a number of valid arguments for employing procedural programming in certain cases. So if you're just beginning to research OOP, make sure you investigate all your development options, to make the best possible decisions for each part of your project.

Sample Questions

1. The class that is inheriting another class is known as the:

    A. Child class

    B. Superclass

    C. Subclass

    D. Base class

2. For methods within objects, what does the keyword `this` specifically refer to?

    A. The object itself

    B. The method

    C. The movie clip containing the object

    D. The root Timeline

3. Which of the following lines of code will create a new object named `myObj`?

    A. `myObj = Object();`

    B. `myObj = new Object();`

    C. `new Object.myObj();`

    D. `new Object(myObj);`

4. Which of the following methods is best for removing an object named `myObj` from memory?

    A. `myObj = 0;`

    B. `remove myObj;` *removeMovieClip()*

    C. `delete myObj;`

    D. `myObj = null Object()`

5. Interfaces can contain what elements?

    A. Only declarations of methods

    B. Declarations and implementations of methods

    C. Only declarations of methods and variables

    D. Declarations and implementations variables

CHAPTER 15

Classes and Objects

In the preceding chapter, we outlined some of the basic concepts that are fundamental to object oriented programming (OOP). In this chapter, we'll take a closer look at the principles of classes and objects—the foundation on which object oriented programming is built.

For newcomers to OOP, coming to grips with the relationship between classes and objects can be a challenge. A good analogy for the concept is to think of a class as a rubber stamp, and an object as the inked impression left behind after the stamp has been used. The rubber stamp (the class), which is found in most places of business, contains attributes specific to the purpose for which it's going to be used. For example, a company may have a rubber stamp that it uses to place the company's contact details (such as name, address, phone number, and Internet URL) on the back of envelopes; these contact details are like the properties of a class. Before a letter is sent off, someone rolls the stamp onto an ink pad and then stamps the back of the envelope. This act of stamping the envelope is equivalent to the OOP concept of instantiating an object (or in-*stamp*-tiating, if you're humorously inclined). The resulting inked impression containing the company's contact details is equivalent to an object. It contains all of the characteristics (members) of the stamp (class) that created it.

Throughout the rest of this chapter, we'll explore classes and objects in more depth, covering these topics:

- Declaring a class

- Rules for packages

- Creating class constructors

- Naming a class

- Designating a classpath

- Instance properties versus static properties

- Working with methods

- Inheritance concepts

Classes

As mentioned several times in earlier chapters, one of the main differences between ActionScript 1 and 2.0 is the way in which classes are created. The prototype-based ActionScript 1 creates prototype objects (classes) via a constructor function, while class-based ActionScript 2.0 creates classes via a *class declaration.*

> **NOTE**
> Throughout the rest of this book, when we refer to a "class" (ActionScript 2.0), we are also referring to the ActionScript 1 prototype object. It's important that you recognize this difference, because the syntax varies between the two. If you're unsure of the syntax, refer to your Help documentation within Flash.

Class Declarations

Before you can use a class, you must define (or *declare*) how that class will behave. In Chapter 6, "Identifiers, Case Sensitivity, and Naming Conventions," we studied the two parts of a class: the *declaration* and the *body*. The declaration is made up of a class statement followed by an identifier (for the name) and a pair of curly braces. The class body is anything that sits neatly between the curly braces.

```
class ClassNameIdentifier{
    // class body
}
```

When you first declare your class, it's important to begin by establishing whether you will work with ActionScript 1 or ActionScript 2.0, because they have different methods of defining a class.

- In ActionScript 1, classes can simply be defined within the Flash IDE on a single frame.

- ActionScript 2.0 is slightly different. When you construct your class, you can only do so in an external ActionScript (AS) file, and the name of your class must be the same as that of the AS file.

Like instance variables, class constructor names have no spaces. Unlike an instance variable, however, a class constructor conventionally begins with a capital letter and has a capital letter at the beginning of each new word.

```
// located within the external CapitalCity.as file
class CapitalCity{
        // CapitalCity class body
}
```

ActionScript 1's prototype-object declarations are slightly different from the class declarations of ActionScript 2.0. If we were to re-create the CapitalCity class within ActionScript 1, it would look like this:

```
function CapitalCity(){        ! ! !
        // CapitalCity prototype-object body
}
```

If you're thinking that this example looks like any ordinary function, you're right—with the exception that the name of the function is capitalized. This telltale sign is often the only indication you'll have that a class rather than a function is being specified.

Packages and Subpackages

Packages are directories that contain one or more class files. They assist in the organization (or housekeeping) of classes that have an element of "commonality." While this element of commonality is not a requirement (i.e. enforced), it is a highly recommended style convention. An example of such commonality would be found in a package called transportationModes. Within this package could be a series of classes called Train, Bike, Car, and Plane. A package can, in turn, contain other packages, called *subpackages*; each subpackage can have its own class files. To reference classes that reside in a package directory, you can either specify its fully qualified class name or import the package by using the import statement.

In a package path, dot notation is used to separate package directory names. Package paths are hierarchical, each dot representing a nested directory. Using our previous example of a transportationModes package, suppose we want to create an instance of the Plane class that resides in a com/localNetwork/transportationModes package. To specify the fully qualified class name, we would do the following:

```
var planeInstance = new com.localNetwork.transportationModes.Plane ();
```

Consistent with other ActionScript naming conventions, package names must be valid identifiers; that is, the first character must be a letter, underscore ( ), or dollar sign ($), and each subsequent character must be a letter, number, underscore, or dollar sign.

Class Constructors

A *constructor* is the special function used to define the properties and methods of a class (or in the case of ActionScript 1, to define the class itself).

In ActionScript 2.0, the constructor function is declared within the body of the class and has the same name as the class that contains it. For example, the following code defines a Dog class and implements a constructor function with the same name:

```
class Dog{
var name:String;
var type:String;
// Dog class constructor function
function Dog (myDogName:String, myDogType:String) {
            this.name = myDogName;
            this.type = myDogType;
    }
}
```

Because ActionScript 1 declares classes (prototype objects) a little differently than ActionScript 2.0, the Dog class/constructor declaration would look like this:

```
Function Dog(myDogName, myDogType){
    this.name = myDogName;
    this.type = myDogType;
}
```

To add a dash more complexity to the mix, the term *constructor* also refers to circumstances where you're creating an instance of a class (an object) using the new operator—just as in our rubber stamp analogy. For example, using our Dog class declaration, we can create (or *construct*) a new dog object as follows:

```
myFriendsDog = new Dog();
```

Now the myFriendsDog object will contain all the same properties and methods (members) of the Dog class.

Within ActionScript 2.0, if a class doesn't contain a constructor function declaration and one is called, the compiler will automatically create an empty constructor function (within the class) for you.

> **NOTE**
> A class can contain only one constructor function.

Class Names

Class names, like the majority of all ActionScript elements, must be valid identifiers. The first character must be a letter, underscore, or dollar sign, and each subsequent character must be a letter, number, underscore, or dollar sign.

> **NOTE**
>
> All class names must be fully qualified within the file in which they are declared; that is, the declaration must include the classpath to the directory in which the class is stored. For example, to create a class named `PlejClass` that is stored in the `myMusicClasses/internationalMusic/nordicLounge` directory, you must declare the class in the `PlejClass.as` file, like this:
>
> ```
> class myMusicClasses.internationalMusic.nordicLounge.PlejClass {
> }
> ```

Classpaths

Unlike the `prototype-object` definitions in ActionScript 1, which can be declared within the Flash authoring environment, classes within ActionScript 2.0 must be defined within an external AS file. In order to import these class definitions at runtime, the Flash compiler must be able to locate them. A *classpath* is a directory tree structure (path) that Flash uses to locate classes that are used within FLAs. Just as we use URLs to locate web pages in a web browser, Flash uses classpaths to locate classes and interfaces.

There are two types of classpath settings used in Flash: a *document-level classpath* and a *global classpath*.

- The document-level classpath (which is empty by default) is set in the Publish Settings dialog box for a particular FLA file (File > Publish Settings > Flash > ActionScript 2.0 Settings), and relates only to FLA files.

- The global classpath applies to both external AS files and to FLA files, and by default, contains one absolute path and one relative path. The absolute path is denoted by `$(LocalData)/Classes` in the Preferences dialog box. Both paths are set in the Preferences dialog box (Edit > Preferences > ActionScript > ActionScript 2.0 Settings).

> **TIP**
>
> It's highly recommended that when you first create your ActionScript 2.0 classes, that you place the new class in a package (or path) that's different from the default global classpath. The reason for this being, that if Flash is ever uninstalled or reinstalled, the default global path classpath may be overwritten (or deleted). If you've stored your classes in the default global classpath, then there's a high probability that your new classes will also be overwritten (or deleted).

doc-level classpath → global classpath → error

Flash first searches the document-level classpath when attempting to resolve a classpath. If the required class can't be found, within the document-level, then the compiler will search the global classpath. If the global classpath search returns empty, a compiler error will occur.

Let's return to the previous Music class example. When the PlejClass is first created and stored within the myMusicClasses/internationalMusic/nordicLounge directory, the classpath to that file must be included when you want to use that class:

```
class myMusicClasses.internationalMusic.nordicLounge.PlejClass {
      //class body goes here
}
```

> **WARNING**
>
> Because Flash uses the absolute global classpath to access its built-in classes, it's extremely important that you understand the implications of modifying the global classpath before you do so. Changing the global classpath will have direct impact on items within the Flash authoring environment, such as components, ActionScript controls, and effects.

> **WARNING**
>
> It also very important not to name your class the same name as any variables used in your Timeline scripts or other classes unless you have purposely created a static class and are using the variable as an object of the class or if the class is stored in a package. All class files that share the local project directory of the FLA are imported automatically *without* the use of the import statement. This can cause confusing compile errors.

Properties

In the rubber stamp analogy to describe classes and objects, it's easy to see how the company's contact details (name, address, etc.) on the stamp can be considered properties of the company (class). The class properties are the unique attributes of that class. The contents (or values) of those properties may change from object to object, but the base attributes always stay the same.

To help reinforce your understanding of this concept, let's look at another example. Assume that all people are object instances of the global PersonClass class. People have many different features or attributes (properties) such as hair color, height, weight, and so forth, whose values are unique for each person, but the fact that these properties exist is common to all people. For many people, there are also behaviors (or methods) that can modify or act on those very attributes, such as dying one's hair or eating too much junk food.

Let's look further at the difference between instance properties and static properties.

Instance Properties

When defining a class, *instance properties* can be added to the class by using the keyword this inside of a method or the class constructor. Instance properties can be manipulated by each object instance without having any impact on their corresponding value within any other object instance.

In the following example, the PersonClass now has an instance property named hairColor whose value by default is set to brown, but which can ultimately be unique for each instance of the PersonClass.

```
//declare the class in an external file
class PersonClass {
      //declare the constructor
      function PersonClass(){
            this.hairColor = "brown";
      }
}
```

Static Properties

A static property is a variable that is attached to the global class definition and whose value can be shared or set without instantiating the class. A static property exists only once in memory, so if the value is changed, it is changed globally (unlike instance properties, which are specific to object instances). By declaring a static property and using the Object.registerClass method correctly, the property will be attached to the class rather than to the object instances. Any ActionScript can access the static property's value by prefacing the class name in front of the property name.

In the next example, there are only 100 eggs available to be shared by all instances of the ReptileClass. Each time the layEgg method is called in any instance, the total eggs available to all instances is reduced by 1.

```
// Declare the Reptile Class using ActionScript 1
ReptileClass = function () {
      trace("New Reptile created!");
      trace("Available Eggs : "+ReptileClass.availEggs);
};
Object.registerClass("ReptileSymbol", ReptileClass);
ReptileClass.availEggs = 100;
ReptileClass.prototype.layEgg = function() {
      return ReptileClass.availEggs;
};
```

Methods

Methods are functions that are associated with a class. For a detailed definition of methods, please refer to Chapter 17, "Methods." Within this section, we'll discuss the prototype keyword and its role in classes and objects.

The prototype keyword is used to attach methods and properties to a class after it has been declared. When an instance of the class is created, the methods attached using the prototype syntax will be available for use in line 1 of the class constructor, and each method or property will be available to other methods using this.methodName();. For example:

```
ClassName.prototype.methodName = function(arg1, etc.)
{
  //statements…
}
```

> **WARNING**
>
> It should be noted that the use of the this keyword does not allow the use of Interfaces and so avoids some of the black box approach to code sharing and development. When coding with ActionScript 2.0, this approach should only be used when absolutely necessary, perhaps to reduce the memory used by a class.

One primary advantage of using the prototype keyword is that there will be only one copy of the method stored in memory, rather than a duplicate for each instance of that object. The following example illustrates how the prototype keyword affects scope within an object:

```
// declare the class…
class SentenceClass {
    //declare the sentence class constructor
      function sentenceClass(noun, verb){
          this._noun = noun;
          this._verb = verb;
      }
}
// declare the combineWords method and attach it to SentenceClass
SentenceClass.prototype.combineWords = function(){
  return this._noun + " " + this._verb;
}
// instantiate the class
var phrase4 = new SentenceClass("Hello", "World")
// call the method 'combineWords'in our new instance
var outCome = phrase4.combineWords();
// trace the returned value.
trace(outCome);
// will output "Hello World"
```

Inheritance

Class inheritance is the act of producing new classes from previously defined (and initialized) classes and is one of the benefits of object oriented programming. The inheritance process can introduce some potential issues, so keep the following points in mind when first starting out in your ActionScript programming career:

- The class that is being inherited is known as a *base class* or *superclass*.

- The class that is inheriting another class is known as the *subclass*.

- A subclass has immediate access to all methods of its base class, as if they were its own.

- The subclass typically defines additional methods and properties, or *extends* the superclass.

- Any base class method can be overridden in a subclass by simply assigning a new method to the same variable name. When this is done, the original, unaffected base class method can be accessed by using the super keyword from within the subclass.

- All built-in objects can be easily extended for any purpose, using inheritance.

- All Macromedia UI components make liberal use of inheritance and provide excellent working models of the principles and concepts of class inheritance.

#initclip num and #endinitclip

The commands #initclip *num* and #endinitclip signify a block of *component initialization actions*. The ActionScript contained within these commands will be initialized or made available immediately before the frame in which the ActionScript resides. If these commands exist within a movie clip that has been set to Export In First Frame, within the Symbol Linkage dialog box, these actions will be made available before Frame 1 of the main movie.

If more than one code block exists for initialization at a single frame, the integer in *num* will determine the order of initialization, beginning with 0 to 1 and so on. In the following example, PersonClass will be initialized *before* Frame 1 of the main movie, and *after* any components with #initclip 0. This number becomes critical when dealing with inheritance. In order to inherit a superclass, it must have already been initialized. So if you have an inheritance chain with five classes in it, each class in the chain must be initialized before another can "subclass" (or inherit) it.

```
//declare the class in an external file
class PersonClass {
    //declare the constructor
    function PersonClass(){
        this.hairColor = "brown";
    }
}
```

> **NOTE**
>
> If you find yourself using many movie clips that are set to export before Frame 1, be aware that you are not only negating the streaming capability of Flash MX 2004, but you won't be able to create a loading animation for your users to see what's going on. One way to overcome this problem is to place most (if not all) symbols into an external SWF file and load it into a main movie at runtime. This process is extremely time-consuming when attempted with the Macromedia UI components, but it is still possible.

Objects

Using our rubber stamp analogy, we discussed how an object is the inked impression left behind after the stamp (class) has been used (instantiated). Here's a more scientific definition of an object: "a discrete container of properties (variables) and the methods (functions) required to manipulate them."

Essentially, objects are made up of data (properties), whose value we can get or set, and methods (code), which we can call as needed. To determine (get) or update (set) an object's properties (or call an object's methods), we need only specify the target object and then the respective property (or method), using dot notation. For example, if we wanted to *set* the value of the myDreamCar object's carType property to equal "Ferrari," the code would look like this:

```
myDreamCar.carType = "Ferrari";
```

> **TIP**
>
> It is considered bad form in OOP to directly access and modify an object's properties. It might seem like the quickest, easiest, and most logical way of manipulating the properties, but in large projects this process can lead to problems. The recommended way of updating an object's properties is via an "accessor" method—or, more specifically, a pair of getter and setter methods.

Creating Objects

After we have declared a class (and its associated constructor function), we're ready to create an instance of that class (an object).

In the following ActionScript 2.0 example, we create an instance of the `Aircraft` class and assign it to the variable `myAircraft`. When we use the `new` keyword, we call the constructor function of the `Aircraft` class, passing as parameters the values "Cessna" and 152.

```
var myAircraft: Aircraft = new Aircraft("Cessna", 152);
```

The `myAircraft` variable is *typed* as an `Aircraft` object. Typing your objects in this way enables the compiler to ensure that you don't accidentally try to access properties or methods that aren't defined in the class.

Believe it or not, you may even have been unwittingly creating objects every time you used Flash. For example, in the Flash authoring environment, when you drag a movie clip symbol out of the Library and onto the Stage, you are actually "instantiating" an "object instance" of the built-in `MovieClip` class.

Extending Flash

Macromedia has gone to great lengths to open up the built-in classes for developers to extend and improve. It is a very simple task to add to the functionality of these native classes, but it can be difficult to improve upon them. For example, if you confidently begin adding a bunch of methods and properties to the `MovieClip` class in order to save yourself some code-writing down the road, it's possible you may have a significant negative impact on system performance—that's because each duplicated movie clip will reference yet more code. A much safer approach in many cases is to *extend* (inherit) the `MovieClip` class in a whole new class, and then use that extended class only when you need the new, additional functionality.

The ActionScript 2.0 `extends` keyword defines a class that is a *subclass* of another class (i.e. a *base* or *superclass*). In the following example, the subclass (`Plane`) will inherit all of the properties and methods that are defined in the superclass (`Transportation`).

```
class Plane extends Class Transportation{
}
```

> **NOTE**
> The `extends` keyword is supported only when used in external script files, not in scripts written in the Actions panel.

Sample Questions

1. Which of the following lines of code will create an object instance of a class named `Organism`?

   A. `Organism = new Class();`

   B. `Organism = new Function();`

   C. `Organism = new Organism();`

   D. `Create new Class(Organism);`

2. Which statement best describes what the `#initclip num` and `#endinitclip` commands indicate?

   A. A block of component initialization actions

   B. A list of methods associated with an object

   C. A block of classes from which to inherit properties and methods

   D. A list of initial property values

3. What keyword is used to attach methods and properties to a class?

   A. `assign`

   B. `prototype`

   C. `inherit`

   D. `Declare`

4. Which of the following is the best definition of a method?

   A. Methods are functions that are associated with a class.

   B. Methods are properties that are associated with a class.

   C. Methods are functions that are *not* associated with a class.

   D. Methods are properties that are *not* associated with a class

5. What keyword is used to call the constructor method of a class?

   A. `this`

   B. `object`

   C. `new`

   D. `function`

CHAPTER **16**

Core, Movie, and Client/Server Classes

The built-in classes that are implemented in the Macromedia Flash Player 7 provide some of the fastest, most robust functionality currently available for rich client applications.

These classes can be implemented and manipulated with more power and flexibility using ActionScript than when using the WYSIWYG environment.

The Flash Player 7 brings further improvement to these built-in classes. They have been completely rewritten in lower-level languages (previously, many of them were written in ActionScript and simply interpreted each time a new instance of the Flash Player was instantiated). As a developer, you can still override and/or extend these classes for more specific purposes, but it is now almost impossible to improve on their performance using ActionScript.

Each built-in object provides another critical piece of functionality. You'll need to study each object closely and gain at least a working knowledge of its capabilities in order to accurately identify not only what is possible, but what development approaches will be most efficient.

Throughout the rest of this chapter, we'll be looking at the range of classes within both Flash and the Flash Player 7 layer, including:

- ECMAScript originating classes which are known as Core classes within ActionScript.
- Movie classes (also known as classes specific to the Flash Player 7)
- Client/server classes

Core Classes

The core classes of the Flash Player 7 and Flash MX 2004 provide a solid foundation upon which a wide variety of tasks can be accomplished. These fundamental core classes are what allow us to act on and manage the movie classes and client/server classes.

Arguments Class

The arguments class is an array that exists at the local scope of every function. It has three properties: callee, caller, and length. The values of the arguments array may exceed the number of values in the function declaration and can be accessed using an indexed for loop.

The arguments class serves two primary purposes:

- *Recursion:* The callee property of the arguments object is frequently used when writing a function that will call itself any number of times to any number of levels of depth.

- *Anonymous callback:* The caller property is used to write functions that will call back to the function that called them without knowing the name or location of that function. This is usually a good way to avoid hardcoding targets into your ActionScript.

The following example shows a very useful implementation of the arguments class that lets you trace the name/value pairs in an object rather than simply seeing "object object" in the Output panel. In an actual implementation, there would be a better special case for arrays, since the for i in syntax doesn't retain the sorting order of an indexed array. Remember, however, that in Flash MX 2004 the typeof() function returns "object" for both classes and arrays. The following code has been written specifically for ActionScript 1:

```
_global.traceObject = function(obj) {
  for(var i in obj) {
    if(typeof obj[i] == "object") {
      // determine whether we're looking at an array
      // or an actual object Object.
      if(typeof obj[i].length == "number") {
        // we've got an array -
        // trace the length and
        // send brackets to wrap the indexes with -
        trace(arguments[1] + i + " : array.length = " +
obj[i].length);
        arguments.callee(obj[i], arguments[1] + i + "[", "]");
      } else {
        // we've got an object Object -
        // will output : [object Object]
        trace(arguments[1] + i + " = " + obj[i]);
        arguments.callee(obj[i], arguments[1] + i + ".");
      }
    } else {
      // if the current property is not an object -
      // trace the current prefix, property and value
      trace(arguments[1] + i + arguments[2] + " = " + obj[i]);
    }
  }
}
function init() {
  // Create a complex example object that nests other objects within
it.
  var obj = new Object();
  obj.prop1 = "myProp1";
  obj.prop2 = "myProp2";
  obj.prop3 = new Object();
  obj.prop3.test1 = "myTest1";
  obj.prop3.test2 = new Object();
  obj.prop3.test2.inner1 = new Object();
  obj.prop3.test2.inner1.val1 = "myVal1";
  obj.prop3.test2.inner1.val2 = "myVal2";
  obj.prop3.test2.inner1.val3 = "myVal3";
  obj.prop3.test2.inner1.val4 = "myVal4";
  obj.prop3.test2.inner2 = "myInner2";
  obj.prop3.test2.inner3 = "myInner3";
  obj.prop3.test2.inner4 = "myInner4";
  obj.prop3.test3 = "myTest3";
  obj.prop4 = "myProp4";
  obj.prop5 = "myProp5";
  obj.prop6 = "myProp6";
  obj.prop7 = new Array();
  obj.prop7.push("hello1");
  obj.prop7.push("hello2");
  obj.prop8 = new Array();
  obj.prop9 = new Object();
  // Call the function that we've created from anywhere in the movie
  // passing in an object that exists in the local scope
  traceObject(obj);
}
init();
```

> **NOTE**
>
> Take note of the `for` loop syntax `for(var i in obj)`. By prefacing the incrementer variable (`i`) with the `var` keyword, that variable and its value will be limited to each instance of the `traceObject()` function scope. That variable will also be destroyed after the function has finished execution. The most important reason to do this, especially with incrementers, is so that the same variable name can be used simultaneously in a *recursive* function, as in the preceding example, without the risk of colliding with a simultaneously running loop.

Array Class

An array is simply a collection of variable values that are indexed by an integer. Arrays in Flash MX 2004 can have any number of "dimensions"—meaning that any item in an array can contain another array to any level of depth.

In most programming languages, there are generally two types of arrays:

- *Indexed:* An indexed array is a collection of values that are indexed by integers. The indexed array is most often used when the order of the data is inherently important, and also when the data set may contain duplicate values.

- *Associative:* An associative array is a collection of values that are indexed by strings. The most useful thing about associative arrays is that they are extremely efficient when you are attempting to set or retrieve a specific value at a known location in the array.

In Flash MX 2004, there's no compelling reason to create associative arrays because you lose access to most of the methods and properties that make an array useful. In cases where you *would* use an associative array, it is recommended that you use an instance of the Object object instead, because it has less overhead. The only exception is when you need to access the sortOn method of the Array object.

The following examples will return two functionally identical objects. The only true difference between the objects is that one will be an instance of the Array class (which inherits the Object object), while the other is directly an instance of the Object object. The Array class contains a number of additional methods and properties, many of which will not work for an associative array—the only exception being the sortOn method.

```
function getAssocArray() {
    // NOTE - the following accessors are
    // horrible practice, but was done to
    // show that the items can be accessed
    // in either of two manners -
    // a) as object properties - .name
    // b) as object property indexes - ["string"]
```

```
    var arr = new Array();
    arr.item1 = "value1";
    arr.item2 = "value2";
    arr["item3"] = "value3";
    arr["item4"] = "value4";
    return arr;
}
function getObject() {
    var obj = new Object();
    obj.item1 = "value1";
    obj.item2 = "value2";
    obj["item3"] = "value3";
    obj["item4"] = "value4";
    return obj;
}
trace(" — — — —");
trace("display an object in the output window");
traceObject( this.getObject() );
trace(" — — — —");
trace("display an associative array");
traceObject( this.getAssocArray() );
```
⎫ X *work but not well*
⎭

The Array class is an essential part of any valid programming or scripting language
and lends itself to organizing and quickly manipulating data. This class has a large
number of methods and properties, explained in detail in the Macromedia
ActionScript Dictionary in your Help documentation.

Here's an example showing the construction and simple manipulation of some
arrays using ActionScript 1.

```
function getTopScore() {
    // call the other function that
    // creates and returns the array
    var highScores = this.getHighScores();
    // sort the array
    highScores.sort();
    // get the last index
    var highestScore = highScores.length - 1;
    // return value for highestScore
    // (last item after sort)
    return highScores[highestScore];
}

function getHighScores() {
    // create a new array
    var arr = new Array();
    // push values into it
    arr.push(4665);
    arr.push(6146);
    arr.push(7321);
    arr.push(5461);
    // return the entire array.
    return arr;
}
// Call the getTopScore function and trace it's return value.
trace("TOP SCORE : " + this.getTopScore());
```

WARNING

You can not use such array methods, within ActionScript 2.0, on objects whose property are set with implicit `get` and `set` methods. Refer to the following technote for more information:

`http://www.macromedia.com/support/flash/ts/documents/`
`usecustomclassobj.htm`

NOTE

In terms of CPU usage, creating and modifying arrays is very expensive. So in the foregoing example, it would be bad practice to create and populate the `highScores` array each and every time you wanted to access it. A more efficient decision would be to create the array during initialization and then store it in a more persistent variable scope.

Boolean Class

The Boolean class is a top-level "wrapper object" that can contain only one of two values: `true` or `false`. This class requires no constructor and exists anytime the literal value of `true` or `false` is placed in a variable. Because logical `if` statements evaluate their arguments to a Boolean `true` or `false` in order to function, you don't need to use an additional `== true` syntax when evaluating Boolean values.

NOTE

"Wrapper object" is used here to mean a simple class that is "wrapped" around a primitive data type and that adds very little (if any) additional functionality.

```
// if statement with a string value:
var myValue = "SomeString";
if(myValue == "SomeString") {
  doSomething();
}
// if statement with a boolean value:
var myValue = true;
if(myValue) {
  doSomething();
}
```

Another useful construct related to Boolean classes is the logical NOT operator. By prefacing a Boolean variable with the `!` character (logical NOT), the opposite value will be returned. In the following example, a movie clip instance named `item_btn` will become "unclickable" after it is clicked once.

```
this.item_btn.onRelease = function() {
  this.item_btn.enabled = !this.item_btn.enabled;
  this.item_btn.useHandCursor = item_btn.enabled;
}
```

> **CAUTION**
>
> If you plan to make an expression Boolean, it is essential that you are absolutely certain that the expression will never need any additional values (three or more). Booleans are for "on/off" logic, not "one of two" logic. In cases where you are unsure, try using integers instead. Once many ActionScript references have been made with the assumption that a variable will be Boolean, changing it can be time-consuming.

Date Class

The Date class provides access to date and time information. There are primarily two ways in which you can determine dates: by using Coordinated Universal Time *UTC* (formerly Greenwich Mean Time); or by using time data that is relative to the operating system on which the Flash Player 7 is running. In many cases, the choice between the two methods is determined by whether you are communicating with a server that might be in another time zone (this calls for using UTC methods), or whether you are just trying to display or manipulate local date and time data to a user (this calls for using local methods).

The following example code will display the current date and time to the Output panel based on the end user's operating system date and time. The example getLocalFullDate() function will present the exact local date and time for each time another script calls it.

```
function getLocalFullDate() {
  // instantiate the date object
  var myDate = new Date();
  var yyyy = myDate.getFullYear();
  var mm = myDate.getMonth();
  var dd = myDate.getDate();
  var hh = myDate.getHours();
  var mi = myDate.getMinutes();
  var ampm = "AM";
  // hh will be an integer from 0 thru 23
  // translate this for 1 thru 12 with ampm...
  if(hh > 12) {
    hh = hh - 12;
    var ampm = "PM";
  } else if(hh == 0) {
    // accommodate 12am
    hh = hh + 12;
  }
  return allMonths[mm] + " " + dd + ", " + yyyy + " " + hh + ":" + mi
  + " " + ampm;
}
```

(continues on next page)

```
function setMonths() {
  // this function just assembles all months
  // in a zero-based array that can be instantly
  // accessed by the results of Date.getMonth()
  var arr = new Array();
  arr.push("January");
  arr.push("February");
  arr.push("March");
  arr.push("April");
  arr.push("May");
  arr.push("June");
  arr.push("July");
  arr.push("August");
  arr.push("September");
  arr.push("October");
  arr.push("November");
  arr.push("December");
  return arr;
}
function init() {
  // put the allMonth list into the _global scope
  _global.allMonths = this.setMonths();
  // Display 'TODAY' to the user -
  trace("Today is : " + this.getLocalFullDate());
}
// begin the scripts -
init();
```

> **NOTE**
>
> We have noticed that each region of this planet seems to have decided on its own way to present numeric date information—[YYYY, MM, DD], [DD, MM, YYYY], or [MM, DD, YYYY] are just a few examples. If you plan to make a truly global Flash application, regional preferences should be taken into consideration. At a minimum, numeric "months" should be translated into their string equivalents to avoid dramatic misunderstandings.

Keep in mind that working with dates can be very complex, especially when you are trying to perform math operations. Read the ActionScript Dictionary Date entries closely before doing any planning, because there can be some functional variation from one client operating system to another, from one region to another, and from one project to another.

Function Class

A detailed description of the Function class can be found in Chapter 8, "Functions." It discusses the time saving use of blocks of ActionScript code that are defined once, and then "called" whenever they are required to be executed.

Error Class

The Error class, which is new to Flash MX 2004, can be used to display custom error messages relating to an error that has occurred in a script. Error objects are created using the Error constructor function. Typically, you "throw" a new Error object from within a try code block, which is then "caught" by a either a catch or finally code block. The following example illustrates an incorrect script execution (which results in an error), while the second block of code represents a correct script execution.

```
//create a function to display the top speed of a particular car
function displayPorcheModelTopSpeed(number){
        if (typeof number != "number"){
                //the value passed across is not a number object so
                //create an error object and associated error message
                throw new Error("Incorrect model number");
        }else{
                //the value passed across is  a number object so
                //so display its top speed properties
                trace("Maximum speed of the Porche 964 Turbo is 280km")
        }
}
//The folowing statement will throw an error
//because it is an incorrect object format (i.e. a string)
try{
        displayPorcheModelTopSpeed("Porche 964");
}catch(newError){
        trace(newError.message);
}
//The folowing statement will display the correct data
//because it is of the correct object format (i.e. a number)
try{
        displayPorcheModelTopSpeed(964);
}catch(newError){
        trace(newError.message);
}
```

Math Class

The Math class is a top-level (static) class that you don't instantiate to use. You simply call its methods or properties from anywhere in your Flash movie. The Math class provides a wide variety of methods and properties that can be separated into two primary groups:

- **Geometry methods** are mostly related to geometry and used most often when scripting complex animation or movement.

- **Simple methods** provide some basic calculations that make life much easier when performing simple and often redundant mathematical operations. The following table includes a list of the simple methods.

METHOD	DESCRIPTION
Math.ceil(Number)	Returns the closest integer that is greater than or equal to Number. (If Number has a trailing decimal value that is greater than zero, the next sequential integer will be returned.)
Math.floor(Number)	Returns the closest integer that is less than or equal to Number.
Math.max(Number1, Number2)	Returns the larger of two Numbers.
Math.min(Number1, Number2)	Returns the smaller of two Numbers.
Math.random()	Returns a decimal value between 0 and 1.
Math.round(Number)	Evaluates Number and returns the closest integer.

For a detailed description of these Math methods, examine the ActionScript Dictionary.

Number Class

The Number class is a top-level wrapper class for the primitive Number data type. Just as its name suggests, this class provides a variety of methods and properties that allow us to manipulate numbers.

The most important thing to know about the Number class is that you don't need to manually instantiate it with a constructor. This statement:

```
var myNum = 5;
```

is the same as

```
var myNum = new Number(5);
```

The Number class also contains a variety of useful constants, each of which can be accessed as follows:

```
var max = Number.MAX_VALUE;
```

> **NOTE**
> The Number object should not be confused with the Number() function, which is typically used to convert strings that represent numbers into actual numbers.

Object Class

The Object class is your primary gateway to more powerful, reusable, and efficient ActionScript. It is this class that exists at the root of the ActionScript class hierarchy. Creating instances of the Object class is an excellent way to preserve variable name spaces (and thus to avoid collisions), and also to extend the built-in functionality of the Flash Player 7. Many examples throughout this book implement the Object class.

Following is an example of how to use the Object class similarly to an associative array. If an indexed array were used, any access to the data would require at least a partial loop of the entire data set. In cases where the requesting script has access to the needed International Standard Book Number (ISBN), there is very little processing required to learn everything else about that book, and the key becomes an important part of the data itself. This approach would not be applicable if there were two books that had the same ISBN, because the last record added would over-write the first one.

```
function getBookList() {
    // construct dummy data object
    // these values will usually be pulled from
    // a server-side script using xml or flash remoting
    var obj = new Object();
    // simple record 1
    obj["0-8070-1423-0"] = new Object();
    obj["0-8070-1423-0"].title = "Walden";
    obj["0-8070-1423-0"].author = "Henry David Thoreau";
    // simple record 2
    obj["0-679-78330-X"] = new Object();
    obj["0-679-78330-X"].title = "Anna Kerenina";
    obj["0-679-78330-X"].author = "Leo Tolstoy";
    // simple record 3
    obj["0-14-044417-3"] = new Object();
    obj["0-14-044417-3"].title = "War And Peace";
    obj["0-14-044417-3"].author = "Leo Tolstoy";
    // simple record 4
    obj["0-553-21035-1"] = new Object();
    obj["0-553-21035-1"].title = "The Death of Ivan Ilyich";
    obj["0-553-21035-1"].author = "Leo Tolstoy";
    // return all records...
    return obj;
}
function getISBNByTitle(title) {
    // find ISBN by title and return it.
    // notice that the for/if loop requires no
    // brackets - each statement contains only
    // a single 'item' in its body
    for(var i in this.bookList)
        if(this.bookList[i].title == title)
            var result = i;
    // if result was not found - return 000000
    // else return the result (isbn)
```

(continues on next page)

```
      return (result == undefined) ? "0-000-00000-0" : result;
    }
    function getAuthorByISBN(isbn) {
      // instant index by isbn
      return this.bookList[isbn].author;
    }
    function getTitleByISBN(isbn) {
      // instant index by isbn
      return this.bookList[isbn].title;
    }
    function init() {
      // create the BookList object - from dummy data function
      this.bookList = this.getBookList();
      // begin searching data for specific values -
      var myISBN = this.getISBNByTitle("War And Peace");
      trace("myISBN : " + myISBN); // output : myISBN : 0-14-044417-3
      var myAuthor = this.getAuthorByISBN(myISBN);
      trace("myAuthor : " + myAuthor); // output : myAuthor : Leo Tolstoy
      var myTitle = this.getTitleByISBN(myISBN);
      trace("myTitle : " + myTitle); // output : myTitle : War And Peace
    }
    // begin the series of scripts
    init();
```

> **NOTE**
>
> Object creation and deletion tend to be the two most CPU intensive tasks in most Flash applications (and in most OOP languages, for that matter). You lighten the burden dramatically by resisting the urge to create classes that have a physical or visual representation in the form of movie clips, and instead creating only the required visual classes as they become needed. Data can be stored in instances of the Object object. Even with this approach, you should be cautious in the timing and placement of most creation and deletion operations. For example, don't create a function like `getBookList()` in the previous example and then call it from every frame in a looping movie clip!

The String Class

The String class is a top-level object wrapper for the primitive String data type. This class allows us to access and manipulate strings using ActionScript. Just about every method and property available will most likely find its way into each and every Flash application that you build. This is primarily due to the need for form validation. If your Flash application lets users enter text data, it's likely you will need to validate it using the String object rules.

> **CAUTION**
>
> Although some dramatic performance improvements have been made in Flash MX 2004, excessive use of strings can causes problems with playback performance, especially when rendering strings to the screen inside text fields.

The following example shows a simple implementation of the String class methods for basic email address validation:

```
function isEmail(str) {
  // find @ symbol index -
  var atIndex = str.indexOf("@");
  if(atIndex > -1) {
    // if @ index is found - look for dot index
    var dotIndex = str.indexOf(".");
    // if dot index is actually after @ index, we're good.
    if(dotIndex > atIndex)
      return true
  }
  return false
}
// create 3 email address variables / records
var email1 = "person@companyXYZ.com";
var email2 = "companyXYZ.com";
var email3 = "person@companyXYZ.co.uk";
// check each record against the function
trace("email1 : " + this.isEmail(email1)); // output : email1 : true
trace("email2 : " + this.isEmail(email2)); // output : email2 : false
trace("email3 : " + this.isEmail(email3)); // output : email3 : true
```

Movie Classes

The built-in classes that fall into the Movie classification (not to be confused with MovieClip objects) are primarily Flash-specific classes that provide rich interactivity. These classes are typically more complex than the core classes and are often found only in Macromedia Flash, as opposed to other ECMA-262 implementations such as JavaScript.

Accessibility Class

The Accessibility Class is a static class that handles the communication with screen reader hardware. A full description of the Accessibility object and its implementation details can be found in Chapter 4, "Accessibility and Usability Best Practices."

Button Class

The Button class is a simpler (more efficient and focused) movie clip with its enabled property of the movie clip set to true. The methods, properties, and events available to instances of the Button class are a small subset of those available to movie clips.

There are primarily two cases in which it makes sense to use Button instances rather than movie clip instances for interactivity:

- **For the hit area:** When using a Button instance, a separate frame can be used to define a hit area that is different from the actual displayed shape.

- **Automatic button states:** When using a Button instance, the Timeline will automatically change frames depending on the mouse state in relation to the instance. This makes Button objects very easy for designers to work with when rollovers are kept simple.

> **TIP**
>
> Button, MovieClip, and Graphic symbol instances can be treated interchangeably by using the appropriate Property inspector for any instance in a keyframe. For example, you can drag a MovieClip symbol out of the Library and, once it is placed into a keyframe, tell Flash to treat this particular instance like a button. Alternatively, you can drag a Button symbol out of the Library and tell Flash to treat it like a single-frame graphic. Among these three symbol types, the variety defined in the Library is truly only describing a default type.

Color Class

The Color class lets you set and subsequently retrieve the color transform of movie clips. The Color class constructor requires a target to a movie clip instance in order to perform as expected. Here are the two primary modes of the Color class, each of which contain a getter and setter method:

- **RGB:** The RGB methods accept or return a hexadecimal numeric value. The following example uses setRGB to change the color of a movie clip:

```
// set the RGB value of a mc
function doRGB(mc, rgb) {
  // if the mc already has a color class -
  // don't waste cycles creating another one.
  if(mc.curColor == undefined)
    mc.curColor = new Color(mc);
  // set the rgb of the color class.
  mc.curColor.setRGB(rgb);
}
// call the method passing in:
// an mc target and a Flash hex color value.
this.doRGB(this.item_mc, 0x333366);
```

- **Transform:** The `Transform` methods accept or return a Color Transform object, which is an instance of the Object class that contains the following properties: ra, rb, ga, gb, ba, bb, aa, and ab. The first character of each of these properties represents either red (r), green (g), blue (b), or alpha (a). The second character in each of these properties represents either an amount (a), at –100 to 100, or an offset (b), at –255 to 255. For example, the myTransform.ra property determines the "red amount" and will be between –100 and 100.

The `getTransform` method call returns only the object that was passed in from the last valid `setTransform` call. Any call to `setTransform` must contain a valid and complete Color Transform object that contains each of the specified properties. The following code example uses the `setTransform` method to change the color of a movie clip:

```
// create a default color transform class
// in a function so that it only has to
// be written out once.
function getTransformClass() {
  var obj = new Object();
  obj.ra = 100;
  obj.rb = 0;
  obj.ba = 0;
  obj.bb = 0;
  obj.ga = 0;
  obj.gb = 0;
  obj.aa = 100;
  obj.ab = 0;
  return obj;
}
// perform color transform upon request
function doTransform(mc, trs) {
  // if the mc already has a color class -
  // don't waste cycles creating another one.
  if(mc.curColor == undefined)
    mc.curColor = new Color(mc);
  // call the setTransform method of the color class.
  mc.curColor.setTransform(trs);
}
// get a new transform color class from our custom function
var trs = this.getTransformObject();
// call the method passing in:
// a movie clip target
// and a transform object
this.doTransform(this.item_mc, trs);
```

Notice that in both examples a function was created that checked for and created a new instance of the Color class *only* if an instance didn't exist. This is because massive and unnecessary class instantiation is usually what adversely affects Flash movie performance. Once the instances of the Color class have been created, they consume comparatively little resources. These functions would help immensely in an application that was constantly or frequently changing the color of the same movie clip instances.

> **TIP**
>
> In order to easily determine how the many seemingly complex `Transform` properties will affect a movie clip, select a movie clip instance on the Stage in Flash MX; in the Properties panel's Color menu, choose Advanced and then press the Settings button. The resulting menu provides exactly the same eight `Transform` parameters, with `Amount` appearing on the left and `Offset` appearing on the right.

ContextMenu Class

The ContextMenu class is a new class to Flash MX 2004 that provides runtime control over items contained within the Flash Player context menu. The context menu is the set of options that appear when a user right-clicks (in Windows) or Control-clicks (in Macintosh) on Flash Player. The ContextMenu class is usually used in conjunction with the ContextMenuItem class to create custom menu items for display in the Flash Player context menu. Each ContextMenuItem object has a caption property (text item identifier) that's displayed in the context menu, and a callback handler (a function) that's invoked when the menu item is selected. The specified function is called when the user selects the context menu, but *before* the menu is actually displayed. To add a new item to a context menu, you add it to the `customItems` array of a ContextMenu object.

Using the methods and properties of the ContextMenu class, you can add custom menu items, control the display of the built-in context-menu items (for example, Zoom In and Print), and create copies of menus. Using the `menu` property of the Button, MovieClip, and TextField classes, you can even attach a ContextMenu object to a specific button, movie clip, or text field object, or to an entire movie level. The "Settings" and "Flash Player 7" menu titles cannot be removed from the context menu.

The following code example adds a custom menu item to the context menu and then traces a message to the Output panel once the option is selected. Notice how the new item is added to the `customItems` array of the `contextMenu` object.

```
myCustomContextMenu = new ContextMenu(menuHandler);
myCustomContextMenu.customItems.push(new ContextMenuItem("Select Me!",
itemHandler));
function menuHandler(obj, menuObj) {
    menuObj.customItems[0].enabled = true;
}
function itemHandler(obj, item) {
    trace("Flash MX 2004's new context menu class rocks!");
}
_root.menu = myCustomContextMenu;
```

Key Class

The Key class is a top-level class that doesn't need to be instantiated and can be accessed from anywhere in your Flash movie. A number of constants—unchanging properties—that represent keystrokes commonly used in games have been added to the Key class.

The most important methods of the Key class are getCode and addListener. The getCode method returns the Key code of the last key pressed, and the addListener method allows you to set up a custom class whose methods will be called whenever the onKeyUp or onKeyDown event is triggered.

The following example sets up a custom class and tracks all keypresses in sequence throughout a session:

```
function init() {
  // create a new array to store key strokes
  _root.keyHistory = new Array();
  // create a new custom class for event tracking
  var obj = new Object();
  // create onKeyDown method
  obj.onKeyDown = function() {
    // Each time onKeyDown is called, add keycode to key history
    _root.keyHistory.push(Key.getCode());
    trace("keyHist: " + _root.keyHistory);
  }
  // add custom object to the key listener
  Key.addListener(obj);
}
// call our init function
init();
```

> **TIP**
>
> The ActionScript Dictionary provides an example implementation of the Key object that makes use of the MovieClip.onEnterFrame event to continually check for the key status. This approach would be effective when building a game, but the addListener approach should always be used in any other circumstances. Using addListener doesn't consume system resources until (and only when) the tracked event is triggered. In contrast, using onEnterFrame sometimes consumes significant system resources for the duration of the movie.

LocalConnection Class

The LocalConnection class allows two different SWF files, residing in two different applications, to communicate without the use of the fscommand() or JavaScript. LocalConnection objects can communicate only between SWF files that are running on the same client machine, but they can be running in two different applications— for example, a SWF file running in a browser and a SWF file running in a projector.

Mouse Class

The Mouse class is a top-level class that doesn't require instantiation and is available anywhere in your Flash movie. The Mouse class provides a small number of reasonably important features:

- `Mouse.hide`: This method hides the cursor.

- `Mouse.show`: This method shows a previously hidden cursor.

- `Mouse.addListener(listenerObject)`: This method adds a specified listener object whose methods are called whenever one of the three mouse events is triggered.

- `Mouse.removeListener(listenerObject)`: This method removes a previously specified listener.

The Mouse class events are triggered while users interact with your application. Be careful to limit the number of scripts that get executed from these events. It's very easy to accumulate a bunch of scripts listening for mouse events and then suddenly take a major performance hit because every time the mouse moves, the player has to execute a few hundred lines of ActionScript.

The following example shows how to add a listener object to the Mouse class:

```
function init() {
    // create a new custom object
    var obj = new Object();
    // add onMouseMove method
    obj.onMouseMove = function() {
        trace(" — ·");
        trace("_xmouse : " + _root._xmouse);
        trace("_ymouse : " + _root._ymouse);
    }
    // add onMouseDown method
    obj.onMouseDown = function() {
        trace("mouse down");
    }
    // add onMouseUp method
    obj.onMouseUp = function() {
        trace("mouse up");
    }
    // call addListener method of the Mouse object
    // and pass in our new custom object
    Mouse.addListener(obj);
}
// call init function
init();
```

the method of ListenerObject (handwritten annotation)

MovieClip Class

The MovieClip class is quite simply the foundation upon which Flash movies rest. This class lets you organize your files into their smallest logical components and present each of those components visually as needed. Movie clips are used throughout any Flash application and can be nested within one another to any level of depth. Compared with any other built-in class, the MovieClip class has an extraordinary number of properties, methods, and events. Each movie clip also provides its own Timeline that executes independently of any other Timeline.

Keep the following issues in mind when working with `MovieClip` objects:

Events: MovieClip objects contain a variety of event triggers that can be overridden with custom functions that are called when those events take place. When using MovieClip events with ActionScript, it is critical to remember that the contents of that function will be executed as if they were written *within* that movie clip's Timeline.

Drawing: There is now a Drawing API that allows you to create vector shapes at runtime within MovieClip instances. These shapes can be any combination of vector lines, fills, or gradients, and they have an extremely low processor overhead. This API completely transforms your ability to implement complex data visualization.

Interaction: By simply setting `movieClipInstance.enabled` to `true`, that instance will also trigger all the events of a Button class. It doesn't automatically display Frame 2 for rollover events and Frame 3 on press events, but this setting is still incredibly helpful—it means you are no longer required to put hidden buttons inside movie clips and change frames to enable or disable them.

Streaming: Movie clips don't stream. Each time the playhead encounters an instance of the MovieClip class, that movie clip and *all* of its contents must be completely downloaded in order to present the first frame to the user.

Performance: Each instance of the MovieClip class references a comparatively vast and complex native class. Creating and deleting these instances will result in the most significant performance hits for end users. Most situations that seem to require intense MovieClip instantiation can be constructed differently using the Drawing API or another less-intensive operation. In spite of its performance hit, however, the MovieClip class has managed to successfully maintain the balance between robust features, processor efficiency, and ease of use. Just be aware of the danger of excessive duplication or instantiation.

Instantiation: Because MovieClip instances can be nested, they are usually very complex, and each instance can play independently of all the others. Movie clips can be instantiated only by using one of the unique capabilities in the following list. Simply calling var myClip = new MovieClip(); doesn't usually provide the desired or expected results.

- Dragging an instance into a keyframe in Flash MX: For all intents and purposes, this is similar to calling the attachmovie method, except that the symbol in question need not have its Symbol Linkage Export property set.

- Using attachMovie: Reference a symbol in the Library by its Symbol Linkage Export property and instantiate it within the targeted Timeline.

- Using duplicateMovieClip: Create a new instance of a symbol from the Library that is identified by another instance that already exists on a Timeline.

- Using createEmptyMovieClip: Create a brand-new (empty) instance of the MovieClip class within whatever instance is targeted.

- Using LoadMovie: Replace an existing MovieClip instance with the contents of the targeted SWF file. This is one of the only ways you can stream visual and/or functional content into a MovieClip instance.

> **NOTE**
>
> In spite of the fact that they tend to be underutilized, the createEmptyMovieClip method combined with the Drawing API are arguably the most significant enhancements provided in Flash MX. They give engineers the ability to instantly create a majority of their Flash movies using only ActionScript.

PrintJob Class

The PrintJob class lets you print content that is rendered dynamically and in multipage documents. It is discussed in more detail in Chapter 25, "Printing."

Selection Class

The Selection class is a top-level class that can be accessed anywhere in your Flash movie and doesn't require a constructor. This class lets you discover and determine which TextField instance is currently selected (or focused). Once a text field is selected, the Selection class provides precise feedback and control over the selection span (the characters that are selected) within that text field. Selection spans are represented using zero-based indexes. (The first character in a text field is represented as the character for zero [0].) The Selection class also provides a standard listener interface of addListener and removeListener.

The methods and events available in the Selection class can be divided into two logical groups:

- *Focus:* These methods deal strictly with determining or setting the currently focused text field. They include setFocus, getFocus, and the onSetFocus handler.

- *Selection span:* These methods deal with selection span and require that a text field is currently focused. They are listed in the following table:

METHOD	DESCRIPTION
Selection.setSelection(begin, end)	Selects the text between the specified indexes. If no end index is passed in, the text from begin to the end of the text field will be selected.
Selection.getBeginIndex()	Returns the beginning index of a selection.
Selection.getEndIndex()	Returns the ending index of a selection.
Selection.getCaratIndex()	Returns the index of the carat within a selection.

SharedObject Class

Shared objects are a data storage feature (similar to cookies), introduced with Flash MX. Remote shared objects are used with Flash Communication Server (FCS), discussion of which is beyond the scope of this book. Primarily, they allow data to be stored or used across several remotely connected users—within a chat application, for example.

The primary purpose of shared objects is to maintain local persistence. There are two types of shared objects: local and remote. Local shared objects enable the saving of data to a user's hard drive (like the storing of a cookie). For example, usernames and passwords are ideal candidates for local shared objects because they contain unique data, which may be required anytime a user logs into a website.

Although you can't use ActionScript to specify (or modify) local storage settings for a user, you can display the Local Storage panel for the user by using System.showSettings(1).

To create a local shared object, use the following syntax:

```
// Create a local shared object
mySharedObject = SharedObject.getLocal("objectName");
```

> **NOTE**
>
> By default, Flash can save locally persistent, remote shared objects up to 100KB in size. When you try to save a larger object, Flash Player displays the Local Storage dialog box, which lets the user allow or deny local storage for the domain that is requesting access. It is important to ensure that your Stage size is at least 215x138 pixels, because this is the minimum size required by Flash to display the dialog box.

Sound Class

The Sound class controls the loading, playing and volume of sound within a movie. A detailed description of the Sound class can be found in Chapter 13, "Rich Media."

Stage Class

Stage is a top-level class that doesn't require a constructor and can be accessed anywhere in your Flash movie. This class is new in Flash MX and available only in the Flash Player 7.

The methods, events, and properties available in the Stage class give you far more precise control than ever before over the rendering of a Flash movie. Previously, you had two options when designing Flash content:

- **Percent:** You could scale an entire Flash movie along with (unfortunately) all its contents to a defined percentage.

- **Fixed Size:** You could define the specific pixel dimensions of the output Flash movie within its HTML document, and the dimensions would be adhered to in the Flash movie.

With the introduction of the Stage class and a few simple settings, in Flash MX you can create Flash content that will scale to make use of higher resolutions when available, will present acceptably on lower resolutions, but will never scale assets that you don't want scaled. Flash content can finally receive layout control similar to that of HTML tables. An important note about this feature is that in order to maintain flexibility, the responsibility for "laying out" Flash elements rests firmly on the developer's shoulders. Implementation of the Stage class isn't well documented and seems to be fairly unknown in the developer community.

Instructions for using this feature are as follows:

1. Open the Publish Settings dialog box.

2. Choose the HTML tab.

3. In the Dimensions menu, choose Percent.

4. Add the following ActionScript to a keyframe (usually Frame 1) in your movie.

```
function init() {
  // create an object to register with the Stage object
  var obj = new Object();
  // add an "onResize" method to our custom object.
  obj.onResize = function() {
    // trace out the new Stage dimensions...
    trace(" — —·");
    trace("Stage.width : " + Stage.width);
    trace("Stage.height : " + Stage.height);
    // align a movieclip to the lower right corner
    // of the stage -
    _root.corner_mc._x = Stage.width - (_root.corner_mc._width +
20);
    _root.corner_mc._y = Stage.height - (_root.corner_mc._height +
20);
  }
  // set the scalemode property so that nothing "auto-scales"
  Stage.scaleMode = "noScale";
  // set the align property so that everything aligns to the
  // upper left...
  Stage.align = "tl";
  // register our custom object with the Stage object.
  Stage.addListener(obj);
  // call our new init function
init();
```

5. Create a movie clip containing a 200x200-pixel square shape. Put it anywhere on the main Timeline and give it an instance name of corner_mc.

The square movie clip you created will appear in the bottom right-hand corner of the Stage, and the Stage dimensions (width and height) will be traced to the Output panel. If you resize the Stage the dimensions will automatically update in the Output panel.

System Class

System is a top-level class containing the Capabilities object, which provides a series of properties that describe details about the current user's system. These properties are available primarily so that you can present customized content to a variety of users based on their system's hardware and configuration. The Capabilities object need not be instantiated to be used.

The following example determines whether the current user can play back audio files and then automatically loads the appropriate SWF file:

```
function getSoundAndArt() {
  // call will return a boolean true for most users…
  if(System.capabilities.hasAudio) {
    // user has audio - get file with sound...
    this.loadMovie("bgAudio.swf");
    } else {
    // user has NO audio get smaller file...
    this.loadMovie("bgSilent.swf");
  }
}
getSoundAndArt();
```

> **CAUTION**
>
> The preceding example has some inherent limitations. The `capabilities.hasAudio` property will return `true` by default. It will only tell you whether someone has a sound card, not whether they have speakers plugged in and turned on. It certainly won't programmatically tell you if someone "wants" to hear your noise.

TextField Class

The TextField class lets you create and manipulate dynamic and input text fields. Similar to the MovieClip class, the TextField class is unique in that instances are tied to a visual representation rather than just existing as ActionScript. Along the same vein, TextField instances consume far more system resources than strictly "virtual" classes. The TextField class has a large number of methods, properties, and events that are well described in the ActionScript Dictionary.

Entirely new instances of the TextField class can be instantiated from the `createTextField` method of the MovieClip class. In Flash MX, TextField instances can be treated similarly to MovieClip instances in that they have comparable methods and properties. Many of the visual properties of a TextField instance can be quickly manipulated using the TextFormat class.

The following example stretches the visible area of a dynamic TextField instance to display all the text that appears within it:

```
this.myText_txt._width = this.myText_txt.textWidth + 10;
```

Like the `MovieClip` object, TextField instances can also now be created at runtime using ActionScript:

```
this.createTextField("display_txt",2,100,100,200,50);
this.display_txt.text = "Hello World";
```

TextField.StyleSheet Class

The TextField.StyleSheet class, available only in Flash Player 7 and later, allows you to create a style-sheet object containing text formatting rules such as font size, color, and other formatting styles. These rules can then be applied to a text field that contains HTML or XML formatted text. The text contained by the TextField object is then automatically formatted according to the tag styles defined by the style-sheet object. You can use text styles to define new formatting tags, redefine built-in HTML tags, or create style classes that can be applied to certain HTML tags.

To create a TextField.StyleSheet object, you simply use the new keyword to call the TextField.StyleSheet's constructor. To add new text styles, you use the setStyle() method of the TextField.StyleSheet class. This method accepts two parameters: the name of the style, and an object that defines that style's properties.

```
//create a new style sheet object
var myStyleSheetObj = new TextField.StyleSheet();
//Add a new style for the headline tags
myStyleSheetObj.setStyle("headline",
  {fontFamily: 'Arial,Helvetica,sans-serif',
  fontSize: '24px'}
)
//Add a new style defintion for the bodyText tags
myStyleSheetObj.setStyle("bodyText",
  {fontFamily: 'Arial,Helvetica,sans-serif',
  fontSize: '12px'}
)
```

To apply styles to a TextField object, assign the style-sheet object to a TextField object's styleSheet property.

```
myTextObj_txt.styleSheet = myStyleSheetObj;
```

You can also create your own style sheets externally, in any standard text editor, and then load that style sheet, using the load() method of the TextField.StyleSheet class, into a style-sheet object at runtime.

TextFormat Class

The TextFormat class lets you store and manipulate character format information. TextFormat instances are created using the new constructor. One nice feature of this class is that it ignores null properties, so you don't need to set each and every value in order to make it work.

The following example makes the word *hello* bold in the text field:

```
function makeSubstringBold( begin, end ) {
  // avoid excessive object creation -
  if(this.myFormat == undefined) {
    // instantiate a new TextFormat object
```

(continues on next page)

```
    this.myFormat = new TextFormat();
    // set the bold property to true
    this.myFormat.bold = true;
  }
  this.display_txt.setTextFormat( begin, end, this.myFormat );
}
this.display_txt.text = "Hello World";
this.makeSubstringBold( 0, 5 );
```

> **TIP**
>
> In addition to formatting an entire TextField, a TextFormat object can return and/or be applied to a substring within a TextField.

TextSnapshot Class

The TextSnapshot object allows you to work with static text contained within a movie clip. Using the various methods of the TextSnapshot object, you can lay out text with greater precision, count the number of static text characters within a movie clip, or even select a range of characters. By using the `hitTestTextNearPos()` method, you can determine which character within a TextSnapshot object is on or near specified *x, y* coordinates of the movie clip.

Client/Server Classes

The client/server classes provide a way to retrieve or transmit data between a running Flash movie and whatever server is hosting that movie. These classes are critical when creating data-driven Web applications using Flash MX 2004.

Here in this chapter, we'll examine the appropriate usage of these classes: when and why you might instantiate a particular class. Detailed information about the client/server classes and their features can be found in Part 5, "Dynamic Data Integration." For complete descriptions and code samples showing many variations for each specific class, refer to the ActionScript Dictionary.

The built-in classes can be separated into four distinct groups, based on the manner in which they are accessed or instantiated.

Static Classes

In some specific cases, you don't need to instantiate the built-in classes. You simply access the static methods and constants provided within a single, global instance of the built-in class. A good example of such a class is the Math class. Because the class definition contains only static methods and properties (constants), and it exists in the _global scope, you can simply access its methods as follows:

```
var myNum = Math.ceil(Math.random() * 10);
```

This example first calls the random method of the built-in Math class. This method returns a pseudo-random decimal number between 0 and 1; you then multiply that number by 10 and round the result by using the ceil method of the Math class (which will always round a decimal value up to the next integer). The resulting value of myNum is an integer between 1 and 10.

Instance-Specific Usage

Most built-in classes are simply class definitions that must be instantiated in order to be used. These classes are available for instantiation from any scope in a Flash movie, but they require instance-specific properties in order to perform as expected.

One good representative of this type of class is the Color class. In the following example, a new instance of the Color class is created and attached to the temporary variable referenced by myColor. This new instance will affect a movie clip that resides on the _root Timeline and has an instance name of myClip_mc.

```
var myColor = new Color(_root.myClip_mc);
myColor.setRGB(0xFFCC00);
```

Automatic Instantiation

Some of the built-in classes are wrappers that provide additional functionality to primitive data types. These classes don't require any constructor, but instead are automatically instantiated whenever the Flash interpreter encounters the appropriate primitive data type. This variety of instantiation is applied to the Number, String, and Boolean classes. For example:

```
var myNum = 5;
```

is the same as

```
var myNum = new Number(5);.
```

Custom Instantiation

Every instance of the MovieClip class must be uniquely instantiated. This is due primarily to the extremely complex nature of the MovieClip class; it has properties identifying its visual representation as well as its physical relationship to all other movie clips in your Flash movie. As a result, the only way to create a new instance of a movie clip effectively is to call one of the specified methods that are attached to an existing movie clip instance. (In spite of some functional peculiarities, the main Timeline can be treated as an instance of the MovieClip class.)

The methods available for creating movie clip instances are as follows:

METHOD	DESCRIPTION
createEmptyMovieClip	This is the only way in ActionScript to create a MovieClip instance without previously defining it in the Library on a Timeline or in an external file.
attachMovie	Attaches a new instance of a symbol that exists in the Library and whose Symbol Linkage Export property has been given a String value.
duplicateMovie	Requires a MovieClip instance target, and creates a new instance of the symbol from which the targeted instance was created. This new instance appears identical to and contains only values that reside in the Library symbol. It does not carry forward values that have been set in the duplicated instance.
loadMovie	Loads an external SWF (or JPEG) file and places it inside a defined movie clip target.
loadMovieNum	Loads an external SWF (or JPEG) file and places it inside a defined _level.

Though not technically accurate, each of these MovieClip instance-creation methods can be thought of as "constructors" for the MovieClip class, only because they let us instantiate new instances of the MovieClip class. In addition, they are the only ways to perform this task using ActionScript.

Sample Questions

1. What is the key difference between indexed arrays and associative arrays?

   A. Associative arrays can have values of any type; indexed arrays contain only numbers.

   B. Indexed arrays contain only one type of data; associative arrays can have multiple types of data.

   C. Associative arrays contain value pairs; indexed arrays contain single values.

   D. Indexed arrays contain values indexed by integers; associative arrays contain values indexed by strings.

2. In which of the following situations would it be best to use the Coordinated Universal Time (UTC) method when creating a Date object?

   A. When calculating elapsed time on the user's machine

   B. When communicating with a server in an unknown geographical area

   C. When accuracy to the millisecond is needed

   D. When converting dates to strings

3. Which of the following is *not* true about the Capabilities object?

   A. It is a property of the System class.

   B. It is intended primarily for the development of content intended for persons with disabilities.

   C. It provides access to information about the user's machine.

   D. It doesn't have to be instantiated to be used.

4. What is the primary purpose of the Stage class?

   A. To size the Flash movie

   B. To layer objects on the Stage

   C. To position objects on the Stage

   D. To load objects on the Stage

5. What is the default maximum file size for locally persistent, shared objects?

   A. 50KB

   B. 100KB

   C. 1Mb

   D. Unlimited

CHAPTER **17**

Methods

In Chapter 14, "Object Oriented Programming Basics," we described some of the fundamental concepts supporting object oriented programming (OOP). In this chapter, we will take a more detailed look at the methods (behaviors) of a class.

One of the benefits of ActionScript 2.0 is that it is a more "strongly typed" language than its predecessors. It gives us the ability to provide built-in *enforcement* for what is known as public and private scope. Developers can thus define the specific methods of a class as being either available (public) or invisible (private) to other external classes. A private method is one that can be accessed or modified only by the class that contains it; a public method is one to which other, external classes have access. When defining a class and identifying the methods that will be assigned to it, the developer should try to at least visually separate its methods into public and private groupings, and then take responsibility to enforce that organization.

Throughout this chapter, we will discuss methods in more detail, including:

- The various method types
- The process of attaching methods to a class definition

Method Types

Methods are functions that are associated with a class. They represent what can be done by instances of that class. For example, the method definitions outlined in the following code establish that all object instances of the Robot class have the ability to crush, kill, and destroy.

```
//declare the Robot class in external AS file
class Robot{
    //declare the crush method
    function crush(){
        //crush cars and trucks
    }
    //declare the kill method
    function kill(){
        //kill all living beings
    }
    //declare the destroy method
    function destroy(){
        //destroy buildings and man-made structures
    }
}
```

Getter/Setter Methods

Getter and Setter methods are special kinds of methods that are defined within a class and are accessible outside the class as properties. They are often referred to as *accessor* methods. One of the advantages of using accessor methods is that they allow you to create (class) members that work like properties external to the class. But unlike standard properties, accessors can have sophisticated logic built into them.

When naming the variable that stores the property's value, it's important to note that the property name cannot have the same name as the accessor method. Generally speaking, to differentiate between the two, the name of the Getter and Setter variables is preceded with an underscore (refer to the following examples for clarification).

Good coding practices dictate that Getter methods should never directly accept parameters (as they're contained within a class) and should always return a value. Just like other methods, a Getter method, can be modified with the public or static keyword. But due to the fact that they're considered *accessors*, Getter methods can't be declared as private. The syntax for a Getter method is as follows:

```
function get myExternalPropertyName():ReturnType {
// Method definition and return statement placed here.
}
```

The next example demonstrates a simple Getter method that returns the value of _speedInKnots as the property currentSpeed.

```
public function get currentSpeed():Number {
return _speedInKnots;
}
```

On the other side of the coin, we have the Setter method. Which, on the surface, appears very similar in syntax to Getter methods, but delve a bit deeper, and the differences become clear. Setter methods should always accept a parameter, never return a value, and use the set keyword instead of get. Like Getters, Setters too can be modified to be either static or public, but not private. Outlined next is a the syntax for a Setter method:

```
function set myExternalPropertyName(parameterName:DataType):Void {
// Method defintion.
}
```

The following example demonstrates a Setter method that assigns a new value to the private property _speedInKnots. Notice that it checks to make sure the value is 0 or greater. If not, it uses the default value of 0.

```
public function set currentSpeed(speedInKnots:Number):Void {
    if(speedInKnots >= 0) {
        _speedInKnots = speedInKnots;
    }
    else {
        _speedInKnots = 0;
    }
}
```

Private Methods

As mentioned in the introduction, private methods are methods that are accessed only by the class in which they reside, and they usually perform small parts of larger tasks.

Public Methods

Public methods are available for use by any other classes or instances and will typically manipulate or return the state of the class. These methods most often call a series of private methods that perform subsets of the requested task. When combined, a class's public methods make up its interface.

Methods Usage

To illustrate how methods are attached to a ActionScript 1 class definition, we will take a single class and work on it through a series of examples adding methods and interfaces.

1. Define the ActionScript 1 class.

```
//- - - - - - - - - - - - - - -·
// Declare the Reptile Class
ReptileClass = function(){
   trace("NEW REPTILE CREATED at : " + this._name);
   this._x = 0;
   this._y = 0;
   this.init();
}
Object.registerClass("ReptileSymbol", ReptileClass);
```
??

2. Next, create a private method for the class.

no param

```
ReptileClass.prototype.init = function(){
   trace("Name : " + this._name);
   trace("_x : " + this._x);
   trace("_y : " + this._y);
}
```

> **NOTE**
>
> The only practical difference between a public method and a private method is whether or not the method is called by other classes. In Flash, public and private methods are syntactically identical, and it is entirely up to the developer to decide to use or enforce this standard.

3. Now, create a public interface method, which will allow other objects to affect this object's behavior.

with parameters

```
ReptileClass.prototype.move(x, y){
   this._x = x;
   this._y = y;
}
```
→ *class level*

4. Assuming an instance of the ReptileClass has been instantiated into the variable lizard using attachMovie, we call the move method.

```
lizard.move(24, 45);
```

We need a method for the lizard instance to move relative to its existing location, but other reptiles (instances of ReptileClass) do not need this behavior. In this case, we are not attaching the method to the class, but rather to the instance itself.

(attach methods to class

```
lizard.moveX = function(x){
  this._x = this._x + x;
}
```

(attach methods to instance

TIP

A class method can be attached at runtime by assigning a new or existing function to a new or existing variable reference within an object instance. A method assigned to an object instance will not automatically be available within any other instances.

---

5. A new method can be attached to (and subsequently removed from) a class from anywhere in a Flash movie. The following code (regardless of its location) will append a new method named moveXY to the ReptileClass class definition. All existing and new instances of this class will have access to the new method within their own local scope.

```
ReptileClass.prototype.moveXY = function(x, y){
  this._x = this._x + x;
  this._y = this._y + y;
}
```

Sample Questions

1. Which of the following statements is true about ActionScript 2.0 in regard to the enforcement of private scope and public scope?

    A. It is weakly typed.

    B. You cannot manually set the scope of methods as either private or public.

    C. Methods of public scope are only accessible outside the object.

    D. There is strict enforcement of the private and public scope with ActionScript 2.0.

2. Which of the following is *not* a good idea when working with methods?

    A. Try to minimize the number of tasks that an individual method provides.

    B. Use methods as an interface for use by other objects.

    C. Only write one method per object.

    D. Ensure your method names are descriptive.

3. Which of these statements best describes a method?

   A. A method is a function that is associated with a class.

   B. Methods are attributes of a class.

   C. A method is a variable assigned to a class instance.

   D. A method is a series of events contained within a function.

4. How many parameters does a "get" method take/pass?

   A. 1

   B. 2

   C. Unlimited

   D. None

PART 5

Dynamic Data Integration

The majority of Internet and intranet applications have two parts: The first part resides on the server side and usually consists of a database and the scripts necessary to access and manipulate that data source. The second part runs on the client side and provides the interface needed for the user to interact with the server side.

Historically, user interfaces have been created in HTML. Even technologies such as ASP and JSP are nothing but methods to produce HTML dynamically. The end-user interface is essentially just a series of HTML views that must be refreshed whenever any interaction is needed between the user interface and the server-side data source.

Flash can provide a rich alternative to HTML for developing data-driven Web intranet and Internet applications. Flash does not require constant refreshing to include dynamic data and communicate with the server. All this can be handled while simultaneously providing the user with a consistent and continuous user interface.

Throughout the rest of this chapter, we will look at aspects of client-server communication, including:

- Overcoming HTTP protocol limitations

- Requesting specific information from a server

- Loading variables from the server

- Using data components to access remote servers

Communicating with Server Applications

Flash has evolved from a simple animation tool to a true application development environment. One major factor responsible for this shift has been Flash's ability to load and use data from dynamic sources. This allows the content of your movies to change as new data becomes available. To get the most out of this feature, it is necessary to understand a little about web servers and the technologies they employ.

Limitations of the HTTP Protocol

The World Wide Web runs primarily on the HTTP protocol. When designing web applications, the developer must understand some inherent limitations to this HTTP system.

Maintaining State

HTTP is a stateless protocol. It contains nothing that allows the server to keep track of what the user has done in the past and what state the application is currently in. Traditionally, the absence of state information has been overcome with the introduction of *session variables* provided by most of the server-side scripting options, including ASP and JSP. Session variables allow important variables that are specific to a particular client session to be stored on the server and used to maintain state in the application.

In lieu of session variables, state can be maintained by passing critical variables from page to page. It is then necessary to construct the HTML pages so that any important variables will be included in each and every new page request. This can quickly become a nightmare when designing a complex application. Any failure to pass critical variables leaves the application in an inconsistent state.

Flash overcomes these limitations with little effort on the part of the designer. Because Flash is a true client-side application capable of maintaining its own internal state between repeated data calls, there is no need to deal with the constant page refreshes that are a part of the classic HTML-based web application. This negates the need for most session variables, except possibly those related to security, which are still best left to the server-side components.

Pushing versus Pulling Data

HTTP is designed in such a way that the client application must make a request to the server-side application in order to get (*pull*) updated data. There is no facility provided for the server to *push* data at the client without the client requesting it. In most applications, this is not a problem—the client application usually only needs to request updated data in response to a user interaction. In other situations, such as a chat application or multiplayer game, it is important for the client application to have access to the most current data available. Without the ability for the server to push new data at the client as it becomes available, it is necessary for the client application to *poll* the server (make frequent, repeated requests) for new data.

Flash's XMLSocket object makes it possible for the server to push data at the client application. The XMLSocket object employs a rather unique system of client-server communication. For more on the XMLSocket object, see Chapter 19, "XML."

Understanding Request Methods

Flash uses two methods for passing variables along with a server request: the GET method and the POST method. Both methods are supported on all standard web servers. Your choice of which one to use depends more often than not on the amount of data you are passing.

GET Method

When you make a request to a server, you are requesting a resource, a page, an image, or some other resource that resides on the server. This request is familiar to anyone who has used the Web more than once; it looks something like this:

```
http://mywebsite.com/index.asp
```

The GET method appends variables to the end of this request. So if we want to pass two variables that will be used to pull a certain record from the database at mywebsite.com, the request might look like this:

```
http://mywebsite.com/index.asp?section=diningroom&subsection=chairs
```

Using the GET method, all the variables (called the *query string*) are passed along with the request. The query string is created by appending a question mark to the end of the request. Each variable is sent as a URL-encoded name=value pair, separated by an ampersand. An example:

```
http://mywebsite.com/index.asp?section=dining%20room&subsection=chairs
```

The biggest limitation on the GET method is one of size. Web servers have specific limits on the maximum size of a query string. If you need to pass more than a few variables, or very large variables, you should use the POST method.

POST Method

The POST method differs from the GET method in that the data is included as the content of the request rather than as part of the URL. There is no inherent limit to the maximum size of data that can be passed in the HTTP protocol, but individual servers may vary in what they will accept. In addition, it is good practice to set a maximum accepted size within your server-side scripts to help prevent potential hacker attacks.

The data sent in a POST is most often in the form of name=value pairs, much like the GET method, but this is not a requirement. In the case of the XML object, when you use the XML.send or XML.sendAndLoad methods to send data to the server, your data is sent in the body of a POST as a single XML document without a name.

Binding with MovieClip

Loading Variables from the Server

Flash can load data from the server in several ways. XML is natively supported using the XML and XMLSocket objects. Here we will focus on loading URL-encoded name=value pairs using the loadVariables and loadVariablesNum methods of the MovieClip object, as well as the LoadVars object that was introduced with Flash MX.

Due to security restrictions, Flash is limited to loading data from the same domain as that from which the SWF was loaded. Flash Player 7 implements exact-domain matching rules rather than superdomain matching rules (which exist in Flash Player 6). Therefore, the file being accessed (even if it is published for a Player version earlier than Flash Player 7) must explicitly permit cross-domain or subdomain access. For example, a SWF loaded from http://myserver.com would not be able to load data from http://otherserver.com. The load operation would fail. There are a number of tricks that can be employed to load data from remote domains, but all require the use of server-side scripts.

Both variations of the loadVariables method and the LoadVars object are designed to load data from the server in URL-encoded format. This data can be in the form of a text file that you have hand-coded, or a dynamically generated page (using middleware such as ASP or PHP) that pulls its values from a database.

XML is covered in more detail in Chapter 19, "XML."

URL-Encoded Data Source

URL encoding requires that all nonalphanumeric characters are replaced with a percent sign (%) followed by two ACSII encoded hex digits. The hex digits for a period character are 2E, so a period would become %2E.

The following example is a simple ASP page that uses the `Server.URLEncode` method to create a data source usable by Flash:

```
producer=<%=Server.URLEncode("bessie D. cow")%>
```

When run on the server, this page will output the following URL-encoded data:

```
producer=bessie+D%2E+cow
```

Generally, your data sources will consist of more than one variable. Multiple variables are separated by ampersands (&). The following data source illustrates a single product record being returned that contains three fields: `product_name`, `producer`, and `unit_price`.

```
product_name=<%=Server.URLEncode("milk")%>
        &producer=<%=Server.URLEncode("bessie D. cow")%>
        &unit_price=<%=Server.URLEncode("2.50")%>
```

Any spaces or line breaks preceding the first variable name will be assumed by the Flash Player to be part of the name of the first variable. In addition, any spaces or line breaks following the last value will be assumed to be part of the last variable value. This can have disastrous effects when you try to use your newly loaded data. As a general rule, it is a good idea to start and end your data source with ampersands to help prevent any unwanted spaces. Using the last example, the modified script would look like this:

```
&product_name=<%=Server.URLEncode("milk")%>
        &producer=<%=Server.URLEncode("bessie D. cow")%>
        &unit_price=<%=Server.URLEncode("2.50")%>&
```

The *loadVariables()* Function and *MovieClip.load* Variables

There are two ways to use loadVariables. It can be used as a function, or as a method of the MovieClip object. Both techniques work the same, but they require different arguments.

In a function, it is necessary to supply a target movie clip that will hold the loaded variables. The following example illustrates the use of loadVariables as a function. Notice that the second argument is the identifier for a movie clip instance:

```
loadVariables("http://127.0.0.1/variables.txt",myMovieClipInstance);
```

When instantiating a movie clip method, the target is optional. If the target is omitted, the data will be loaded into the caller instance. The following example shows the movie clip instance's method being called. The result of the following call would be identical to the function call previously shown.

```
myMovieClipInstance.loadVariables("http://127.0.0.1/variables.txt");
```

Both the function and method forms of loadVariables return immediately, but the data will not become available until sometime in the future. Either your script must watch and wait for the data to arrive, or you can use the onData event handler of the MovieClip object to be notified when the data has loaded and is available for use.

To use the following example, create a movie clip instance on the main Timeline and name it productMC. This movie clip will have two frames. The first frame contains a stop action. The second frame is named displayData and contains three dynamic text fields associated with the variables product_name, producer, and unit_price.

On the main Timeline, add the following code:

```
productMC.onData = function(){
    this.gotoAndStop("displayData");
}
productMC.loadVariables("variables.txt");
```

The first part of this code overrides the default onData handler for the movie clip. This will be called when the data from our loadVariables action becomes available. The second part of this code block loads the data source variables.txt. This is just a text file with the following line:

```
&product_name=milk&producer=bessie+D%2E+cow&unit_price=2%2E50&
```

which results in the loading of the data file and display of the record.

Sending Variables to the Server with *loadVariables*

Up to this point, we have just requested a data source and accepted whatever was returned. Often, you will want to send data to the server as part of your request. The server can then customize the data returned.

Using the productMCexample in the preceding section, we can modify the script in the main Timeline to include an extra variable that will be sent to the server. Replace the script in the main Timeline with the following script:

```
productMC.onData = function(){
    this.gotoAndStop("displayData");
}
productMC.SKU = 2;
productMC.loadVariables("http://127.0.0.1/variables.asp","POST");
```

Notice that there is now a variable, SKU, that is set prior to loading the data. Also, we have added to the loadVariables call an argument that specifies the format in which we will send our variables to the server (in this case, POST). When Flash makes a loadVariables call, all variables that exist in the target movie clip will be sent to the server using the specified method. Since we added an SKU variable to the movie clip, it will be sent along as part of the request. There is nothing else that we need to do to qualify the data requested.

We can also modify the data source to allow us to specify which product we want returned. Since this is not a dynamic data source, we cannot use a text file. We must use a dynamic page that will be served over a web server. The example here is a simple ASP page that contains three products we can choose from. The SKU variable refers to the array index of the product we are interested in:

```
<%
product1 = Array("milk","bessie D. cow","2.50")
product2 = Array("bread","Olde McDonald","3.75")
product3 = Array("Korn","PhytoBioWizardy, Inc.","47.95")
products = Array(product1,product2,product3)
selectedItem = products(Request.form("SKU"))
Response.write "&product_name="&Server.URLEncode(selectedItem(0))& _
    "&producer="&Server.URLEncode(selectedItem(1))& _
    "&unit_price="&Server.URLEncode(selectedItem(2))&"&"
%>
```

send back

Now we can request the data for a particular product by changing the value of the SKU variable to 0, 1, or 2.

LoadVars Class

```
send AndLoad ( ... );
send ();
load ();
```

The LoadVars class allows the loading of data to be separated from the MovieClip class, and also adds a few features of its own. It is the preferred approach to loading URL encoded data.

> **NOTE**
>
> By moving the variable loading functionality from the MovieClip class to the LoadVars class, it is easier to isolate the variables you would like to send to the server. When selecting a GET or POST operation, Flash sends all the enumeratable variables that exist in the movie clip to the server.

In many ways, LoadVars works the same as the `loadVariables` function/method described in the earlier sections, and all the information regarding URL encoding remains true for the LoadVars class.

We can quickly modify the `loadVariables` example shown earlier to use the LoadVars class instead. The main difference in the following example is that the variables will now be loaded into the specified object, in this case the LoadVars class instance, rather than into a movie clip.

```
myVars = new LoadVars();
myVars.onLoad = function(){
   trace("data is loaded");
   for(var i in this){
     trace(i + " = " + this[i]);
   }
}
myVars.SKU=2;
myVars.sendAndLoad("http://127.0.0.1/variables.asp",myVars,"POST");
```

This example loads data from the ASP page we constructed for the earlier example. When this code runs, it will load the record for the product with an SKU of 2 and trace the values of the variables loaded.

The data source URL and method arguments are the same here, but a new second argument specifies the object that will receive the loaded variables. Unlike the `loadVariables` method of the MovieClip class, the `sendAndLoad` method of the LoadVars class can load incoming variables to any object other than the one that made the call.

Although the `sendAndLoad` method of the LoadVars class is most similar to the `loadVariables` method of the MovieClip class, the LoadVars class also contains several other methods that are not present in the MovieClip class. The `send` method provides the ability to send variables to the server without receiving any return value, and the `load` method does the opposite, loading variables from a data source without sending any data.

A Word about Data Components

Data components are explained in more detail in Chapter 22, "Data Classes and Components," and Chapter 23, "Functional Testing Methodologies," but they bear brief mention here as a form of client/server communication.

Flash MX Professional 2004 contains a series of new data components that allow unprecedented access to remote data sources such as databases and web services. For example, the RDMSResolver component combines user settings with changes made to a DataSet component to create an XML update packet. This packet can be parsed by an external data source such as a web service, servlet, or ASP page to update a relational database.

Sample Questions

1. Which of the following is the key advantage of Flash's being a true client-side application?

   A. It uses a stateless protocol.

   B. It supports the use of ASP and JSP.

   C. It provides rich support of server-side session variables.

   D. It can maintain its state without help from the server.

2. When should you generally use the POST method instead of the GET method?

   A. When the query string contains periods (.)

   B. When the query string contains spaces ( )

   C. When the query string is particularly long

   D. When the query string has only one variable

3. The data pulled by a loadVariables() function is stored where?

   A. The targeted array

   B. The targeted movie clip

   C. The main Timeline

   D. Any of the above

4. Which of the following is the key advantage of using LoadVars instead of `loadVariables`?

   A. Data can be loaded into any object, other than the one making the LoadVars call.

   B. LoadVars can handle more variables.

   C. LoadVars is supported by Flash Players 4 through 7.

   D. LoadVars loads variables faster than `loadVariables`.

5. URL encoding requires that all nonalphanumeric characters are replaced with which character?

   A. &

   B. $

   C. %

   D. #

XML is a tag-based markup language that is used to describe data. Unlike the URL-encoded methods described in Chapter 18, "Client/Server Communication," XML has a structure that allows you to describe the relationships between data. The structure of XML makes it ideal for describing large and complex data sets.

The beauty of XML is that it makes it easy for developers to create their own unique interoperable dialects of markup languages, based on logical content rather than on formatting. Because of this "user friendly" form of markup, humans (and computers) can more easily search for specific content-based information within a document, rather than just searching the entire text of a page.

This chapter explores the different elements of XML, including:

- The structure of XML documents

- Working with XML formatted data with the XML class

- Server connectivity with XML Sockets

- Connecting components and external XML data with the XMLConnector component

XML Rules

XML (like HTML) has its roots in Standard Generalized Markup Language (SGML). Unlike HTML though, XML's defining document structure is far simpler. While at the same time providing enhanced flexibility for data and document management. The following sections explore some of the facets of this enhanced flexibility.

While XML is a much more "user friendly" form of scripting language, there are still some rules you need to adhere to. In contrast to HTML, which is very loose in its implementation of rules, an XML document must follow XML rules if it is to be logical, or "well formed."

> **NOTE**
> An XML document that follows the structural rules of XML is called "well formed."

Two of these rules are

- All tags must be closed.
- All attributes must be quoted.

The combination, of a set of opening and closing tags, represents a single XML *element*. Here's an example of an `image` tag in HTML, which is an unclosed tag and written like this:

```
<img src=/images/logo.gif>
```

For this to be well-formed XML, we need to close the tag and quote the attribute. Closing a tag can be done in one of two ways: with another tag that begins with a slash (/), or by ending the opening tag with a slash. Here are examples of both techniques.

```
<img src="/images/logo.gif"></img>
<img src="/images/logo.gif"/>
```

Because XML is a rather verbose syntax, the second example helps to eliminate the unneeded bulk of a second tag. Obviously, this is appropriate only when the tag being closed is empty—that is, when it contains no nested tags.

Another important rule is that an XML document can contain only one outermost element, which is usually named for the document type. For example, an XML document that contains a list of products might look like the following:

```
<warehouse>
  <product>
    <name>Big Green Vase</name>
    <price currency="USD">17.95</price>
  </product>
  <product>
    <name>Plush Couch</name>
    <price currency="USD">275.00</price>
  </product>
</warehouse>
```

While the previous XML document contained 14 tags in total, they form the basis of the seven elements (i.e. one warehouse element, two product elements, two name elements, and two price elements).

Defining an XML Document Type

If you know HTML, XML will seem very familiar to you, because they share a common history. But unlike HTML, which has specific elements already defined (such as the table and br elements), XML has no predefined elements. You're free to create whatever elements you deem necessary to describe your data.

Defining a new XML document type can be a very simple process. If you're passing a simple data set, you're free to wrap your data in appropriate tags and load it into Macromedia Flash MX/MX 2004. As long as your document is well formed, Flash can load and use your new data source.

If you're working with a more complicated data set, it's worth giving serious thought to the design of your new XML document type. To define it, you create your own *Document Type Definition (DTD)* or *schema* that defines the structure of your XML document. These schemas let you establish a set of rules for creating XML documents based on your new document type.

When you create a DTD, you're essentially defining a new markup language. You're establishing what elements and attributes are "valid" within the scope of your document type. (Even HTML is being rewritten as XML, with the creation of a DTD that defines HTML as a subset of XML. This new XHTML markup language will soon serve as a true XML version of HTML.)

> **NOTE**
> An XML document that conforms to the rules of its assigned DTD is called "valid."

Flash MX Professional 2004 lets you manually create a schema through the XMLConnector component. This component is a worthy addition to Flash MX; it lets future developers more easily create applications that use your XML data source, as well as allowing you to test the XML for valid output.

A simple DTD for the earlier products example would look like this:

```
<?xml version="1.0" encoding="UTF-8"?>
<!ELEMENT name (#PCDATA)>
<!ELEMENT price (#PCDATA)>
<!ATTLIST price
  currency CDATA #REQUIRED
>
<!ELEMENT product (name, price)>
<!ELEMENT products (product+)>
```

This DTD contains all the information necessary for someone unfamiliar with this format to be able to read and write valid products XML documents.

Working with the XML Class

The XML class, which was introduced in Flash 5, has vastly improved with each release of Flash Player. Using instances of the XML class, developers can modify XML documents, and work with XML formatted data. The following sections provide a more detailed overview of the XML class and how you can work with it.

Constructing an XML Document

The XML class is instantiated like any other Macromedia ActionScript class. The syntax is as follows:

```
myXML = new XML();
```

Using a String

Optionally, the constructor for the XML class takes an XML document as a string argument. If you wanted to create a simple XML class, you could instantiate and populate it in a single step. In the following example, an XML instance is created and populated. The trace statement included in the example will output the name of the first node in the XML class; in this case, the node name is item.

```
myXML = new XML("<item SKU=\"4573\">Large Green Lamp</item>");
trace(myXML.firstChild.nodeName);
```

Sometimes you will want to parse a string that is in XML format and use it to populate an existing XML instance. The XML class provides a parseXML method that allows you to parse a string after initialization. This lets you reuse an existing XML class instance. The following code block is functionally equivalent to the previous one:

```
myXML = new XML();
myXML.parseXML("<item SKU=\"4573\">Large Green Lamp</item>");
trace(myXML.firstChild.nodeName);
```

Using the Document Object Model (DOM)

The XML class provides methods for creating and appending nodes to the XML tree. Using the DOM ensures that your final document will be well formed.

The XML document we've created in this example is fairly simple, but it illustrates several concepts. First, when you create a new node using the createElement or createTextNode method, the node you create is not attached to the XML tree; you must manually append it to the tree using the appendChild method. Second, the example demonstrates that creating attributes is a simple assignment operation.

```
//create XML instance
var myXML = new XML();
//create item node
var itemNode = myXML.createElement("item");
itemNode.attributes.SKU = "457347";
//create name node
var nameNode = myXML.createElement("name");
//createand append text node to name node
nameNode.appendChild(myXML.createTextNode("Wine Rack"));
//append name node to item node
itemNode.appendChild(nameNode);
//append item node to XML instance
myXML.appendChild(itemNode);
```

Create   Append   stack

The XML produced by this sample code would look like this if traced:

```
<item SKU="457347"><name>Wine Rack</name></item>
```

Navigating XML Nodes

You can target nodes in an XML document using relative or absolute paths. Following is the XML document that we are using for the upcoming examples of identifying nodes in an XML document:

```
<?xml version="1.0" encoding="UTF-8"?>
<store_locations>
  <location name="Bait and Tackle">
    <address>1845 W. Tenth St.</address>
    <city>Westerville</city>
    <state>CA</state>
  </location>
  <location name="Fly Fishing Outlet">
    <address>4354 Templeton</address>
    <city>BoomTown</city>
    <state>CA</state>
  </location>
  <location name="Bait Stop">
    <address>24634 157th Ave.</address>
    <city>Oakley</city>
    <state>CA</state>
  </location>
</store_locations>
```

This next code will load the document:

```
myXML = new XML();
myXML.onLoad = myOnLoad;
myXML.ignoreWhite = true;
myXML.load("locations.xml");
```

by default, xml class doesn't ignore white spaces.

Targeting Nodes Using Relative Properties

The XML class and each XML node contain properties that target other nodes in a relative way. The properties firstChild, lastChild, nextSibling, previousSibling, and parentNode target nodes relative to the current node.

The following example illustrates targeting the address for the third location using entirely relative targeting. The keyword this refers to the XML instance; the first firstChild is the root node of the document (store_locations); the second firstChild is the first location node; the first nextSibling is the second location node; and the second nextSibling is the third location node. The end of the target path, firstChild.firstChild.nodeValue, targets the address node, the text node inside of it, and finally returns the value 24634 157th Ave.

```
function myOnLoad(){

trace(this.firstChild.firstChild.nextSibling.nextSibling.firstChild.
firstChild.nodeValue);
}
```

As you can tell, this is not the most efficient or most readable way of getting to the value.

> **NOTE**
> As a general rule, if you're trying to target more than three nodes, it's a good sign that you might want to restructure your code into more steps.

Targeting Nodes Using ChildNode Arrays

A good alternative to the relative targeting method is to access nodes as an array, by using the childNodes property. The childNodes property contains an array of all the child nodes of the current node, and can be likened to absolute targeting.

The following example targets the same value as the relative version, but this one uses the childNodes method. Again, this is not the most readable approach, but it illustrates another way to access a node:

```
function myOnLoad(){
   trace(this.childNodes[0].childNodes[2].childNodes[0].childNodes[0].
→  nodeValue);
```

It's usually best to combine the relative and array methods of targeting nodes. A third version of the myOnLoad() function uses both systems to target the address value.

```
function myOnLoad(success){
  var documentElement = this.firstChild;
  var locations = documentElement.childNodes;
  var thirdLoc = locations[2];
  var address = thirdLoc.firstChild.firstChild.nodeValue;
  trace(address);
}
```

CAUTION

Text is a special type of node called a text node. It doesn't have tags, but it's still treated like a node. In the example

```
<animal>dog</animal>
```

the text dog is a text node that is a child of the animal node. To get the value dog would require this path:

```
XMLInstance.firstChild.firstChild.nodeValue
```

The first firstChild targets the animal node, the second targets the text node inside, and nodeValue returns dog.

If XML processing in your project becomes any more complex than the examples we've shown you here, it's a good idea to break up the processing into steps. This lets you focus on what's required in each step and prevents excessively long targeting paths like those shown.

The following example uses the same XML document but traces all the information about each location:

```
function myOnLoad(success){
  var documentElement = this.firstChild;
  doStoreLocations(documentElement);
}
function doStoreLocations(storeLocationsNode){
  var locations = storeLocationsNode.childNodes;
  for(var i=0;i<locations.length;i++){
    doLocation(locations[i]);
  }
}
function doLocation(locationNode){
  trace("_____");
  trace(locationNode.attributes.name);
  var kids = locationNode.childNodes;
  for(var i=0;i<kids.length;i++){
    trace(kids[i].nodeName + " " + kids[i].firstChild.nodeValue);
  }
}
```

Loading an XML Document

When loading an XML document, you have the option of sending data to the
server at the same time. It is also possible to send data without requesting any data
in return. The XML methods load, send, and sendAndLoad allow you to choose
whether data will be loaded, sent, or both.

The methods for loading data are asynchronous—that is, the loading methods
(load and sendAndLoad) do not return that data at the time they are called. Your
scripts must rely on the onLoad event to know when the data has returned and is
available for use.

XML.onLoad   *XML.onlaad*

The XML class has an onLoad handler that is called when loading of the XML
document is complete. By default, the onLoad handler does nothing; you must
override the handler with your own function. You should override the onLoad
handler before calling the load or sendAndLoad method of the XML class.

The onLoad handler is passed a single Boolean argument that indicates whether
the load operation was successful.

Within the body of the onLoad handler, the keyword this refers to the XML class.
In the next example, the onLoad handler traces the XML document that just
loaded—or, in the case of an error, it traces the word error.

```
myXML = new XML();                    ？  How to  determine the value?
myXML.onLoad = function(success){
  if( success ){
    trace(this);
  }else{
    trace("error");
  }
}
myXML.load("http://localhost/test.xml");
```
test

XML.load *(URL)*

The simplest method of loading an external document is by using the load method.
This method loads and populates the XML class with the loaded XML document.
The load method takes a single argument: the URL of the document to be loaded.

The file being loaded can be a static XML document or a dynamically generated
document produced by a server-side script. Dynamic generation lets your scripts
pull the requested data from a database and create a custom XML document for
your request. In this case, you typically need to provide the script with the variables
it will need to fulfill your request. These variables can be passed in the query string
of the URL.

If you're creating an Active Server Pages (ASP) document, for example, that will query a database for a particular product and return the details of that product in XML format, your script might look like this:

```
myXML.load("get_product_info.asp?SKU=" + SKU);
```

with query string

XML.sendAndLoad

The sendAndLoad method of passing variables to the server by using the query string is called the get method. The XML class doesn't provide a method to post simple variables to the server, but it does allow you to post an entire XML document.

> **CAUTION**
> The XML document is sent as the body of the post, not as a named variable. This affects the way your server-side scripts access the data.

The following ActionScript creates two XML documents—one that will be sent to the server and one that will hold and trace the returned value:

```
myXMLout = new XML("<test>this is a test</test>");
myXMLin = new XML();
myXMLin.onLoad = function(){
  trace(this);
}
myXMLout.sendAndLoad("http://localhost:8080/test.asp", myXMLin);
```

retrieved

send out

The following sample ASP page will read the posted XML data, save it to the hard drive, and echo it back at your movie. Note that you will need to have Microsoft XML 3 (MSXML3) installed on your server for this page to function properly.

```
<%@LANGUAGE="VBSCRIPT" CODEPAGE="1252"%>
<%
Response.ContentType = "text/xml"
Dim xmldoc
Set xmldoc = Server.CreateObject("Msxml2.DOMDocument.3.0")
xmldoc.load(Request)
'Save the XML document
xmldoc.save(Server.MapPath("sample.xml"))
'echo the document back to Flash
Response.write xmlDoc.xml
%>
```

↓ myXMLout

ASP

↓ myXMLin

↓

flash

XML.send

Sometimes you may want to send an XML document to the server without requiring any response. The XML send method lets you simply post the XML document to a specified URL.

An optional window argument lets you specify where any returning data will be displayed. Unlike XML.load and XML.sendAndLoad, the data is not loaded by your movie; rather, it's up to the server-side scripts to determine what will be returned to the window specified:

```
myXML = new XML("<item SKU=\"4573\">Large Green Lamp</item>");
myXML.send("http://localhost/test.asp");
```

> **TIP**
>
> It's generally a good idea to use **sendAndLoad** to pass an XML document to the server. This allows the server to easily pass back a message telling your movie the status of the operation. If something goes wrong, your server-side script could respond with an error code, and then you could repeat the operation or handle the error in some other way.

XML.ignoreWhite

One of the powers of XML is that it's flexible enough to handle all kinds of data. You, the developer, get to decide what nodes there will be and what information they will contain. Text is a valid node type. The XML parser makes no attempt to strip out meaningless spaces between nodes; they are interpreted as data and are added to the XML tree structure as text nodes.

The XML class in Flash contains a property, ignoreWhite, that lets you tell the parser that white space between nodes should be ignored and not added to the XML tree. In most cases you should set this property to true, unless the white space in your document is in fact data. By default, the ignoreWhite property is set to false; that is, white space will be added to the XML tree as text nodes.

In the following example, the ignoreWhite property is not set, so any white space in the document will be parsed. The document loaded in this example looks like this:

```
<item SKU="4573">WHITE_SPACE
WHITE_SPACE<name>Large Green Lamp</name>WHITE_SPACE
</item>
```

The white space in this document consists of a carriage return at the end of the first two lines, as well as the spaces used to indent the second line. Without the ignoreWhite property set to true, the item node will contain three child nodes: the return and indentation spaces, the name node, and the return at the end of the second line. As you can imagine, this would make targeting very difficult.

When the same document is loaded with ignoreWhite set to true, the item node will contain a single node, the name node. In addition to easier targeting of nodes, this technique achieves a performance gain. If your XML document is formatted in such a way that there is a return at the end of each node, then by setting ignoreWhite to true you can nearly reduce by half the number of nodes that must be created during parsing.

The XMLSocket Class   *Stateful protocol*

HTTP, the backbone protocol of the Internet, was originally intended for transferring simple text documents. Today, many of the sophisticated websites served across HTTP are more correctly called web *applications*. To help overcome the limitations of HTTP, developers have patched together a number of frameworks centered around the XMLSocket class, for developing web applications.

Push versus Pull

As was outlined in Chapter 18, "Client/Server Communication," HTTP is a one-way, request-and-response protocol. Everything begins with the client requesting a resource from the server. The server responds and sends the requested resource. There is nothing in HTTP that lets the server initiate the transfer of information. Should a resource change during a client session, the server has no way to inform the client of this change; the server must wait for the client to request the resource again.

Take, for example, a chat application. With HTTP, each client must regularly request an update from the server. This repeated requesting is called *polling* the server. If the client polls too slowly, the user's experience suffers. If the client polls too frequently, the server gets inundated with data requests. Either way, the server must work hard at answering all the polls, whether or not any new information has become available.

The XMLSocket class uses a two-way socket that is *persistent*; in other words, an unlimited number of messages can be passed through a single connection. Once the client connects to the server, the connection remains until either the client or the server chooses to terminate it. Anytime during this connection, the server can push data at the client. There is no need to poll the server; the server can inform the client when data becomes available and then the information can be pulled from the server.

The strength of the XMLSocket class and its persistent two-way connection is for applications that require real-time updates. Applications such as chat, collaborative white boards, or real-time charts are perfect candidates for the XMLSocket.

Creating a Socket Server

The XMLSocket class requires a special server. There are several commercial servers on the market that can be used with the XMLSocket class. Each has its own system for handling messages; always refer to the documentation of the server you choose.

You can write a program for your own server as well. The requirements for a basic server are fairly simple. Servers have been developed in Java, Perl, VisualBasic, and a number of other languages. Sockets are the foundation of networking and a standard part of most languages.

Requirements for *XMLSocket*

The basic requirements of an XMLSocket server are very simple:

- The server must accept a socket connection on a port greater than 1024.
- Messages are terminated by a zero byte.
- Connections are persistent (an unlimited number of messages may be passed through a single connection).

Although the XMLSocket was designed for passing XML, you can also use the socket to pass any text-based messages, as long as they're terminated by a zero byte.

XMLSocket Events

Boolean

onConnect(success). The onConnect() method is called when the connection is made to the server. The *success* argument is Boolean—true if the connection was successful and ready for use, false if it failed.

onClose(). This event is called when the connection is closed by the server or killed by network error. Overriding this method allows your application to handle unexpected socket closures.

by default
onData calls onXML

onData(StringData). The onData() method is called when the server has received a message, before the message is parsed into XML. If you want to use plain text in your messages instead of XML, you will override this method instead of the onXML handler. The default implementation of this method parses the incoming string into XML and calls the onXML handler. If you choose to override this onData method, onXML will no longer be called unless you choose to call it in your implementation.

onXML(XMLData). This handler is called after data has been received and parsed. If you override the onData handler, onXML will not be called unless you call it in your implementation of onData. The parameter passed to this handler is a parsed XML document.

XMLSocket Methods

connect(host,port). The connect() method is used to initiate a socket connection with a specified server. The *host* argument is a fully qualified domain name or IP address. The *port* argument is the port on the host to which you wish to connect;

connect (host, port) → send (data) → close ()

this port must be greater than 1024. The connect method returns a true to indicate whether the first stage of the connection was successful. You must still wait for the onConnect handler to be called in order to know whether the connection is ready for use.

close(). The close() method closes the socket connection. The onClose handler is not called when the connection is closed by the client.

send(data). The send() method sends data to the server. When you call send(), the method passes your data and appends a zero byte to indicate to the server that the message is complete. The data passed to the server is passed as plain text; there is no attempt to convert your data to XML before sending it to the server. If you choose to use the XMLSocket to send plain text, you can still use the send() method as you would for XML.

Following are three examples of calling send(). The first sends an XML class as a message, the second sends an XML string as plain text, and the third sends plain text.

```
mySocket.send(new XML("<data>" + input.text + "</data>"));
mySocket.send("<data>" + input.text + "</data>");
mySocket.send(input.text);
```

xml & plain text

> **NOTE**
>
> As far as the server is concerned, every incoming message is just a series of characters. Whether you send an XML class, an XML string, or just plain text, the server will receive the data as text. It's up to the server to determine how to respond to the incoming data.

The *XMLConnector* Component

Connector components, in Flash MX 2004, are used to provide a simple means of communicating with external data sources. The XMLConnector provides easy access to external data sources that return (or receive) XML through HTTP post or get operations. The XMLConnector implements a set of methods, properties, and events encapsulated within the RPC (Remote Procedure Call) Component API.

RPC

A good way to think of the XMLConnector component is as a power double adapter that's constructed of ActionScript, or a data binding. This adapter allows you to "plug-in" components to external XML sources, and at the same time, to read and write XML.

The document that outlines the structure of an XML document, and the various data elements which can be bound to, is known as the *schema*. The schema is by far the simplest way to connect to an external XML file and consume its parameters and results within your application. The new schema browser panel within Flash MX Professional 2004 simplifies this process even further.

> **NOTE**
> Although the `XMLConnector` component has properties and events (like other components), it is not visible at runtime. *trigger () method*

Sample Questions

1. Which of the following is *not* true about Document Type Definitions (DTDs)?

   A. They give you a means of testing your XML for valid output.

   B. They must be referenced when instantiating an XML object.

   C. They make your XML data sources more understandable.

   D. They let you create new markup languages.

2. What does the `childNodes property` contain?

   A. The number of child nodes for the current node.

   B. The number of child nodes in the current document.

   C. An array of all the child nodes for the current node.

   D. A `true` or `false` value indicating whether the current node has child nodes.

3. What is the primary difference between the `XML.sendAndLoad` method and the `XML.load` method?

   A. The `XML.sendAndLoad` method has additional properties for checking load status.

   B. `XML.load` loads documents slightly faster because there is no error checking on the client side.

   C. `XML.sendAndLoad` allows you to send specific XML data to the server.

   D. An entire XML document can be sent to the server using `XML.sendAndLoad`.

4. Which of the following is *not* true about the XML.ignoreWhite property?

   A. If the ignoreWhite property is true, all spaces in the XML document will be ignored.

   B. Carriage returns are treated as data if the ignoreWhite property is set to false.

   C. With the ignoreWhite property set to true, you can reduce the number of nodes that need to be created during parsing.

   D. The default value for the ignoreWhite property is true.

5. How does an XMLSocket server know when a received message is complete?

   A. The XMLSocket.onXMLLoad method is called by the client.

   B. The XMLSocket.onLoad method is called by the client.

   C. A zero byte is received.

   D. The XMLSocket server is unable to determine when a received message is complete.

CHAPTER 20
Flash Remoting

Remoting is a product that provides the connection between Flash and your web application server. This feature actually refers to three separate components that, when combined, make up *Flash Remoting*. In order to test or deploy Flash Remoting, you must do the following:

- Install and configure a supported web server application environment (Macromedia ColdFusion MX, Sun Microsystems J2EE, or Microsoft .NET).
- Download and install the server-side (runtime) remoting components.
- Download and install the Flash MX 2004 (author-time/runtime) remoting components.

Once these three requirements have been met, your system is fully configured to begin testing and deploying Macromedia Flash Remoting applications.

Throughout the rest of this chapter, we'll be discussing Remoting concepts, including

- An overview look at Flash Remoting, its drawbacks and advantages
- Technologies available for server-side implementation
- Implementation of Flash Remoting using ActionScript

The Role of Flash Remoting

The Flash Remoting package was created so that developers can focus more closely on implementing features in a language that they understand (ActionScript), rather than marshaling data from one format to another using technology that may be unfamiliar. Conceptually, this is an admirable goal, and for the most part Macromedia has done a good job of implementing it.

Flash Remoting allows you to transmit and retrieve data from a server-side application in native ActionScript format (from the perspective of your local scripts). This includes communication with Java servers, ColdFusion MX, and .NET applications. The Flash Remoting components are armed to dynamically marshal and unmarshal native ActionScript data types into a variety of *other* supported types. As we shall see, this is done with varying degrees of success.

That said, one of the greatest drawbacks in building a complex distributed application using Flash Remoting is that there is no efficient way to *stub* the back end. In the past, when you used a standard XML request model, you could create a stub server out of a directory of static XML documents, and then toggle the Flash application to either load the static documents or request data from the live web application. For those of you unfamiliar with the concept of stubs, a stub is simply a small programmatic routine that replaces a larger program, possibly to be loaded later or that is located remotely. Primary, they are used for the purpose of short-term efficiency.

With Flash Remoting, a significant amount of work on the client side can't begin until the server-side application is nearly complete. Additionally, any adverse change to the staging build of the server-side application can immediately halt development on the client side. This issue alone can prove far more time-consuming than marshaling some XML documents.

One big question remains about Remoting: Why do you need it? The simple answer: You don't—not *really*. There are, nonetheless, a few advantages to Remoting in some scenarios. For example, the WebServiceConnector component cannot send the same range of complex data types to all middleware solutions. Also, some types of processing can be a little faster with Remoting because it does not have the same overhead as the WebServiceConnector component. In addition, you can deploy application server solutions that are not based on Web Services and access them with Flash Remoting.

Server-Side Technologies

As a Flash developer, you shouldn't be required to concurrently develop and deploy the server-side aspects of an enterprise-class web application (see the next Note). Certainly for the purpose of the Flash MX 2004 certification exam, you don't have to worry about being an expert on ColdFusion MX, much less on Java. Therefore, implementation details for these technologies won't be covered here. You should, however, have at least enough familiarity with these technologies to speak intelligently with whomever is implementing them in your project.

> **NOTE**
>
> Throughout this chapter, the term *enterprise class* will be used to describe an application that can contain *n* number of pages, where *n* is technically limitless, or so large that it might as well be. In this context a "page" is simply a unique "view" of a certain data set. For an example of an enterprise-class web application, consider www.macromedia.com, where *n* exceeds 20,000.

ColdFusion MX

ColdFusion MX implements a reasonably easy-to-learn tag-based language and can be used for rapid prototyping or deploying smaller web applications. There are some inherent problems with performance and true scalability for ColdFusion in an enterprise environment. But if you're looking to learn about Flash Remoting and don't know much about server-side applications, ColdFusion MX is the ideal environment in which to get your feet wet.

J2EE

The latest Java offering from Sun Microsystems is an obvious candidate for deploying any large-scale application. Beware that if you're unfamiliar with this technology, it can prove daunting (to say the least) to a novice with no outside direction. If you've been assigned to build an enterprise-class system, it's highly recommended that you hire a professional Java developer to build your server-side application. Don't just pick up a book and expect to construct a robust, scalable web application unless you have a fair bit of experience.

Flash Remoting can be used to communicate with a Java application without using ColdFusion MX. This process does have some significant obstacles when you consider complex data mappings. If ColdFusion MX is used as a gateway, these complexities and transformations increase tenfold. In most cases, it will prove far more useful to integrate a Simple Object Access Protocol (SOAP) or other XML-based communication API, where marshalling data types isn't performed automatically by the Remoting gateway but rather by the Web Service Description Language (WSDL) document.

One of the most stunning decisions Macromedia has made regarding integration with Java has to do with the marshaling of data types. Java is known as a *strongly typed* language, and subsequently supports a broad variety of very specific data types. To allow communication between these two very different technologies, Macromedia must cast each data type in each language into a similar data type in the other. In many cases this results in the generic ActionScript data being forced into some semi-appropriate *specific* Java data type. For example, ActionScript supports only one primitive Number object. Java supports size, byte, short, int, long, float, and double. Each of these requires a different quantity of system resources for storage.

All ActionScript numbers are subsequently cast as a Java double. This can wreak havoc on a server-side system that was constructed without this limitation in mind. Another huge issue concerns the process of transmitting, retrieving, modifying, and subsequently retransmitting ActionScript objects.

The anticipated ease of this process is one of the most effective reasons to use Flash Remoting. In theory, you can now retrieve an object directly from the server, modify it, and seamlessly return it to be persisted. All of this can supposedly be done without manual data transformation. This is a compelling idea, but unfortunately, the reality isn't nearly so simple. The current implementation of the Flash Remoting gateway performs the following inexplicable transformation:

- An Object object is transmitted from ActionScript to Java. The object will be marshaled into a Java Map data type. *AS object → Java map*

- The same object is requested back from Java. The object will be marshaled by the Remoting gateway into an ECMA Array (effectively, an instance of the Array object in ActionScript, only with string keys).

- This object (an *associative array*) is transmitted back to Java. That same object now becomes an ArrayList data type in Java. If there are any server-side data validation routines, as there should be, the submission will fail.

For more information about data transformation between Flash MX 2004 and Java, see

```
www.macromedia.com/support/flash_remoting/ts/documents/presalesfaq.htm
→ #datatypes.
```

Details regarding this issue are covered here only because your Java programmer will look directly at you, the Flash guru, and want to know why you're now transmitting an ArrayList when you originally gave them a Map.

Active Server Pages .NET

Active Server Pages (currently ASP.NET) is the server-side technology provided by Microsoft for Internet Information Server (IIS). Microsoft has provided extensive support for Web Services in its .NET strategy, and ASP.NET is no exception. This is an ideal platform for deploying Flash MX 2004 Remoting with Web Services integration as long as your client is running IIS. ASP syntax tends to be somewhat closer to English than that of other programming languages, but learning it can be frustrating if you're already familiar with ActionScript's ECMA syntax.

Flash MX 2004 Remoting Tools

The Flash MX 2004 Remoting package ships with some tools that provide support to ease the configuration and debugging of the connection with the server side of your Remoting application. Not surprisingly, some of these tools tend to work most effectively (or, in some cases, *only*) when combined with ColdFusion MX running on Macromedia JRun.

Flash Remoting Server

To implement Flash Remoting, you need to run the appropriate installer for your server configuration—on the server. This requires that you have administrator- or root-level-access privileges on that machine. You can get the appropriate files at www.macromedia.com/software/flashremoting/. Just download the evaluation version, install it, and begin testing.

Flash Remoting Classes

A package of Flash components extends the Flash MX 2004 authoring environment to enable Flash Remoting. The classes include the following:

- **NetServices Class:** These are external ActionScript files that should be #included in the first frame (or at least a frame prior to their being called) of any movie that will use Flash Remoting. These classes provide a variety of features and are critical additions in order to use remoting at all. The createGatewayConnection() method of the NetServices class is used to set the location of the application server.

- **Service Browser:** After installing the Remoting components, you should be able to access this tool from Window > Service Browser. This component lets you define a valid gateway URL and service name. Once these items have been entered correctly, the available API will be displayed with whatever descriptions exist. This feature works only when combined with ColdFusion MX and JRun on the server.

- **NetConnection Debugger:** This component can really help when you're trying to determine whether or not your requests and responses are actually transmitting the data that you expect them to—and whether they're transmitting anything at all. This panel monitors and displays any communications that pass through the Flash Remoting interface.

RecordSet [handwritten]

- **RecordSet Class:** This class is used to create and modify SQL query results that are contained within RecordSet objects returned from a server. RecordSet objects contain an array of records, the names of the columns (within the record), and a reference to the application server. The methods of the RecordSet class can be used to add, modify, create or delete these RecordSet items. The following example demonstrates the instantiation of a RecordSet object via the use of the RecordSet constructor. We have also declared two column headings `FriendName` and `PhoneNumber`, but haven't populated the datset with any data.

```
myFriendRecordSet = new RecodSet(["FriendName", "PhoneNumber"]);
```

DataGlue [handwritten]

- **DataGlue Class:** The DataGlue class is used to bind (or "stick") RecordSet objects to array based UI components such as the ComboBox or ListBox. Traditionally, data has been added to these components via the `addItem()` method, but the DataGlue class is a much simpler way of performing this. The DataGlue class contains two methods (the `BindFormatStrings()` and the `bindFormatFunction()`) that act in a similar manner to a data provider and a data consumer. They respectively provide information about the RecordSet object containing that data to be used, and the instance name of the component on which the data is to be bound to.

info [handwritten]

ActionScript Implementation

Regardless of which server-side technology will be supported, the ActionScript process that is used to implement Flash Remoting is effectively the same.

1. `#include` the appropriate NetService classes.

> **TIP**
>
> On Windows XP, after the Flash Remoting tools have been installed, the NetService classes can be `#included` in a Flash movie that exists anywhere on your file system, without your having to manually copy the files into your current working directory.

2. Declare the current or default gateway using ActionScript.

   createGateway Connection () [handwritten]

3. Instantiate a new NetServices object that will be used to represent the server-side interface locally.

4. Manually or dynamically create an identical local API with unique functions for each method name followed by `_Result` and `_Status`. The `methodName_Result()` function is called after data has been successfully retrieved from the server-side method of the same name;

`methodName_Status()` is called whenever an exception has taken place at some point on the server.

If your application requires only a handful of simple API calls, certainly the most efficient methodology would be to manually duplicate the server-side API with the appropriate `_Result` and `_Status` methods. Alternatively, if you are building a robust, scalable, and expansive application that has a broad range of different and changing APIs, it might make more sense to make use of proven software *design patterns* (see sidebar) to dynamically generate the requisite methods when they're needed.

Design Patterns

One of the inherent design challenges with regard to server-side communication in Flash is that the connection is asynchronous. This means you can make any number of concurrent method calls on the server, and their results may be returned in any order. If the same server-side method is called more than once prior to receiving the first result, you may have difficulty determining what to do with the results when they do start to arrive.

Fortunately, software engineers have tackled many of these issues by instituting and using *design patterns*. To learn more about the wide variety of problems that have been solved using these techniques, read *Patterns in Java: A Catalog of Reusable Design Patterns Illustrated with UML*, 2nd Edition, volumes 1 through 3, by Mark Grand. This is an excellent series of books that clearly describe the problems, solutions, and implementations of an extremely wide variety of design patterns. The *Patterns in Java* books contain extensive descriptions combined with UML (Unified Modeling Language) diagrams and code samples written in Java. (The Java syntax is similar enough to ActionScript that it won't look completely foreign to you.)

The following example is an extremely simple implementation of Flash Remoting that would work for a small server-side API. This example should reside on the main Timeline of your Flash movie, and assumes that there is a single Remoting service configured on the server with a single method available. The service name is `myService`, and the remote method name is `methodName`.

```
// include Macromedias Netservice Codebase -        ⑦
#include "NetServices.as"
#include "NetDebug.as"
// Initialize the gateway connection -             ⓔ
function init() {
    // set the default gateway URL. -
    NetServices.setDefaultGatewayUrl("http://localhost:8500/
    → flashservices/gateway");
```

(continued on next page)

```
    // connect to the gateway
    this.gatewayConn = NetServices.createGatewayConnection();
    // get a reference to a service
    this.myService = this.gatewayConn.getService("/googleService", this);
    this.inited = true;
}
function doMethodName() {
    // This function would be called by a user event
    // such as a button click - and will actually call
    // the remote method.
    this.myService.methodName(myArgument);
}
function methodName_Status(result) {
    // Handle Exceptions here...
    trace("methodName_Status called with: ");
    for(var i in result)
        trace(i + " : " + result[i]);
}
function methodName_Result(result) {
    // Called with successful result data...
    // pass result data and send to view here -
    for(var i in result)
        trace(i + " : " + result[i]);
}
if(!this.inited)
    this.init();
```

It's essential to note that using Flash Remoting is an entirely data-oriented process. In the Model View Control (MVC) pattern, the Flash Remoting data is effectively your model and should not inherently be tied to any physical or visible objects, such as MovieClips, that consume resources while drawing to the screen. This means you can create a new ActionScript class that will behave as a local, centralized, singular implementation of the remote API (in the world of design patterns, this is known as a *singleton*). This new class should *not* extend the MovieClip object, but should instead extend only the Object object, and would normally be instantiated into the global scope of your movie. The following example is a real implementation of such a class.

```
#initclip 0
//———————————————————————————————————————
// Initialize the new Instance -
//———————————————————————————————————————
function BrokerClass()
{
    this.init();
}
Object.registerClass("BrokerClass", BrokerClass);
//———————————————————————————————————————
// init step 1
BrokerClass.prototype.init = function()
{
    // Initialize the Broker Class -
    // add isBusy property getter / setter
```

(continued on next page)

```
  this.addProperty( "isBusy", this.getIsBusy, this.setIsBusy );
  // set isBusy
  this.isBusy = false;
  // create the methodQueue array -
  this.methodQueue = new Array();
  // initialize the services for this application...
  this.getServices();
}
//— — — — — — — — — — — — — — — — — — — — — — — — —
// init step 2
BrokerClass.prototype.getServices = function()
{
  // Set the default gateway URL -

NetServices.setDefaultGatewayUrl("http://localhost:8500/flashservices/
→ gateway");
  // Connect to the gateway -
  this.gatewayConnection = NetServices.createGatewayConnection();
  // Connect to a service -
  this.javaConn = this.gatewayConnection.getService("/googleService",
  → this);
  // All additional services would be
  // initialized here - at this time.
}
//— — — — — — — — — — — — — — — — — — — — — — — — —
// Public Broker method to call server-side methods -
//— — — — — — — — — — — — — — — — — — — — — — — — —
BrokerClass.prototype.doMethod = function(service, method, cb, arg1,
→ arg2, arg3, arg4, arg5)
{
  // set up callback - if CB == a function then it's OK -
  // Else - callback to the function that calls this method - sending
  → results -
  this.callback = (typeof(cb) == "function") ? cb : arguments.caller;
  if(this.isBusy) {
    // The broker is currently waiting for a response -
    // Put the method into the queue
    trace("PUTTING METHOD INTO QUEUE");
    this.queueMethod(service, method, this.callback, arg1, arg2,
    → arg3, arg4, arg5);
  } else {
    // The broker is not busy - execute the method call -
    trace("— — — — — — — — — — — — — — — — — — —·");
    this.isBusy = true;
    // Create a _Result method with the current method name -
    this[method + "_Result"] = function(result) {
      trace("Server Response Successful");
      this.isBusy = false;
      trace("— — — — — — — — — — — — — — — — — —·");
      this.callback(result);
    }
    // Create a _Status method with current method name -
    this[method + "_Status"] = function(result) {
      // track and handle errors - do not return control
      // to the caller...
```

(continued on next page)

```
      trace("Server Communication Failed : Captured in Broker Object");
      trace("_Status Called with : " + result.description);
      for(var i in result)
        trace(i + " : " + result);
        this.isBusy = false;
        trace(" — — — — — — — — — — — — — — — —·");
      }
    trace("Broker transmitting to : " + method + " AT : " + service);
    eval("this." + service + "." + method)(arg1, arg2, arg3, arg4,
    → arg5);
  }
}
//— — — — — — — — — — — — — — — — — — — — — — — —
BrokerClass.prototype.queueMethod = function(service, method, cb,
→ arg1, arg2, arg3, arg4, arg5)
{
  // add method call to the end of the queue...
  this.methodQueue.push( { service : service, method : method, cb :
  → cb, arg1 : arg1, arg2 : arg2, arg3 : arg3, arg4 : arg4, arg5 :
  → arg5 } );
  if(this.queueID == undefined)
    this.queueID = setInterval(this, "checkMethodQueue", 500);
}
//— — — — — — — — — — — — — — — — — — — — — — — —
BrokerClass.prototype.checkMethodQueue = function()
{
  if(this.methodQueue.length <= 0) {
    // If there are no more items in the queue,
    // stop looping -
    clearInterval(this.queueID);
    delete this.queueID;
  } else if(!this.isBusy) {
    // The broker is available - send the next
    // method call to the server -
    var item = this.methodQueue.shift();
    this.doMethod(item.service, item.method, item.cb, item.arg1,
    → item.arg2, item.arg3, item.arg4, item.arg5);
  }
}
//— — — — — — — — — — — — — — — — — — — — — — — —
// isBusy property getter / setter
//— — — — — — — — — — — — — — — — — — — — — — — —
BrokerClass.prototype.setIsBusy = function(busy)
{
  // call appropriate methods to enable / disable
  // global interactions - and update artwork
  // to notify user that the application is
  // transmitting...
  if(busy)
    _root.disableInteraction();
  else
    _root.enableInteraction();
  this.isBusy = busy;
}
//— — — — — — — — — — — — — — — — — — — — — — — —
```

(continued on next page)

```
BrokerClass.prototype.getIsBusy = function()
{
  // this.isBusy getter method -
  return this.isBusy;
}
// — — — — — — — — — — — — — — — — — — — — — — — —
#endinitclip
```

Assuming the preceding example resided in a MovieClip symbol with its linkage property set to Export for ActionScript and Export in First Frame, the following code could exist on the _root Timeline to implement it:

```
// include Macromedias Netservice Codebase -
#include "NetServices.as"
#include "NetDebug.as"
function init() {
  // instantiate the BrokerClass into the _global scope
  _global.Broker = new BrokerClass();
  // Test the new Broker Class
  this.testBroker();
  this.inited = true;
}
function testBroker() {
  // Call the custom Broker Instance and pass in:
  // 1) Service Name : javaConn
  // 2) Method Name : doSearch
  // 3) Custom Result function : this.doSearch_Result
  // 4) opt. Argument : "luke bayes"
  Broker.doMethod("javaConn", "doSearch", this.myDoSearchResult,
  → "luke bayes", 0);
  // NOTE : This object can now be called from within any timeline at:
  // Broker.doMethod(args);
}
function myDoSearchResult(result) {
  // Custom function to handle results that does not need
  // to follow any specific naming convention -
  trace("myDoSearchResult called with:");
  for(var i in result)
    trace(i + " : " + result[i]);
}
if(!this.inited)
  this.init();
```

The New Flash MX 2004 Data Components

Since its inception, Flash Remoting has been promoted by Macromedia as the single best way to get data into the Flash Player, while that is still true, it's not the only way to import dynamic data since the introduction of the new data components in Flash MX Professional 2004 (see Chapter 10, "v2 Components"). Although Flash Remoting is a simple and efficient mechanism for the manipulation of data, it can prove more time-consuming when you take into account the management of the workflow challenges.

Sample Questions

1. Which of the following steps is *not* required in order to test or deploy Flash Remoting?

   A. Install and configure a supported web server application environment.

   B. Download and install the server-side remoting components.

   C. Download and install the Flash MX 2004 Remoting components.

   D. Implement a Macromedia UI component.

2. Which of the following external ActionScript files must you #include in your movie in order to use Flash Remoting?

   A. URLRemote.as

   B. Gateway.as

   C. NetServices.as

   D. GetRemote.as

3. Flash Remoting *cannot* do which of the following?

   A. Access data directly from a remotely hosted web service

   B. Integrate seamlessly with existing Macromedia UI components

   C. Translate SOAP XML data into native Flash objects

   D. Marshal native Java objects into Flash objects

4. Which Flash Remoting class binds RecordSet objects to Flash components?

   A. NetServices class

   B. DataGlue class

   C. NetConnection class

   D. DataBinding class

   [handwritten: Bind Format String()
   Bind Format Function()]

5. Which panel monitors and displays any communications that pass through the Flash Remoting interface?

   A. Services Browser

   B. NetConnection Debugger

   C. Gateway Connection

   D. Marshaling Gateway

CHAPTER 21

Web Services

Over the last couple of years, Web Services has emerged as the next generation of Web-based technology for exchanging information. Web services are self-describing, self-contained modular applications that are accessible over the Internet. To better facilitate accessibility to these self-contained applications, the World Wide Web Consortium (W3C) has begun describing and documenting a framework to allow web services to communicate more consistently with one another, known as *interoperability*. (See www.w3c.org for more information.)

If you're building a Flash application that submits or retrieves data from a server, you're in fact building a *distributed* application. Using either the Flash Remoting gateway or its new Web Services data-connectivity components, you can provide a seamless marshaling interface for XML documents based on the industry-standard SOAP protocol. (SOAP stands for Simple Object Access Protocol.)

Macromedia has recently added support for Web Services in the form of its WebServiceConnector component and Web Service classes. These features are only available in Flash MX (via Flash Remoting), and Flash MX Professional 2004, and they both make it possible to access remote methods exposed by a server, using the SOAP protocol.

Throughout the rest of this chapter, we explore some of the elements of Web Services technology, as well as the new Flash MX Professional 2004 Web Services data-connectivity components, including:

- Understanding the Web Services technologies: SOAP, UDDI, and WSDL
- Accessing Web Services with the Web Service classes: Log, PendingCall, and SOAPCall
- Using the `WebServiceConnector` Component
- Lazy decoding

Web Services Technologies

One of the main benefits of using web services is their substantial and far-reaching presence. Because these applications are provided over the Internet, they are accessible from anywhere and use an existing infrastructure. Furthermore, because of the standards with which web services are developed, they work well with existing security systems such as firewalls.

> **NOTE**
> The new cross-domain security rules released with Flash Player 7 also apply to Web Services.

SOAP   (Simple Object Access Protocol)

Simple Object Access Protocol (SOAP) is an XML-based protocol for exchanging information in a decentralized, distributed environment. The protocol defines a mechanism by which to pass commands and parameters between clients and servers. Like Web Services as a whole, SOAP is independent of the platform, object model, and programming language being used.

SOAP's particular advantage over earlier protocols, such as Internet Inter-ORB Protocol (IIOP) for CORBA or Java Remote Method Protocol (JRMP) for Java Remote Method Invocation (RMI), is that it uses XML and is therefore text-based. This makes SOAP-based applications easier to debug, because it is obviously easier to read XML than to read a binary stream. Additionally, text-based protocols such as SOAP over HTTP are firewall friendly and tend not to create the same security issues as proprietary protocols.

Because SOAP is an XML-based framework, it is entirely platform and device independent, and subsequently can be used with the majority of server-side technologies

XML-based, device independent, secure, firewall-friendly

(with varying degrees of simplicity, based on their particular implementation of Web Services).

UDDI *(Universal Description, Discovery and Integration)*

The Universal Description, Discovery, and Integration (UDDI) protocol is one of the major building blocks required for successful Web Services implementations. You could consider UDDI the "Yellow Pages" for Web Services. It is an information database of web services; descriptions about companies and the services they offer are stored in a common XML format. Just as businesses list their products and services in a telephone directory, web service brokers use the UDDI specification to register web services that requesters can then discover and invoke. Web-based applications interact with a UDDI registry using SOAP messages.

Conceptually, the data in a UDDI registry can be divided into three different types of telephone directories: a "white pages" section that provides business contact information, a "yellow pages" section that categorizes businesses and services, and a "green pages" section that provides technical information about the services offered by a business. A typical example of UDDI usage is a stock-ticker application that can automatically locate a web service that offers stock quotes using a standardized API.

WSDL *(Web Services Description Language)*

The Web Services Description Language (WSDL) is the metadata language of web services. It acts as a "user manual" for the services, defining how service providers and requesters communicate with each other about the services.

Like XML, WSDL is extensible to allow the description of endpoints and their messages, regardless of what message formats or network protocols are used for communicating. WSDL can be used to design specifications to invoke and operate web services on the Internet and to access and invoke remote applications and databases.

Typically, if you want to create an application that communicates with a particular web service, all you need is that service's WSDL file. In this way, WSDL files are similar to the Interface Definition Language (IDL) used by RPC and CORBA systems.

WSDL files are accessible using an everyday URL. In Flash MX Professional 2004, you can view the schema of any web service by entering the URL for its WSDL file using the Web Services panel or directly into the WSDLURL parameter of the component itself. Once you identify a WSDL file, the web service itself is available to any application you create.

Web Service Classes

WebService Connector component

Web Service class

Flash MX Professional 2004 comes with two new features for connecting to Web Services. The first of these is the WebServiceConnector component, which is discussed later in this chapter. The second, is a set of Web Service classes that utilize SOAP to access remote Web Services. These classes, which can be found in the mx.services package, can only be used with ActionScript and, unlike their UI counterparts, don't have a visual element to them.

The main advantage of using the Web Service classes over the WebServiceConnector component is that you have greater control over the interaction between Flash and the Web Service. This is achieved via the Web Service object methods, that relate to operations within the WSDL URL that have been passed across. Additionally, Web Service object debugging is more detailed (than with the WebServiceConnector component) due to the log class.

Unfortunately, both the Web Service classes, and the WebServiceConnector component, have an issue that causes long delays when returning large datasets. This is due to the fact that converting the returned data into ActionScript objects can be quite processor intensive. This problem can be partially overcome by enabling *Lazy Decoding*, which defers the data processing process (and is discussed later in this chapter).

Currently, the most effective method of returning large data sets from a Web Service is via Flash Remoting. Unlike Flash, Flash Remoting returns data sets as Action Message Format (AMF) instead of XML. AMF has a much faster transfer speed due to the fact that it's a compressed binary format similar to SOAP.

Log Class

The new web services logging feature in Flash MX 2004, allows developers to view interactions between Flash and the remote Web Service in a step by step manner, as they occur. The log is very useful when trying to locate potential bugs within Web Service code. The following code creates a new log object.

```
//Create a Log object that outputs all events that occur
//when calling a web service.
displayWebServiceLog = new Log(Log.VERBOSE);
displayWebServiceLog.onLog = function(txt) {
    trace(txt);
}
```

The log object has 3 levels of reporting:

- Log.BRIEF: The log records primary life-cycle event and error notifications.

- Log.VERBOSE: The log records all life-cycle event and error notifications.

- Log.DEBUG: The log records metrics and fine-grained events and errors.

In this example, we have set the level of reporting to Log.Verbose, which records everything. The Log object also takes a second parameter called logname, that can be helpful if need to log events of two web services at the same time.

PendingCall Class

The PendingCall object is an automatically returned object that is returned when you initially call a method on a WebService object. The onResult and onFault callbacks of the PendingCall object are subsequently used to manage the asynchronous responses from the WebService method.

If there's been a problem in connecting to the Web Service, for example if the server is not responding, Flash Player calls the PendingCall.onFault callback and passes a SOAPFault object. This object can contain a verbose error message, relating to the XML SOAP fault. On the other hand, if the Web Service connection is successful, Flash Player will call the PendingCall.onResult callback, and pass a result object composed of XML. The result object will then be deserialized into ActionScript. As mentioned previously, this action can be processor intensive if the returned object is quite large.

problem → on Fault → SOAP Fault

SOAPCall Class

sucessful → on Result → XML object

The SOAPCall object is a descriptor that describes the operations that occur within the WSDL URL of the Web Service. The object contains information that is specific to each operation within the WDSL, for example the structure of the XML. The SOAPCall object for any given WDSL operation can be returned by using the getCall(operationName) function.

The WebServiceConnector Component

The WebServiceConnector component, which is available only in Flash MX Professional 2004, allows developers to quickly and easily connect to remote web services. Data from the WebServiceConnector is returned as an object which can be bound to other components within a Flash application. Additionally, if the WebServiceConnector component receives multiple records of data from a Web Service, it converts them into an ActionScript array so that they are more easily consumed within your application.

To use the WebServiceConnector component, simply drag an instance of it onto the stage (from the Data Components library), set the URL for the web service (within the Component Inspector panel or the Web Services panel), and trigger it.

drag → set URL → trigger

> **NOTE**
>
> When you first use the `WebServiceConnector` during application authoring, it will appear on the Stage for easy access and configuration. After the application is compiled, the component will not be visible in the runtime application

Using Lazy Decoding

As previously mentioned, when record sets are returned from a remote source (such as Web Service), the conversion of the returned XML/SOAP data into a format more easily consumed by Flash (such as an ActionScript object) can be extremely processor intensive task. This load on the system can sometimes cause considerable delays in the extraction of data. To help alleviate this issue, the WebServiceConnector component contains a feature called *lazy decoding*. The lazy decoding (algorithm) allows the process of converting the returned data to be delayed, by placing it into an `ArrayProxy` object. This allows the data to be called and translated only as it's needed, rather than in one large block. By default, lazy coding is enabled within Flash. To disable lazy coding, the `SOAPCall.doLazyDecoding` property needs to be set to `false`.

Sample Questions

1. The World Wide Web Consortium (W3C) has begun describing and documenting a framework, which allows self-contained applications to communicate more consistently with one another. What is this capability otherwise known as?

   A. Compatibility

   B. Interoperability

   C. Interconnectivity

   D. Intercommunicabilty

2. Simple Object Access Protocol (SOAP) is based on what protocol?

   A. HTML *firewall friendly*

   B. TEXT *text-based*

   C. XML *device-independent*

   D. ColdFusion *easy to debug*

3. The Web Service classes of Flash MX Professional 2004 are located in which package? *mx. services*

   A. `flash.webSevices`

   B. `mx.services`

   C. `macromedia.eng.remoteServices\`

   D. HTML

4. How are WSDL files accessed?

   A. XML *WSDL is a ~~descriptor~~ metadata language*

   B. URL *of web services, defining how services'*

   C. Flash Remoting *providers and requesters communicate*

   D. `sockets` *with each other.*

5. Lazy decoding is a feature of the `WebServiceConnector` component. Why is it called "lazy"?

   A. It is more tolerant of "loosely typed" code and permits developers to be less strict with coding standards.

   B. It permits the `WebServiceConnector` to randomly (or "lazily") poll connections to a web service.

   C. Because you need to use a different instance of `WebServiceConnector` for each operation you want to call.

   D. It allows developers to defer the conversion of multiple records of data from XML/SOAP into ActionScript native data.

SOAPCall. doLazyDecoding

Data Classes and Components

The new *data binding classes* and *data connection components* in Macromedia Flash MX Professional 2004 allow developers to create dynamic data-driven applications rapidly using data sources such as web services and application servers. Unlike most of their counterparts, these classes and components have no visual appearance at runtime and are characterized only by their respective icon when placed on Stage at author time. These new features dramatically enhance Flash's position with the web application development community. Using the data connection components, you can now quickly connect to an external data source simply by entering that data source's URL. Once the data is returned, you can use the data binding properties of the components to display the data or manage it in local record sets and UI controls.

Data binding functionality has also been improved in the latest version of Flash. You can now seamlessly match up the properties of various user interface components and link them to the data on your server via the data components or the data component classes.

This chapter touches on the various elements of the data component set, including:

- The seven data binding classes
- Data warehousing with the `DataHolder` component
- List-based class communication with the DataProvider API
- Handling data collections with the `DataSet` component
- Updating relational databases with the `RDBMSResolver` component
- Reading and writing XML documents with the `XMLConnector` component
- XUpdate standards and the `XUpdateResolver` component

> **NOTE**
> The majority of the data classes and components require Flash Player 7 or later.

Data Binding Classes

As mentioned, data binding is not new to Flash. It was first introduced in Flash MX in early 2003 when Macromedia acquired the Firefly Components from CyberSage Software, and then bundled them into the Flash MX Data Connection Kit. With the release of Flash MX Professional 2004, data binding functionality has been enhanced and incorporated into the Flash IDE in the form of a set of classes and components.

For those of you not familiar with data binding, simply put, it relates to the concept of connecting components together and allowing them to share and update data. This is achieved via the component's properties, which allow data to be passed in and out of the component. A *binding* is a statement that says "When property X of component A changes, copy the new value into property Y of component B."

Developers transitioning from other object-oriented languages such as Java and C++ will be familiar with data binding, since it is one of the key features of Rapid Application Development (RAD).

The point-and-click data binding actually works by utilizing a runtime data binding API, which can also be accessed via ActionScript, provided that you include the required assets in your movie. Including the assets involves simply adding a copy of the data-binding classes symbol from the Classes common library, found in the Flash menu bar in Window > Other Panels > Common Libraries > Classes. Data binding is carried out within the authoring environment using the Bindings tab of the Component Inspector panel. From here you can add, view, and remove bindings for a component. Alternatively, you can programmatically create and configure bindings using the classes in the `mx.data.binding` package.

> **NOTE**
> In order to use any of the data binding classes at runtime, the `DataBindingClasses` component must be added to the library of the FLA file.

There are seven data binding classes, all of which are available only in Flash MX Professional 2004. These classes are located within the `mx.data.binding` package.

Binding Class

The Binding class defines the connection between a data *source* and a data *destination*. Essentially, it listens for changes to the data source and copies the modified data to the destination endpoint every time a change is detected. Once instantiated, the Binding class can be used to bind data to any ActionScript-based object, as long as the object emits events and has properties.

ComponentMixins Class *why*

The ComponentMixins class defines and automatically adds data binding–specific functionality (by way of properties and methods) to components or objects that are the source or destination endpoint of a binding. The objects or components are specified by calling the ComponentMixins.initComponent() method.

CustomFormatter Class

The CustomFormatter class contains two methods that allow you to transform data values from one specific data type into a String, and vice versa. The format() and unformat() methods, by default, don't do anything until they've been implemented in a subclass of the mx.data.binding.CustomFormatter. The CustomFormatter class is handy for converting numeric values (for example 1, 2, 3) into an English string equivalent (for example "one", "two", "three").

CustomValidator Class

If you wish to validate data fields contained within components, you must first create a custom validation class. This is done by creating a subclass of the CustomValidator class. Once it's created, you can implement the validate() method, which examines and validates the data that is passed across in the form of a parameter. From here you can use the validationError() method to display an appropriate error message.

DataType Class

The DataType class enables read/write access to the data fields of a component property. The main advantage to using DataType object methods when getting and setting component data field values is that these values are automatically processed (and converted, if possible) to the format that is specified on the field's schema settings. This offers data transfer functionality that is superior to directly getting (or setting) values onto the component instance—primarily because when data is entered in this way, it exists in a "raw" form (rather than based on the schema settings).

EndPoint Class

As outlined previously, the Binding class defines the *connection* between a data source endpoint and a data destination endpoint. When the Binding class constructor is called, it requires two EndPoint objects to be passed across. These objects define a data source and destination for the respective binding, and they contain properties that can be used to either obtain or assign data.

TypedValue Class

The TypedValue object is used to assist in the type conversion of data that is passed to the DataType class. When the DataType.getTypedValue() method is called, a TypedValue object is returned, which contains a data value along with information about the value's data type.

DataHolder Component

The DataHolder component acts as a data warehouse for storing data received from data sources. It can also be used to facilitate the connection between other components, using data binding. Using either bindings or ActionScript code, you can assign various types of data to a DataHolder property. When the value of the data contained within the binding or property changes, the DataHolder component will broadcast an event with the same name as the property (or binding) associated with the changed data.

DataProvider API

List-based classes (such as Arrays, RecordSets, and DataSets) communicate with data sources using a series of methods and properties that are contained within the DataProvider API. DataProvider-compliant classes are created by implementing all the methods and properties described within the DataProvider API. These classes can then become data providers for List-based components.

A *data provider* is a linear collection of items similar to an array. Each item within the data provider is an object that's composed of several fields of data. These objects can be accessed by their index number, just as you would within an array. Using the methods of the DataProvider API, you are able to update and query the data in UI components that display data (such as the DataGrid, ListTree, and so on). This window into the data (using the component) is more commonly known as a *view*. Just as in a house, several windows may overlook the same courtyard; so too is it possible to have multiple views of the same data provider.

DataSet Class

The DataSet class contains a series of properties, methods, and events that allow you to you work with data as collections (or *sets*) of objects.

There are far too many class members (properties, methods, and events) to be covered in any detail here. A full definition of the DataSet class can be found in the Flash Help documentation under Using Components > DataSet Class.

> **NOTE**
>
> One property of the DataSet class that rates a special mention, because you're very likely to encounter it when working with data within Flash, is the `DeltaPacket` property. A `DeltaPacket` represents any changes that have been made between `dataSets`. The `DeltaPacket` property, which is returned as an object, is critical in mapping any changes that have been made to a `dataSet` collection and its items.

DataSet Component

The `DataSet` component is the foundation upon which data-driven applications within Flash MX 2004 are created. This component facilitates working with data as collections of client-side objects that can be searched, sorted, modified, and indexed, just like traditional server-based objects.

Working with data via the `DataSet` component is accomplished with `DataSetIterators` and `DeltaPackets`. A `DataSetIterator` is a set of methods that allows complex data sets to be traversed and modified, as compared to a `DeltaPacket`, which is a set of interfaces and classes that facilitates the updating of data collections. Consistent with solid OO design, these classes are never read or modified directly. Rather, they are updated through a set of *accessor* methods, including `addItem()`, `applyUpdates()`, and `removeAll()`, all of which are found within the DataSet class.

Generally speaking, the `DataSet` component is used in conjunction with several other components, such as a `Connector` or `Resolver`, to modify a data source.

RDBMSResolver Component

The `RDBMSResolver` component creates an XML update packet that can be passed across to an external data source, such as an ASP/JSP page, servlet, or web service. This passage is accomplished via a connector component such as the `XMLConnector` or `WebServiceConnector`. The passed XML update packet can then be translated into SQL statements that can be used to update any standard SQL relational database.

Through the use of bindings, the RDBMSResolver component is connected to a DataSet component's DeltaPacket property, which provides the RDBMSResolver with any updates in the data packets. The RDBMSResolver then sends an XML update packet to a connector component. If errors occur during this communication process, the RDBMSResolver will pass them back to the DataSet component.

XMLConnector Component

Think of the XMLConnector component as a power double-adapter that's constructed of either ActionScript or a data binding. This adapter allows you to connect components to external XML sources. It has the ability to read or write XML, via HTTP post or get operations.

To send and receive parameters and results to and from external data sources, the XMLConnector implements a set of methods, properties, and events encapsulated within the RPC (Remote Procedure Call) Component API.

The structure of an XML document that outlines the various data elements to which the document can be bound is known as the *schema*. The schema is by far the simplest way to connect to an external XML file and consume its parameters and results within your application. The new schema browser panel within Flash MX Professional 2004 simplifies this process even further.

XUpdateResolver Component

XUpdate is an industry standard for describing updates that have occurred to an XML document. The standard is supported by a variety of XML databases, including Xindice or XHive.

The XUpdateResolver component is used to convert changes made to a DataSet component into XUpdate statements. The updates from the XUpdateResolver component are then sent, in the form of an XUpdate data packet, to the database (or server) through a connection object.

Using bindable properties, the XUpdateResolver component receives a DeltaPacket from a DataSet component, sends its own update packet to a connector, receives server errors back from the connection, and communicates them back to the DataSet component.

Sample Questions

1. When Macromedia acquired the data binding components from CyberSage Software in 2003, what was their original name?

   A. FireStar

   B. Firefly

   C. FireStarter

   D. FireBug

2. What is data binding?

   A. The connection of SWF files

   B. The concept of component connection with data sharing and updating

   C. The linking of data to a single component instance

   D. The connection/association of dataSets

3. What is represented within a DeltaPacket?   *a property of DataSet*

   A. Changes made within a dataset

   B. A list of connections to a relational database   *DataSet Iterator*

   C. Definitions of an event, for which a Binding object listens

   D. Connections among other components and external XML data sources

4. Which component acts as a data warehouse for storing data received from data sources?   *DataProvider API*

   DataHolder

   A. List component

   B. DataSet component

   C. DataHolder component

   D. RDBMSResolver component

5. The RDBMSResolver component is used in association with which other data component?

   A. DataSet component

   B. XUpdater component

   C. DataHolder component

   D. XMLConnector component

PART 6

Testing, Implementation, and Deployment

CHAPTER 23

Functional Testing Methodologies

Within this chapter, we'll examine some of the best practices and options available for testing the functionality of your Macromedia Flash MX 2004 applications. These testing options include some of Flash's built-in tools, but for the most part, identifying and resolving bugs depends 99 percent on your own finely tuned problem-solving skills.

Here are some of the topics we'll explore:

- Using Flash's built-in tools for debugging: trace statements and the Error class

    - Automatic exception handling

    - Compiler error messages

    - The Flash Debugger

    - The Service Browser and the NetConnection Debugger for Remoting issues

- Four different approaches to testing:

    - Modular architecture

    - Isolating the issues of concern with guide levels and multi-line comments

    - Focusing on network communication

    - Version control

Flash's Built-in Testing Tools

With Macromedia's latest release of Flash, the company has made a concerted effort to assist developers to efficiently debug their Flash code. Though it's not yet in the league of other object-oriented languages (such as Java), ActionScript 2.0 has been a step in the right direction. Let's take a look at some of Flash's built-in tools for testing code.

trace Statements

If you plan to build anything at all with ActionScript, you should be intimately familiar with the trace() function. This function lets you send string values to the Output panel, and the code will be displayed in test mode. A good habit to get into when creating a new class, method, or function, is to insert a trace statement in the first line of code, like this:

```
MyCustomClass = function(arg) {
   trace(" — — — — —");
   trace("My Custom class instantiated");
   this.init(arg);
}
MyCustomClass.prototype.init = function(arg1) {
   trace("My Custom class inited with : " + arg1);
   this.getObj();
}
```

I don't think so.

To test the constructs in this example, simply instantiate the newly defined class:

```
var myCustom = new MyCustomClass("hello world");
```

The Output panel will display the following:

```
— — — — —
My Custom class instantiated
My Custom class inited with : hello world
```

Notice how the argument values are being output within these statements. Once it is confirmed that the methods do in fact work, immediately comment the trace line, but leave it in there. This way, if the application becomes complex and difficult to debug, you can simply uncomment a bunch of trace statements and clearly see which functions are called, in what order, and what values are being passed into them. With this method you can find out approximately where any new issue exists.

Limitations of trace

The trace feature is your single most powerful ally when you want to debug a Flash movie. Unfortunately, there are some inconvenient limitations to be considered.

First, keep in mind that trace will *not* automatically output the keys and values of any object instance. If the following code appeared immediately beneath the MyCustomClass class declaration:

```
MyCustomClass.prototype.getObj = function() {
  var obj = new Object();
  obj.item1 = "value1";
  obj.item2 = "value2";
  obj.item3 = "value3";
  trace("my obj : " + obj);
  return obj;
}
```

and if the new method were called, the Output panel would display the following:

```
my obj : [object Object]
```

This is completely unacceptable if you're trying to determine whether some complex data has been retrieved or transmitted correctly.

There are a number of ways you can introspect ActionScript objects using tools that Macromedia provides. Unfortunately, not one of these tools lets you explicitly define a single specific object for introspection. Instead, the tools either show *all* (List Objects, List Variables, and the Debugger, each of which will be described shortly) or nothing. To get around this limitation, you can create a custom routine that augments the trace action and recursively outputs any object methods and properties.

TIP

The recursive function being referred to makes use of the `for i in` construct. This is a looping statement that cycles through each variable in an object and assigns its name to the value of `i`. The `i` variable can then be used to access that object's methods and properties as follows:

```
for(var i in myObj) {
  trace(i + " : " + myObj[i]);
}
```

TIP

The `trace()` function should be used liberally, but it's your responsibility to manage when and why you call it. If you find the Output panel is getting completely filled with meaningless `trace` statements, none of them is doing you any good. As a courtesy to whomever else may see your code, always comment unnecessary `trace` statements before delivering builds.

Using the Omit Trace Actions Setting

If your application includes a large number of trace statements that remain active for one reason or another, you can have a decent impact on reducing file size and an even bigger impact toward improved performance by choosing Omit Trace Actions from the Publish Settings dialog box. But if you do decide to take advantage of this feature, don't forget that you turned it on! There's nothing worse than spending an hour trying to figure out why your most recent trace action isn't working, only to discover that you set this option in Publish Settings.

Built-in Exception Handling

Flash MX has some basic exception (or error) handling built into the compiler. This is the first line of defense for identifying some of the most common and obvious problems with ActionScript.

When you go to test mode, if any of a number of common syntactical or structural errors exist in your movie, extremely helpful messages will be displayed in the Output panel before any other trace actions. These messages will tell you in which movie clip the error exists and specifically what the error is.

Debugger

In previous versions of Flash, the Debugger console received a fair amount of attention due to a bug causing it to function only intermittently. As a result, it was considered pretty much useless for the purpose of bug discovery. Thankfully, these issues were resolved in the last version of Flash (MX).

Using the Debugger, you can set and manage breakpoints. You can step through, inside, or over all of your ActionScript, and view a hierarchical representation of the SWF file's objects at any given moment during playback.

The Debugger is enabled by pressing Ctrl+Shift+Enter to test your movie. You'll notice an additional file in your working directory, fileName.swd,; this is where the debugging information is stored. Be aware that if you compile a debug build on a movie that employs substantial ActionScript, the actual SWF file is also slightly larger.

Although the Debugger's features can be very useful for discovering many technical problems, keep in mind that it requires considerably more system resources to present real-time debugger data. If your Flash application is already experiencing performance problems, previewing it in Debugger mode will certainly aggravate those problems. Application performance in a Debugger build will almost always be worse than when compiled only for the Macromedia Flash Player 7.

When a Debugger build is compiled, you're immediately presented with the Debugger interface. The movie then pauses so that you can use the combo box on the right of the interface to set and manage breakpoints. When the playhead encounters a breakpoint, it stops interpreting and awaits your interaction. You can make any of a number of selections in the Debugger interface.

Remoting: Service Browser

The Remoting service browser is actually a SWF file that is played back in a panel in the Flash MX editing environment. This panel is installed along with the Remoting services after you download them from Macromedia. Basically, You can point the service browser at a valid Remoting gateway and identify the services. If they are available, you can then clearly see the available API calls. This tool is very handy when setting up Flash Remoting connections, especially if you're new to Flash Remoting.

Remoting: NetConnection Debugger

The NetConnection debugger is an extremely useful tool that lets you view and manipulate the Flash Remoting connection settings. It also displays Remoting events combined with output of any data that is transmitted into or out of the Flash Player. if you're transmitting large quantities of data through a Remoting connection, this tool may present a significant performance hit.

Bandwidth Profiler

This tool is accessed by first pressing Ctrl+Enter to test your movie (or Ctrl+Shift+Enter to bring up the Debugger and test), and then choosing View > Bandwidth Profiler (or Ctrl+B). You will be presented with a frame-by-frame accounting of your movie along with some global file-size data. For those experiencing problems with streaming data, the Bandwidth Profiler used to be a perfect place to get more information.

A significant problem with this tool is that it wasn't updated when Macromedia introduced the new and improved compilation algorithm in Flash MX. For example, if you drag every single UI component from UIComponent package 1 into a new movie and look at the Bandwidth Profiler, it will tell you that your SWF file is 96KB. However, the actual SWF file produced is 27KB. If you had to choose between a *much* smaller SWF file and a compliant Bandwidth Profiler, you would certainly choose the smaller SWF file. So, given the circumstances, Macromedia probably made the right decision to leave the Profiler alone. Just understand that this tool is useless if you're developing content for the Flash Player 6 or 7 and you choose Compress Movie in your publish settings. On the upside, the Profiler is still accurate if you do *not* choose Compress Movie. Also, if you're testing the upload of images, data streams, or external SWF files, the Profiler will show a worse case scenario than what you'd have after compression. When publishing you can also generate a size report which is far better than in the last versions.

Error Class

As outlined in Chapter 16, "Core, Movie, and Client-Server Classes," Flash MX 2004's new Error class allows developers to extract information from Flash Player relating to errors that have occurred within a script.

When monitoring errors, you'll generally use instances of the Error class or its subclasses, combined with the `throw` statement. The `throw` statement generates ("throws") an error that can be handled ("caught") by a `catch{}` or `finally{}` code block. If an exception is not caught by a `catch` or `finally` block, the string representation of the thrown value is sent to the Output panel.

When the `message` property of the Error class is used, a string that contains an error message associated with an error can be displayed within the Output panel. The `error.message` property is commonly used in conjunction with the `try..catch..finally` code blocks.

try..catch..finally

Errors can be captured using a combination of the `try..catch..finally` code blocks. This technique allows developers to test their code for certain errors and then react in a predefined manner when an error occurs. The try code block is always required to be followed by either a `catch` block, a `finally` block, or both.

> **NOTE**
> A single `try` block can have multiple `catch` blocks but only one `finally` block.

If code within the try block doesn't throw an error (that is, if the `try` block completes normally), then the code in the `finally` block is still executed. The `finally` block executes even if the `try` block exits using a `return` statement.

If any code within the `try` code block throws an error (using the `throw` action), control then passes to the `catch` block (providing one has been defined). After executing the `catch` block, control then passes to the `finally` code block (once again, providing one has been defined).

In the following example, the `finally` code block will execute regardless of whether any values have been returned.

```
//define a new iceCream object
var myIceCream = new IceCream()
//test
try {
  var totalFlavors = myIceCream.getIceCreamFlavors();
  if(totalFlavors!= 64) {
    throw new Error("I'm sorry I couldn't find all 64 flavors");
  }
}
finally {
  // Delete the myIceCream object no matter what.
  if(myIceCream!= null) {
    delete myIceCream;
  }
}
```

NOTE

The `finally` block will always execute, regardless of whether an error was thrown.

Error Messages

Macromedia Flash MX 2004 now provides developers with enhanced compile-time error reporting if they are developing with ActionScript 2.0.

The compiler within Flash will generate numeric errors based on the particular event that has occurred. For example, if you neglect to include a class name, the compiler will throw an error 1093, or if you've tried to specify more than one class constructor, error 1153 is thrown.

There are over 100 unique error codes that can be thrown; you'll find them all listed in the Help documentation of Flash MX 2004.

List Objects and List Variables   *for small application*

Two more commands available in test mode are Debug > List Objects and Debug > List Variables. Each of these commands presents information about all objects and/or variables that currently exist in the movie. Though both are useful tools for small Flash movies that don't contain many objects or variables, for complex Flash applications these commands create a huge amount of text information that can obstruct the search for a specific problem.

Approaches to Testing

There are several approaches you can take to help simplify the testing and debugging process. Implementing these practices is not reliant on any particular feature; instead, each represents a different philosophy for specific challenges.

Using a Modular Architecture

Taking a global modular approach is a major design decision that can greatly assist you in locating bugs down the road. First, separate and encapsulate each piece of functionality in your application. When you can successfully isolate features into their own independent classes (or modules), debugging becomes very simple. For any given issue, the list of likely candidates will be narrowed to one.

If you're attempting to "modularize" an application for the first time, the absolute best way to learn about this process is by reading about *design patterns*. Most of the available resources covering design patterns are related to other programming languages (such as Java), but design patterns can easily be applied to ActionScript.

> **NOTE**
>
> *Patterns in Java: A Catalog of Reusable Design Patterns Illustrated with UML, 2nd Edition, volume 1* of a three-volume series by Mark Grand, is a very useful book. The topic of design patterns is a huge one all on its own, but if you can at least become familiar with how other engineers have already tackled the issues of design patterns, you will ultimately save yourself considerable time, money, energy, and possibly even embarrassment.

Isolating the Issues

Assuming you have already built an application that has displayed one or more unanticipated bugs, you need to begin a clearly defined process to determine where the problem exists and what you need to do to fix it. The debugging process can be very fast and efficient, or it can be extremely tedious and time-consuming. A principal factor affecting the time invested in debugging is how effectively you have separated each feature in your application from the others.

If your ActionScript is a long series of linear statements that are buried inside many movie clips, you will have a hard time locating even the simplest problems. If your ActionScript is logically separated into classes and stored in external AS files, you should be able to immediately isolate the most likely cause of the problem and eliminate it. Following are two ways in which you can rapidly filter through the complexity of a movie and isolate a problem:

- **Guide Layers:** If your movies and components make use of multiple layers, you can simply change them to become *guide layers*. This effectively keeps the contents of a layer from being active at runtime. A complex Timeline-based Flash application can quickly be simplified into a couple of key features using this approach.

- **Multi-line Comments:** In the land of #included ActionScript, guide layers don't usually help much. A wise alternative is to refrain from using multi-line comments when writing code. You can always add them later and instantly comment almost all of a complex object, enabling only the methods or properties that you're currently dealing with.

Focusing on Network Communication

One very common place for bugs to appear is in the network communication layer of Flash applications. Since many Flash applications are built without the concept of a network layer, a lot of bugs are introduced within communication processes. If you expect to make your Flash movie communicate with a server, any and all server-side communication should be fed through a single internal network layer. This "layer" doesn't exist in Flash—you have to build it. If you build a single local interface (not a GUI, but an API) through which *all* server-side communication passes, you effectively construct a network communication layer in Flash. This will let you quickly identify and repair connection issues as well as data transformation problems.

Most Flash applications seem to work by simply accessing server-side resources from anywhere and anything in Flash that needs them. The single internal network layer approach described here is for all of those internal scripts that would "like" to access a server-side resource to simply access the local interface. *Then* that local interface deals with any remote interfaces and actual network communication.

Implementing Version Control

If you're developing complex Flash applications, you should definitely be using some form of version control software. Lucky for you, Flash MX Professional 2004 comes with built-in version control. This allows developers to *check out* and *check in* the files that they're working on, helping to reduce the chances of the same file being overwritten or modified by different developers.

If you're not running Flash MX Professional 2004, the market offers plenty of decent third-party version control software (VCS). Just about all of these products can examine standard text documents and provide you with what's known as a "diff." This is a feature that can be fed two different documents (or, more often, two *versions* of the same document) and outputs a listing of each line that has been changed.

This is very useful when you're searching for a problem, especially if you know that it didn't exist before a certain date.

Version control software also usually lets you roll back a single document, a group of documents, or even an entire application to a specified state (either by date or by previously saved states).

One of the most important features of version control software is that it usually allows multiple developers to work safely on the same project without fear of losing one developer's work to that of another hasty developer.

> **NOTE**
>
> Using Test Project in the Flash Project panel is *not* designed to allow the simultaneous compilation and error reporting of multiple FLA files. Users should expect details in the Output panel to reflect what is associated with the main project FLA only. It is better to design, develop, and test any child SWFs before integrating them with the main SWF of the project.

To use the version control features of Flash MX Professional 2004, you need to first define your site within the Flash Project panel. As well as allowing you to view project-related files, the Project panel allows you to specify a local, network, or FTP connection, or custom plug-ins for version control systems.

> **TIP**
>
> In the realm of third-party version control, Concurrent Versions System (CVS) is probably the single best system. CVS is an open-source, freely available, extremely robust version control system. More information can be found at www.cvs-home.org.

> **TIP**
>
> There is currently no version-control package that can introspect binary files to produce diff reports. This means you can implement this feature only on AS files that exist outside the Flash editing environment.

Sample Questions

1. Which of the following cannot be automatically output by the
   `trace` action?

   A. String values

   B. Array values

   C. Object instance values

   D. Date and Time values

2. Which of the following is *not* a result of exporting a movie for a
   Debugger build?

   A. A normal SWF file is created.   *the actual SWF is slightly larger.*

   B. A SWD file is created in your working directory.

   C. The Debugger window appears.

   D. You can step through each breakpoint that you have set in the movie.

3. Which of the following is *not* an effective means of developing
   applications that are easy to debug?

   A. Separating and encapsulating each feature of your application

   B. Avoiding the use of external AS files

   C. Creating different classes for different tasks

   D. Making sure your methods and classes have descriptive names

4. When used within a `try..catch..finally` combination, when does the
   `finally` code block execute?

   A. Only when an error has been thrown

   B. When multiple `finally` blocks have been previously defined

   C. Only when control has passed to it from the `catch` code block

   D. Always

5. Which property of the Error class displays an `error` string to the
   Output panel?

   A. `error.message`

   B. `error.output`

   C. `error.throw`

   D. `error.show`

CHAPTER 24

Usability Testing Methodologies

Usability testing is an often-overlooked part of development. Although almost no one would consider releasing a product without first conducting a little functional testing, most applications are never seen by their intended users until all the code has already been frozen. As a result, many applications are released to the public riddled with usability bugs that make the program ineffective, frustrating, and sometimes completely useless.

Usability testing is a big topic—way too big for one chapter. This chapter attempts to cover only the essentials of usability testing, to dispel possible misunderstandings of what's involved in the usability testing process, and show you just how quickly and easily usability testing can be incorporated into product development.

The topics discussed in this chapter include:

- The benefits of usability testing
- Planning the test
- Conducting the test
- Analyzing and using the test results

Testing for Usability

One of the common issues faced by developers these days is the gap between the developer and the end user. Because a developer spends long periods of time working with and understanding an application, they (the "power" user) may overlook a "normal" user's likely approach to accomplishing common application-related tasks. To help address this issue, it's highly advisable to conduct usability testing with a broad spectrum of end users, at the start, middle, and end of the project. This helps ensure that the product really is *user friendly*—not only for power users, but entry-level users as well.

What Exactly Is Usability Testing?

First of all, you may be wondering what *usability* means. The International Organization of Standards (ISO) defines usability as "the extent to which a product can be used by specified users to achieve specified goals with effectiveness, efficiency, and satisfaction in a specified context of use" (ISO 9241:11, 1998).

To clarify any misconceptions, usability is not just about graphic design. There are many applications and websites out there that are gorgeous to look at but awkward or completely inaccessible from a user's standpoint. An example of this is the ever popular Flash intro that designers love but users categorically hate. Usability issues include everything—from site navigation to button labels—that might affect the user's experience with your application.

So what is usability *testing*? Generally speaking, it is an effort to determine the usability of your application. More specifically, it is discovery of *where* and *how* your application is not as usable as it could be, so that these areas can be improved.

Why Is Usability Testing Necessary?

Often it's the people whose opinions dictate the development process who wonder, "Why bother with usability testing? I know what the customer wants." Or they say, "I'm a user, so if I like it, so will our target users." The task of convincing these people that some sort of usability testing should be conducted often falls on the shoulders of the concerned developer. Here are some reasons why usability testing should always be considered.

- **You obtain real opinions from real users.** As stated earlier, many people believe they know what customers want and how they will use the application. Of course, if these people were always correct, new products and businesses would never fail. By bringing in actual members of your target audience, you discover very important—and unexpected— opinions about how your application is used, as well as the concerns and goals of your customers. You also gain qualitative data about how users feel about your application, how happy they are about using the application, whether they would use the application again, and how their experience of the application differed from their expectations. All this information is valuable and can often be immediately converted into specific improvements.

- **You ensure that the application serves its purpose.** Can users accomplish what the application is purported to do? Note that this is a different issue than "Can everything the application claims to do actually be done?" If the user can't figure out how to use your application before they decide to leave it, then it's not serving its purpose.

- **You determine if the application is easy and predictable to use.** If your application isn't easy to use, it won't be used for long. Though you have slightly more time to show users the application's relevance in the testing phase than, say, on a website, they will nevertheless leave if they can't quickly get to the information they seek or complete the task they want to accomplish.

- **The testing is cheap, easy, and effective.** When people think of product testing, they often imagine marketing experts and expensive labs in which time-consuming tests are conducted and lengthy reports are written. Fortunately, usability testing doesn't have to entail any of this. Anyone willing to try can conduct effective usability testing on a shoestring budget. The only real expense is the day or two of time you invest. Of all the phases of development and all the processes intended to ensure the success of a product, few surpass the return on your investment more than usability testing.

Laying the Groundwork

So when can usability testing begin? The answer varies from product to product, but generally you can start right away. In fact, the sooner you start testing, the sooner and more cheaply you can make meaningful changes to the application. It's even possible to start testing before the first line of code has been written. Effective testing has been conducted with little more than hand-drawn sketches or printouts of a product at different stages of use.

Additionally, any part of the application can be tested independently of the whole. In other words, you can test how well a particular feature fares with your target audience before it's implemented. Or, if your team is debating the best way to implement a feature, you could leave it up to the test audience to make the decision. The beauty of usability testing is that it can be used effectively in many different situations.

Preparing the Test

Although you can begin testing very soon in the development cycle, it's a good idea to put some early thought into how you will conduct the testing. By addressing the following issues, you can ensure that your testing will yield the best results in the most efficient manner.

Identify the Purposes of Your Application

Obviously, there is a reason you're developing this application. List these reasons. You will use them later to determine if the user perceived them. They will also help you determine what sample tasks you can ask your test group to perform.

Identify Your Target Groups

Who do you think will use your application? Does the majority of your audience fit into one category? If not, you will need to define additional groups as well. For instance, if you have an application that will be used by scientists and potential investors equally, both groups should be represented during testing.

The more information you gather about your target groups, the better. Some questions you can ask yourself to help better define target groups include the following:

- Are they experienced computer users? (for example, how comfortable are they using standard computer-based applications such as word processing, Internet browsing, or spreadsheets).

- Under what circumstances will they use the application (for example, will the application be used on a Personal Digital Assistant (PDA) out in the field, or will it be used on a dial-up connection on a home PC)

- How old are they?

- How well do they speak the language (for example, English, Japanese, or an industry-specific vernacular) used in the application?

Once you've answered these and other relevant questions, you will have a better idea of who should participate in your test groups and what types of tasks you want them to try when testing your application.

> **CAUTION**
>
> It's very easy to overestimate the user's ability with your application and their knowledge of your company in general. After all, few know the application as well as you, so your perspective of what a "normal" user knows may easily be unrealistically high. Try to be as objective as possible when identifying your target groups.

Writing the Test

After you've compiled the data from the questions you asked when identifying the purpose of your application and identifying your target group, you should have a good idea of who will be accessing your site and what their intent will be. Now you just need to convert this into practical tasks that you can ask your test audience to perform.

For instance, let's say your application is for a local amusement park, and you've concluded that most people who access the application want to know either how to get to the park, how much it costs, or whether a particular ride is open that day. You now have three tasks for the user to perform: determine how to get to the park, determine how much the tickets cost, and determine whether a particular ride is open that day.

> **NOTE**
>
> User task descriptions should be general in nature. You don't want to give your testers specific instructions on how to use the application. In the example of the amusement park application, you wouldn't want to ask the user to "click on Directions, then enter the starting address to get directions to the park." A better way of designing this task would be to ask the tester, "Can you determine how to get to the amusement park from where you live?"

> **CAUTION**
>
> When designing a usability test, make sure the test group won't be embarrassed if they can't perform the specific tasks. Remember—if they can't use your application as it was intended, it's your problem, not theirs.

Of course, you can add other tasks or questions that are important to the success of your product. For example, you can seek to determine whether the design of your application conveys the feeling you'd like customers to have about your product or company (professional, established, competent, cutting-edge, and so on).

Keep in mind that the test itself on paper doesn't have to be particularly elaborate. Most of the real work will be done by the interviewer conducting the test.

Testing the Test

Now that you have a list of reasonable tasks for the user to perform, it's in your best interest to practice administering your usability test. This will undoubtedly raise issues that would otherwise have caused problems during the real testing.

The practice test can be administered to a colleague who has some free time. You should act as if this is the real test and use the same language and methods you plan on using during the real test. In particular, you should use the same build of the application, since encountering new bugs during usability testing can be very disruptive. Naturally, any problems or questions that arise during the practice test should be addressed before giving the actual test.

> **NOTE**
>
> Generally speaking, the length of a test should be about 30 minutes, although this will vary depending on how your application is used and the type of people who use it.

Gathering Your Test Group

So, you've got your test all ready to go. What next? Fortunately, you've already done the work to identify your target markets, so now it's just a matter of contacting people who fit the target profile and asking them if they'd like to participate.

Each industry and market can be quite distinct from the next, so there isn't just one way to recruit test participants, or one source of participant to tap. However, you can probably find everyone you need by simply asking existing or potential customers, people you know who fit the test group profile, or even people at the local mall to participate. Of course, everyone you ask should fit the target user profile you assembled earlier.

> **CAUTION**
>
> Avoid recruiting fellow employees, because their experience with the application and company objectives will not be typical of your target audience.

Another thing in your favor is that you don't need an army of people to conduct effective usability testing. In fact, studies have shown that five people make an ideal sample group size for usability testing. (See study by Jakob Nielsen and Thomas K. Landauer at www.useit.com/alertbox/20000319.html.) Once you go beyond five people, you start to get diminishing returns. If you need more data, time and money might arguably be better spent on another small test group at a later stage in development.

> **NOTE**
>
> If you're testing with more than one target group, it's a good idea to reduce the size of each group to three or four to make the most of your time and resources.

Compensation ✗

You can compensate your target audience for their time in many ways. Most people will be flattered that you're interested in their opinions and will be satisfied with a simple token of your appreciation. Some possible forms of compensation include any combination of the following: a free copy of the finished application, company logo (T-shirts, hats, and so on), a gift certificate to an appealing retail store, free product training, a pass to an industry event, and/or your sincere appreciation for their time and valuable contribution to your product's success (which should be offered anyway).

> **NOTE**
> You can also pay your testers with a check, if you prefer. The standard rate is $100, although this amount will vary based on their level of experience (for instance, high school students versus medical doctors), the length of testing, and the distance the tester has to travel to participate.

Conducting the Test

Once you have the testing metrics in place and have gathered your test group, you're ready to start testing.

If you are still thinking that usability testing is a necessary evil and hindrance to the flow of a project, try and keep an open mind. The feedback testers provide, even if it generates a considerable amount of (re)work (as is sometimes the case), is of real value to the success of your product. The purpose of the usability text exercise is to assist you in producing a high-quality product, usable by the specified target audience.

Test Scheduling

Assuming the tasks take about 30 minutes to complete, you should be able to conduct a complete test in under an hour. This includes greeting the test user, explaining the test, conducting the test, discussing the test with the participant, answering any questions they may have, and thanking the participant for their time. At the rate of an hour per participant, you could pretty easily complete all five tests in the course of a day.

Role of the Interviewer

Since the interviewer is the one person who will have direct access to the target users, it is essential that she understand the intent of the test. The interviewer must have a clear understanding of how to present the test in an objective manner; for example, she shouldn't imply disappointment if the user can't complete a task and shouldn't inadvertently encourage the user to give positive statements. The interviewer should also be able to record the user's actions, comments, feelings, and so on accurately and in a timely manner.

> **NOTE**
>
> The interviewer need not have an intimate knowledge of the application being tested. Using an interviewer who does not know the application can actually be an advantage, because the interviewer will be less likely to lead the test user.

Guidelines for Effective Testing

It's very important to convey to test users how much their opinions about the application are valued. If users feel as if they're just guinea pigs being told what to do, chances are they will simply give you the answers they think you want to hear. If they perceive that their opinions do matter and may result in the improvement of the product, they will be much more likely to provide you with truthful and valuable comments.

The following are additional guidelines for effective usability testing:

- Ask test users to think aloud as they use the application. Listening to what they say gives you a better idea of what's going on in their minds. You can also get an inkling of what users are thinking by watching their mouse actions. Often people "look" with the mouse, so you can get an idea of how they're attempting to accomplish a given task.

- Avoid leading questions. If you ask questions like "Isn't that cool?" or "That's not very obvious, is it?" you'll get worthless agreement from the user. It's much better to ask open questions such as "What do you think will happen next?" or "Is that what you expected to happen?" or "What do you think this feature does?"

- As mentioned earlier, avoid providing specific instructions such as "Click on this button and enter your e-mail address." Instead, ask the user to perform a task that would require the same steps, such as request an item (such as a brochure), but do not outline the steps of the task for them.

- Take notes on whatever elements you think bear recording: users' comments, actions, mouse movements, sighs, and so on.

- Depending on your testing goals, you may also want to record how long it takes the user to complete the specific tasks. The results can then be compared with earlier (or later) tests or weighed against agreed-upon acceptable times. A sample task for comparison might be, "Get directions to the amusement park from your house."

- Let users know that you're on their side and that you won't be disappointed if they don't like the product or don't use it as intended. In fact, it's their job to find ways in which the product can be improved.

NOTE

Some usability testers prefer to use a video camera to ensure that nothing is lost during testing. The camera is focused on the screen, and the microphone records the users' comments. Although there may be some advantage to this, it isn't really necessary if adequate notes are taken. Also, the camera may intimidate some people and thus influence their performance or comments during the testing.

Analyzing and Acting on Test Results

After you've completed usability tests, you can review the results and look for commonalities between the comments and actions of the test users. At this point, you should already have a pretty good idea about where the application succeeds and fails. If you deem it necessary, at this point you can write up a report citing how the application fared during testing. Based on its meeting expectations, or exceeding or falling short of them—as well as users' comments—you can make educated recommendations on how to improve the application's performance.

It's important to look for big-picture causes of what designers and developers may discern as small, independent problems. For example, designers and developers are often asked by managers to make a button bigger, make it a different color, make it flash, and so on because users might be having trouble finding it. The person requesting the change may be overlooking the fact that the overall button layout is illogical, that the button names are misleading, or that it's unclear whether a button is supposed to be used at all. These possible issues should be considered when deciding what actions to take based on the test results.

Once you've made improvements to the application in response to the usability testing results, you need to decide if another round of testing is necessary. You should base this decision on factors such as deadlines, schedules, scope of the application, and budget. If you decide to perform more testing, most of your preparatory work has already been done. Just be sure to include a new test user group that won't be biased by any previous experience with the application.

Reading Further

Following are a few of the many resources available on the Web that will help you with usability testing tasks.

Macromedia's list of Flash-centric usability-related links:

```
www.macromedia.com/software/flash/productinfo/usability/articles/
```

Usability expert Jakob Nielsen's website:

```
www.useit.com
```

Information and Design's Usability Testing web page:

```
www.infodesign.com.au/usability/usabilitytesting.html
```

Sample Questions

1. Which of the following is *not* a key benefit of usability testing?

   A. To find out how potential customers will use your application.

   B. For direct marketing exposure to test candidates.

   C. To identify areas where the product is difficult to use.

   D. To receive valuable comments from customers on how to improve the application.

2. At which point can you start usability testing?

   A. When some sketches of the product's interface are drawn.

   B. When the application goes alpha.

   C. When the application goes beta.

   D. When the application code is complete.

3. Which of the following is *not* a guideline for conducting effective usability testing?

   A. Avoid leading questions.

   B. Provide helpful, step-by-step instructions on how each task should be completed.

   C. Ask users to think aloud.

   D. Take lots of notes.

4. What is generally considered the ideal group size for usability testing?

   A. 1–2

   B. 3–5

   C. 6–11

   D. 11–20

5. Which of the following is *not* a recommended choice for a test group member?

   A. Student

   B. Co-worker

   C. Homemaker

   D. Engineer

CHAPTER 25
Printing

Printing functionality first appeared in Flash Player 4, release version r20, and has continued to evolve ever since. The latest release of Flash is no exception; it introduces the PrintJob class.

One of the major benefits of printing from within Flash is that you can print text and graphics, which are located off stage and not visible to the user. This is important for printing full A4 PostScript documentation from within the confines of a 468 x 60-pixel banner ad.

Throughout this chapter, we'll discuss some of the new (and existing) aspects of printing from within Flash, including:

- The PrintJob class and its three methods

- Various uses for the Print command

- Implementing printing within the application

- Using the bounding box parameter to specify a print area

The PrintJob Class

[handwritten margin note: PrintJob.start(); PrintJob.addPage(); PrintJob.send();]

The PrintJob class, a new addition to Flash Player 7, offers considerable improvements to the existing print functionality provided by the print() method. This class allows developers to control the printing of dynamically generated content, including that extracted from databases or user-generated input.

Print control is performed via the three methods of the PrintJob class, which carry out the following tasks:

- Displaying system Print dialog boxes to alert users about pages being spooled and added to the print queue , as well as other system print–related tasks

- Adding frames and predefined print areas (in the form of pages) to print queues

- Accessing the user's printer settings and formatting Flash content to match these settings

PrintJob.start()   *[handwritten: return boolean]*

The PrintJob.start() method opens the user's operating system Print dialog boxes and gives them a chance to modify print settings, including paperHeight, paperWidth, pageHeight, pageWidth, and orientation.

After the user clicks OK in the Print dialog box, the printJob.start() method returns true and the player begins spooling a print job to the operating system. If the user clicks Cancel rather than OK, the printJob.start() method returns false and any future calls to PrintJob.addPage() and PrintJob().send will fail. This can be resolved by testing the returned value. If the value is false, there's no need to send the PrintJob.addPage() command.

Irrespective of the returned value, good coding practice dictates that once an object has finished its lifespan, it should be deleted. This is especially important in the case of using the PrintJob object because deleting the PrintJob object clears the print spooler, as shown in the following example:

```
//create a new printJob object
var myPrintJobObject = new PrintJob();
//display the print dialog box
var myReturnedValue = myPrintJobObject.start();
if(myReturnedValue) {
    // check the return value and take the required action
}
//delete the object to clear the print spooler
delete myPrintJobObject;
```

PrintJob.addPage()

The `PrintJob.addPage()` method, working in tandem with the `PrintJob.start()` method, adds content to the print queue after the user clicks OK in the Print dialog box.

This method accepts a few parameters. The following statement includes a few common ones:

```
myPrintJob.addPage(target [, printArea] [, options ] [, frameNumber])
```

- `target` refers to either the numeric value of the level, or the instance name of an object you wish to print.
- `printArea` is an optional parameter that is an object representing the print area bound by the `xMin:topLeft`, `xMax:topRight`, `yMin:bottomLeft`, `yMax:bottomRight` values. When using this object, all four of the preceding properties must be defined in order for the object to be considered valid.
- `options` is an optional Boolean object–based parameter that specifies whether the page prints as a vector or bitmap. *By default, print As Vector*
- `frameNumber` is the final optional parameter for specifying which frame of the movie is to be printed.

PrintJob.send()

The `PrintJob.send()` method sends to the printer all the queued pages gathered from the `PrintJob.addPage()` method.

Print Commands

The following sections discuss the various instances where Print commands can be invoked by the user.

Printing from the Browser's File Menu

If a user doesn't see an immediately recognizable printer interface element in your Flash content, the browser's File menu is most likely the first place they will go to print. Unfortunately, this method is extremely difficult for the developer to control and will have varying results. The most important things to keep in mind about this method of printing are that the user will be printing only (and exactly) what they see at the proportions of the browser window, and that the Flash developer currently has no way to disable this functionality consistently throughout the movie.

Printing from the Flash Player Context Menu

The context menu is the one that appears when the user right-clicks (Windows) or Control-clicks (Macintosh) on an element. In the absence of a visible Print button, this is the second most common choice of many users to print something. The context menu is enabled by default in Flash Player; consequently, if a developer has not invested any time in the printable configuration of a movie, execution of a Print command with this method can prove disastrous. If there are no frames in the main Timeline that are designated as printable frames, the Flash Player will begin printing every single frame.

Fortunately, changing a few export settings can disable the Flash Player context menu. Because this menu exists only for Flash content, and only when developers have not disabled it, many users are still unaware that printing from the context menu is even an option. It is recommended that you not rely on this feature when you want to include the capability to print Flash content.

> **NOTE**
> When a user chooses to print from the context menu, they can only print frames designated in the main Timeline, and they will not be able to print transparencies or color effects.

> **NOTE**
> When a user chooses to print from the context menu and either no frames or two or more frames are designated as printable, the Page Range option of the user's Print dialog box–where they would normally designate the number of pages to print–will actually mean "specified frames."

Using the *print* Action

Direct printing from Flash Player using the `print` action has been available since the distribution of Flash Player revision 4.0.20 This is by far the most desirable way to enable printing in which the Print dialog box displays for the user. Making effective use of the built-in `print` action will give the developer the most robust control over layout, content, and usability. The upcoming section "Implementing `print` Actions" gives examples of `print` actions.

Implementing *print* Actions

Because it provides the developer with the most control over printing, the `print` action should be the preferred method of implementation. The Flash `print` action comes as two primary commands, and each has two variations. The primary actions are Print as Vector (`print`) or Print as Bitmap (`printAsBitmap`). With both, you can choose to print either the contents of a movie clip or a single Flash _level. All four versions of the print action will accept an argument that identifies the print area. If this argument is not given, the main movie Stage dimensions are used.

Here are some examples of print statements:

```
print(_root.myClip, "bmax");
printNum(_level0, "bmax");
printAsBitmap(_root.myClip, "bmax");
printAsBitmapNum(_level0, "bmax");
```

(target, print-area)

Keep in mind that any variant of the print action can (and usually should) target movie clips whose _visible property is set to 0. These movie clips will print correctly, but they will not appear in the Flash Player and therefore can be formatted for the printed page rather than with the browser dimensions.

> **CAUTION**
>
> The use of levels as a targeting mechanism should nearly always be avoided. By targeting movie clip instance names rather than levels, your ActionScript will be more explicit and far easier to debug. The only exception to this rule is in cases when you're attempting to target an item within a known stacking order, and you have no need to identify which movie clip that item is an instance of.

> **CAUTION**
>
> Unfortunately, printing features are often not requested until after a project has already launched or is nearly complete. It can be extremely time-consuming to implement such features during later phases if some attention was not given to them during development. Always assume that certain logical components in every Flash application will eventually need to be printable. Allowing for this will cost very little time and energy up front and will save considerable time and money down the road.

Available *print* Actions

The following sections describe each variation on the print action in more detail.

print

The print action prints high-quality vector-based printouts of all frames of the target Timeline or, if any frames have been identified, only those frames with a #p frame label. This is the best way to achieve extremely clean, high-resolution print output with a minimal amount of network traffic and CPU usage.

> **CAUTION**
>
> The print and printNum actions do not print alpha channels, bitmaps, or color effects.

printNum

The printNum action is the same as the print action, except that printNum prints the specified _level in the target movie clip.

printAsBitmap

The printAsBitmap action prints out a bitmap version of each frame in the target movie clip, or only those frames containing a #p label. Bear in mind that this action prints at the highest resolution available on the end user's printer and as a result can sometimes take an extraordinarily long time to execute.

The printAsBitmap action will print transparencies and color effects as well as bitmap images.

CAUTION

In many cases, the printAsBitmap action provides inferior print quality and much longer print delays than the standard print action and should only be used when absolutely necessary.

---

printAsBitmapNum

The printAsBitmapNum action is the same as printAsBitmap, except that printAsBitmapNum prints only the specified _level.

Specifying a Print Area with Bounding Box Modifiers

The *bounding box* modifier is an optional second modifier available within all four variations of the print action. This modifier defines the outermost limits of the printable area. If a movie clip is identified as the bounding box, the movie clip's dimensions will be superimposed over any printable frames, and any assets that fall outside of those "bounds" will not be printed.

When this modifier is omitted, the main movie Stage dimensions will be used as the bounding box. If this is an undesirable aspect ratio for the printed page (as it will usually be), the modifier can be one of these string values: bmovie, bmax, or bframe.

bmovie

The bmovie parameter designates a specific frame in the movie as the bounding box identifier for the entire movie. The frame designated must contain a frame label of #b.

> **CAUTION**
> If you are duplicating movie clips or attaching them to a Timeline, and you have a frame marked with the #b label, within the duplicated movie clip, it is probable that your duplicated movie clips will also exist in the designated frame, therefore changing the bounds of the printable area.

The following code will print frames in myClip_mc and use the #b frame label to identify the boundaries of all printable frames. The #b frame label must exist within the myClip_mc Timeline.

```
print(_root.myClip_mc, "bmovie");
```

bmax

The bmax parameter will simply determine the largest bounding box out of the frames that have been identified as printable, and it will use this largest bounding box for all frames printed. If no frames contain the #p frame label, then the largest bounding box will apply to all frames in the movie clip.

The following statement will print all frames in myClip_mc and use the largest frame to identify the bounds. This frame will retain proportional sizes from one frame to the next:

```
printAsBitmap(_root.myClip_mc, "bmax");
```

bframe

Using bframe will force each frame to use its own bounding box as the bounds for that particular page. This option is useful if you have different sized objects, in each frame, and you wish to have each object fill the printed page area.

The following code will print all frames in myClip_mc and will use the bounds of each frame for the printable page, thereby scaling assets and destroying any proportional relationships from one frame to the next:

```
print(_root.myClip_mc, "bframe");
```

Sample Questions

1. Which of the following methods provides the most controlled printing of Flash content?

    A. Printing from the Flash Player contextual menu

    B. The Print action

    C. The ExportToPrinter action

    D. The browser's File menu

2. Which of the following is *not* a true statement about the `print` action?

   A. It provides quality vector-based prints.

   B. It prints all frames of the target Timeline unless otherwise specified.

   C. It is CPU-intensive.

   D. It doesn't print alpha channels. *and color effect.*

3. What will be the result of the following line of ActionScript?

   ```
   print(_root.myClip, "bmax");
   ```

   A. The `myClip` and `"bmax"` movie clips will be printed.

   B. A bounding box will be created by the location of the `myClip` and `"bmax"` movie clips, and this area will be printed.

   C. The `myClip` movie clip will be printed, and each frame will be scaled to fill the maximum space on the printed page. *b frame*

   D. The largest printable frame in `myClip` will be used to determine the bounding box for all frames printed. *b max*

4. Apart from being good coding practice, what is the benefit of deleting the `PrintJob` object after it has completed its life cycle?

   A. It removes excess byte code from the Flash Player.

   B. It clears the print spooler.

   C. It allows control to be passed to the printer.

   D. It resets the print bounding box.

5. The `PrintJob.addPage()` method works in conjunction with which other two methods?

   A. `PrintJob.start()`

   B. `PrintJob.cancelPage()`

   C. `PrintJob.clearPage()`

   D. `PrintJob.send()`

PART 7

Appendix

A

Sample Questions and Answers

At the end of each chapter was a series of sample questions that were designed to provide you with an insight to the types of questions that are asked on the certification exam. These questions are meant only as an example. Though every attempt to be all encompassing was made, there is not guarantee that the topics of the sample questions will or will not be included on the actual exam.

Chapter 1

Sample Questions

1. What is the default frame rate of the Timeline in frames per second?

   A. 1

   B. 12

   C. 24

   D. 30

   Answer: B – Although the frame rate can be set from .01 to 120 frames per second, the default is 12 fps.

2. What are the three most common types of symbols in Flash?

   A. Graphic, button, and font

   B. Button, movie clip, and video

   C. Video, font, and graphic

   D. Graphic, button, and movie clip

   Answer: D – While all of the above are symbols, the three most commonly used symbols are the graphic, button, and movie clip.

3. Which of the following CANNOT have a behavior applied to it?

    A. Movie clip

    B. Text field

    C. Graphic symbol

    D. Sound File

    Answer: C – Behaviors can only be applied to movie clips, text fields, and video and sound files.

4. What file formats can be included into a Flash Project?

    A. Only .FLAs

    B. .FLA, .SWF, and .FLP

    C. .XML and .FLA

    D. Any file format

    Answer: D – A Flash Project can contain any Flash or other file type, including previous versions of FLA and SWF files.

Chapter 2

Sample Questions

1. Which of the following is the recommended character to use for separating target path levels?

    A. / (slash)

    B. $ (dollar sign)

    C. _ (underscore)

    D. . (dot)

    E. % (percentage sign)

    Answer: D – Although the slash syntax is still supported, its use is no longer recommended

2. Which keyword is used to implement the functionality of external classes and packages?

    A. `include`

    B. `import`

    C. `attach`

    D. `clamp`

    Answer: B – The `import` keyword is used to include external classes at runtime.

3. In which level does the original movie reside?

   A. 0

   B. 1

   C. 100

   D. 1000

   Answer: A – The original movie will always reside on Level 0. This can be referenced by using `_level0` in your target path.

4. What happens if a SWF is loaded into an already occupied level?

   A. An error is thrown.

   B. The new SWF is rejected and the old one stays.

   C. The old SWF is unloaded and the new one is loaded.

   D. They share the same level.

   Answer: C – The new SWF will replace the old one on the same level.

5. Which of the following is an objective of the `DepthManager` class?

   A. To manage the loading (and unloading) of movie clip instances into particular depths.

   B. To manage relative depth assignments within any document.

   C. To retrieve movie clip instances from a specified depth.

   D. To act as a traffic controller to ensure movie clips on certain depths are not overwritten.

   Answer: C – The `DepthManager` class has two main purposes: to manage the relative depth assignments within any document, and to manage reserved depths on the root Timeline for system-level services such as the cursor and tooltips.

Chapter 3

Sample Questions

1. Which of the following assumptions *cannot* be made when developing an application for intranet deployment?

   A. The connection speed between computers will be generally faster than on the Internet.

   B. Users will have the same version of the Flash Player.

   C. The computers accessing the application will have pretty similar capabilities.

   D. Users will have an Internet connection.

   Answer: B – Although all users on a company intranet will have fast access to the Internet, there's no guarantee that they will all be using the same version of the Flash Player. It's important to check the user's Flash Player version if your application requires specific features from a particular version

2. Which of the following is the most important factor in determining the compatibility of your application?

A. The Flash Player version installed

B. The operating system installed

C. The screen resolution

D. The use of external assets

Answer: A – Since your Flash MX applications won't run on earlier versions of the Flash Player (unless specifically designed and exported for such use), this is the most important factor for determining application compatibility

3. Which of the following is *not* a typical host application for the Flash Player?

A. A browser

B. A Projector

C. A Java executable

D. A third-party wrapper

Answer: C – As of this writing, there is no simple way to host a Flash application from within a Java application.

4. Which object allows you to access information about the user's system?

A. `System.settings`

B. `System.capabilities`

C. `System.status`

D. `System.requirements`

Answer: B – The `System.capabilities` object is used to access information about the system that is running your Flash movie.

Chapter 4

Sample Questions

1. When does the `System.capabilities.hasAccessibilities` method return `true`?

A. When the current Flash movie is in an MSAA-compatible browser

B. When a screen reader is detected

C. When an input device for people with disabilities is detected

D. When Flash content has been designated as Accessible

Answer: B – The `Accessibility.isActive()` method is designed to return `true` only when a screen reader is detected.

2. Which of the following items *cannot* be hidden from screen readers?

   A. Static text

   B. Dynamic text

   C. Buttons

   D. Movie clips

   Answer: A – Since only buttons and objects can be manipulated by the Accessibility panel, and static text is read by screen readers by default, it is the only item on the list that cannot be hidden from screen readers. To hide static text, it must first be converted to dynamic text, and then have its Make Object Accessible option unchecked. Another way to hide the text would be by breaking it apart, although this might not be practical.

3. Which of the following properties can be used to control the order in which the user can tab through the elements in a Flash movie?

   A. `tabOrder`

   B. `tabNumber`

   C. `tabValue`

   D. `tabIndex`

   Answer: D – The `tabIndex` property is designed to provide the Macromedia Flash Player (and screen readers) with a manually determined Tab order. The other "properties" don't exist.

4. To control the reading order of objects on the Stage, you use which of the following properties?

   A. `readingOrder`

   B. `tabOrder`

   C. `tabIndex`

   D. `readingIndex`

   Answer: C – Once again, the `tabIndex` property is designed to provide the Macromedia Flash Player (and screen readers) with a manually determined Reading order. The other "properties" don't exist.

Chapter 5

Sample Questions

1. The value of a variable of Timeline scope will persist until:

   A. The code block in which it was declared finishes executing.

   B. The variable is removed using the clear keyword.

   C. The player moves to a new scene.

   D. The object to which it belongs no longer exists.

   Answer: D – All timelines variables assigned to an object are deleted when the object no longer exists.

2. Which of the following statements creates a new global variable, `birthyear`, with an initial value of 1968?

   A. `new Global birthyear = 1968;`

   B. `global(birthyear) = 1968;`

   C. `_global.birthyear = 1968;`

   D. `global.birthyear = 1968;`

   Answer: C – You must use the `_global` identifier when declaring a global variable. However once declared, you no longer need to use the `_global` identifier to refer to the variable.

3. Which of the following statements should be used to manually dispose of the variable `myVar`, in order to prevent memory leaks?

   A. `delete myVar;`

   B. `remove myVar;`

   C. `myVar = null;`

   D. `myVar = 0;`

   Answer: A – Using the `delete` keyword is the best way to dispose of a variable without causing a memory leak.

4. What is the main benefit of strict data typing?

   A. Assists other developers identify variable data types

   B. Helps avoid data type mismatches

   C. Allows you to more clearly identify compiler errors

   D. Adheres more closely to other OOP-related languages

   Answer: B – Strict data typing helps avoid type mismatches.

Chapter 6

Sample Questions

1. Which of the following characters can be added to the identifier, `mylengthyvariable`, to make it more readable?

    A. A minus sign (for example, `my-lengthy-variable`)

    B. An underscore (for example, `my_lengthy_variable`)

    C. A period (for example, `my.lengthy.variable`)

    D. A plus sign (for example, `my+lengthy+variable`)

    Answer: B – The underscore is the only option listed that will read as one variable by the Flash Player.

2. Which of the following conventions is/are recommended for the name of a constant?

    A. Spaces between each word in the name

    B. All capital letters

    C. A number before the characters

    D. A name followed by `()`

    Answer: B – Using all capital letters is the commonly accepted way to designate an identifier as a constant.

3. What should be inferred from a variable named `birthPlace_str`?

    A. It is a short-term variable and will be disposed of once its script is executed.

    B. It can store multiple values.

    C. It is a string.

    D. It can hold only 64 characters.

    Answer: C – The "_str" suffix is the commonly used method of identifying a variable as a string.

4. Which of the following is most likely a class constructor?

    A. `CLASS_CONSTRUCTOR`

    B. `ClassConstructor`

    C. `classConstructor`

    D. `class_constructor`

    Answer: B – Class Constructors should be title-cased.

5. What value will be displayed in the output panel when the following block of ActionScript 2.0 code is compiled?

```
function personalDetails
(firstName:String,lastName:String,age:Number){
    trace(firstName+" "+LastName+" "+age);
}
personalDetails("Simon","Reid",30);
```

A. Simon Reid 30

B. undefined

C. Simon undefined 30

D. type mismatch

Answer: C – The LastName variable has not been declared (note the capital "L") and will subsequently return an "undefined" value.

Chapter 7

Sample Questions

1. Which of the following if statements is correctly written?

A. if firstName = "George" then {};

B. if {firstName = "George"} then ();

C. if (firstName == "George") {};

D. if (firstName = "George" & lastName = "Lucas") {};

Answer: C – Two equal signs (==) must be used when comparing values. Answer D would also be correct if it incorporated both two equal signs and two ampersands (&&):

```
if (firstName =="George" && lastName == "Lucas"
```

2. In which of the following situations would it be best to use a switch statement?

A. You need to test for two possible values.

B. You want to test for many possible values.

C. You want a loop to run at least once.

D. You only want one thing to happen if a condition is true.

Answer: B – The switch statement is best used when testing for many distinct values.

3. Assuming `myVar` equals "fish," what will be traced by the following code block?

```
switch(myVar){
  case "cat": trace("cat");
  case "fish": trace("fish");
  case "bird": trace("bird");
  default: trace("default");
    }
```

A. `"fish"`

B. `"fish bird"`

C. `"fish default"`

D. `"fish bird default"`

Answer: D – The _str suffix is the commonly used method of identifying a variable as a String.

4. What is the key difference between `while` loops and `do while` loops?

A. `do while` loops cannot get stuck in an endless loop.

B. `do while` loops will always execute at least once.

C. `while` loops are deprecated in Flash MX.

Answer: B – Class constructors should begin with a capital letter.

5. Which of the following statements uses proper `for` loop syntax?

A. `for(i=0 , i<10 , i++){}`

B. `for(i=0 ; i<10 ; i++){}`

C. `for((i=0),(i<10),(i++)){}`

D. `for(i=0 i<10 i++){}`

Answer: B – The `LastName` variable has not been declared (note the capital L) and will subsequently return an `undefined` value.

6. If it takes 2 seconds for an object to move across the Stage within an animation that is playing back at 12 fps, how long will the same animation take if the frame rate is increased to 24 fps?

A. Half a second

B. One second

C. Two seconds

D. Four seconds

Answer: B – The frame rate has been doubled, so any onscreen animation will now play twice as fast.

Chapter 8

Sample Questions

1. Which of the following is *not* a valid function name?

   A. `get_value`

   B. `_getvalue`

   C. `4ever`

   D. `$23`

   Answer: C – A function name cannot begin with a number, although it can contain a number.

2. Which of the following is a *true* statement about functions?

   A. Functions must specify exactly how many arguments they can accept.

   B. Function parameters should be comma-delimited.

   C. Functions can only exist within a pre-defined object instance.

   D. Functions names must begin with a capital letter.

   Answer: B.

3. Functions can be assigned to identifiers at runtime. Assuming `sampleVar` equals `true`, what will be returned by the following function?

   ```
   function sampleFunction (sampleVar) {
       if(sampleVar == true) {
            return "true";
            return "continue";
       }
   }
   ```

   A. Nothing

   B. `true`

   C. `truecontinue`

   D. `continue`

   Answer: B – A function will stop executing once it has performed any return statement.

4. Which of the following is the correct syntax for passing parameters to a function?

   A. `myFunction(param1,param2,param3);`

   B. `myFunction(param1;param2;param3);`

   C. `myFunction(param1:param2:param3);`

   D. `myFunction(param1.param2.param3);`

   Answer: A – The correct syntax for passing parameters is
   `myFunction(param1,param2,param3);`

5. *Recursion* within a function refers to what?

   A. An endless loop

   B. A function calling itself

   C. A function using parameters that have been passed to it

   D. The returning of a value once a loop has been completed

   Answer: B – Recursion occurs when a function needs to call itself.

Chapter 9

Sample Questions

1. Which of the following statements best describes an event handler?

   A. A single, central script that handles all the events that take place and determines the appropriate action to take

   B. A security function, in the root of the Timeline that controls access to events

   C. A means of allowing an object to notify your scripts of a change of state

   Answer: C – Generally speaking, event handlers respond to changes in state (for instance, when something has been clicked or moved, or a movie has finished loading).

2. Which of the following methods is most likely an event handler?

   A. `MouseDown()`

   B. `_mouseDown`

   C. `MouseDown`

   D. `onMouseDown`

   Answer: D – Event handler names should begin with on to distinguish them from the type of event to which they're associated.

3. Which of the following is a true statement about custom event handlers?

   A. Their use should be avoided.

   B. They can cause handler conflicts with native ActionScript handlers.

   C. They can inherit from existing ActionScript classes.

   D. They are not supported by the Flash Player 5.

   Answer: C – Being able to inherit from parent classes allows you to use the parent's existing event handlers as well as any additional ones you may create.

4. True or false? `on()` event handlers can contain locally scoped variables if implicitly defined.

   A. True

   B. False

   Answer: B – `on()` and `onClipEvent()` handlers don't have a locally defined scope.

5. If the following event handler is attached to a three MovieClip instances named `myMovieOne`, `myMovieTwo`, and `myMovieThree`, which are each located on a separate layer, which movie will play when `myMovieTwo` is pressed?

   ```
   onClipEvent(mouseUp) {
           play();
   }
   ```

   A. `myMovieTwo`

   B. The movie located on the highest layer

   C. None of them

   D. All of them

   Answer: D – Because `on()` and `onClipEvent()` handlers don't have a locally defined scope, their contents are scoped to the main Timeline. In this example, clicking *anywhere* on the Stage of the main Timeline (including the MovieClip instances themselves) will cause the event handler method's body to be executed.

Chapter 10

Sample Questions

1. Which of the following is *not* a benefit of using Macromedia's prebuilt v2 components?

   A. Possible time savings by using prewritten code.

   B. Good code examples to learn from.

   C. Macromedia components stream into the Flash Player over the duration of the main movie Timeline.

   D. Simple color and font changes are easier to make.

   Answer: C – UI components dragged to the stage must be loaded prior to frame.

2. What is the downside of Macromedia components making extensive use of inheritance and encapsulation?

   A. Global variables cannot be used.

   B. Increased file size for first component added.

   C. Components cannot be modified.

   D. SWF files cannot be loaded at runtime.

   Answer: B – Adding the first component increases your file size. However, each additional component thereafter will add only marginally to the file size.

3. Which ActionScript method should be used to bring a component from the Library to the Stage?

   A. `attachMovie()`

   B. `addComponent()`

   C. `insertMovie()`

   D. `openComponent()`

   Answer: A.

4. What is the name of the default theme for Macromedia v2 components?

   A. Star

   B. Halo

   C. Blur

   D. Heaven

   Answer: B – Macromedia has included Halo as the default theme for Flash MX 2004.

5. What is a SWC?

   A. A SWF that has been converted into a component

   B. An exported component file format

   C. A component's skin file format

   D. A compiled theme format

   Answer: B – A SWC (Small Web Component) is a component that has been exported for installation on another user's system.

Chapter 11

Sample Questions

1. Which of the following HTML tags is *not* supported within Flash MX 2004?

   A. `<a>`

   B. `<img>`

   C. `<p>`

   D. `<table>`

   Answer: D.

2. How many parameters are accepted by the `setStyle()` method of the `TextField.StyleSheet` class?

   A. 1

   B. 2

   C. 3

   D. None

   Answer: B.

3. What event is used to determine whether an external CSS has finished loading?

   A. `loadComplete`

   B. `loadTrue`

   C. `onLoad`

   D. `onLoadComplete`

   Answer: C.

4. Which method is used to apply the new TextFormat object to a text field?

   A. `setTextFormat()`

   B. `setTextObject()`

   C. `setTextFormatStyle()`

   D. `setStyleFormat()`

   Answer: A.

Chapter 12

Sample Questions

1. Which of the following is *not* a disadvantage of using the `fscommand()` function?

   A. Your movie becomes tied to a particular host application.

   B. You can have only one `fscommand` call in your movie.

   C. Use of `fscommand()` is not supported by Netscape 6.

   D. The host application will not be able to return values to your `fscommand` call.

   Answer: B – You can have as many `fscommand` calls in your movie as you wish, as long as you give them different names.

2. Which of the following is the best reason for using the `getURL()` function, instead of `fscommand()`, when communicating with the host application?

   A. `getURL()` can receive return values from the host application.

   B. You don't have to use JavaScript to interact with the host application.

   C. `getURL()` is supported by the Flash Player 6.

   D. `getURL()` is compatible with more browsers than `fscommand()`.

   Answer: D – `getURL()`'s broad browser support is a key reason to use it instead of the `fscommand` function. Answer C is not a key advantage because both `fscommand` and `getURL` are supported by the Flash Player 6.

3. Which of the following is the correct way to create an alert box using `getURL()` and JavaScript?

   A. `getURL = function ("javascript:alert("Hello World!"));`

   B. `getURL(alert,"Hello World!");`

   C. `getURL(javascript (alert,'Hello World!'););`

   D. `getURL("javascript:alert('Hello World!');");`

   Answer: D.

4. Which command allows you to embed JSAPI commands into ActionScript?

   A. `MMExecute()`

   B. `ExecuteJSAPI()`

   C. `RunMMJSAPI()`

   D. `MMCommandExecute()`

   Answer: A.

5. Which of the following is *not* an advantage of using third-party SWF2EXE applications?

   A. They expand Flash's default `fscommand` set.

   B. They allow you to create SCR (screensaver) files.

   C. They integrate seamlessly into the Flash authoring environment.

   D. They allow access to the host file system.

   Answer: C – Third-party SWFtoEXE applications are stand-alone applications that don't integrate into the Flash authoring environment.

Chapter 13

Sample Questions

1. In general, non-MP3 digital audio that is destined to be imported into the Flash MX authoring environment should first be compressed how much?

   A. 0% (largest acceptable file size)

   B. 50% (medium file size)

   C. 75% (smaller file size)

   D. As much as possible (smallest acceptable file size)

   Answer: A – It's generally best to let Flash compress raw digital audio files using its built-in Sorenson codec.

2. Which of the following is *not* true about FLV files?

   A. They contain video with all the compression selections already applied.

   B. They can be imported into other movies without a significant delay.

   C. They are not compatible with Macintosh OS 9.

   D. When imported, they are treated the same as other imported video files.

   Answer: C – FLV files should work fine on computers running Macintosh OS 9.

3. Which of the following methods can be used to determine if a microphone or a camera is installed on the user's machine?

   A. `System.richMedia()`

   B. `System.accessories()`

   C. `System.capabilities()`

   D. `System.peripherals()`

   Answer: C – Only `System.capabilities()` will tell you if the user has a microphone or a digital camera installed. The other methods don't exist.

4. Which of the following video file formats *cannot* be imported into Flash?

    A. `.avi`

    B. `.mpg`

    C. `.mov`

    D. DIVX

    Answer: D.

5. What is the name of Flash MX 2004's built-in video compression codec?

    A. Sorenson Spark

    B. Sorenson Video Wizard

    C. Sorenson Studio Pro

    D. Sorenson Squeeze

    Answer: A.

Chapter 14

Sample Questions

1. The class that is inheriting another class is known as the:

    A. Child class

    B. Superclass

    C. Subclass

    D. Base class

    Answer: C – The class that is being inherited *from* is called the base class or superclass.

2. For methods within objects, what does the keyword `this` specifically refer to?

    A. The object itself

    B. The method

    C. The movie clip containing the object

    D. The root Timeline

    Answer: A.

3. Which of the following lines of code will create a new object named `myObj`?

    A. `myObj = Object();`

    B. `myObj = new Object();`

    C. `new Object.myObj();`

    D. `new Object(myObj);`

    Answer: B.

4. Which of the following methods is best for removing an object named `myObj` from memory?

   A. `myObj = 0;`

   B. `remove myObj;`

   C. `delete myObj;`

   D. `myObj = null Object()`

   Answer: C – Although setting `myObj` to `null` will remove any references to the object, the memory allocated to `myObj` will not be freed, thus creating a memory leak.

5. Interfaces can contain what elements?

   A. Only declarations of methods

   B. Declarations and implementations of methods

   C. Only declarations of methods and variables

   D. Declarations and implementations variables

   Answer: A.

Chapter 15

Sample Questions

1. Which of the following lines of code will create an object instance of a class named `Organism`?

   A. `Organism = new Class();`

   B. `Organism = new Function();`

   C. `Organism = new Organism();`

   D. `Create new Class(Organism);`

   Answer: C – When creating a new instance, it is necessary to cite the object from which the instance is being created.

2. Which statement best describes what the `#initclip num` and `#endinitclip` commands indicate?

   A. A block of component initialization actions

   B. A list of methods associated with an object

   C. A block of classes from which to inherit properties and methods

   D. A list of initial property values

   Answer: A – The ActionScript between these tags will be initialized or made available immediately before the frame upon which the code sits.

3. What keyword is used to attach methods and properties to a class?

   A. assign

   B. prototype

   C. inherit

   D. Declare

   Answer: B – The prototype keyword helps eliminate the need for duplicate methods.

4. Which of the following is the best definition of a method?

   A. Methods are functions that are associated with a class.

   B. Methods are properties that are associated with a class.

   C. Methods are functions that are *not* associated with a class.

   D. Methods are properties that are *not* associated with a class

   Answer: A.

5. What keyword is used to call the constructor method of a class?

   A. this

   B. object

   C. new

   D. function

   Answer: C – The new keyword is used to call a class's constructor function.

Chapter 16

Sample Questions

1. What is the key difference between indexed arrays and associative arrays?

   A. Associative arrays can have values of any type; indexed arrays contain only numbers.

   B. Indexed arrays contain only one type of data; associative arrays can have multiple types of data.

   C. Associative arrays contain value pairs; indexed arrays contain single values.

   D. Indexed arrays contain values indexed by integers; associative arrays contain values indexed by strings.

   Answer: D – Indexed arrays contain values indexed by integers; associative arrays contain values indexed by strings.

2. In which of the following situations would it be best to use the Coordinated Universal Time (UTC) method when creating a Date object?

    A. When calculating elapsed time on the user's machine

    B. When communicating with a server in an unknown geographical area

    C. When accuracy to the millisecond is needed

    D. When converting dates to strings

    Answer: B – Using the Universal Coordinated Time (UTC) method gives you one common time reference, thus removing any uncertainty between applications in different time zones.

3. Which of the following is *not* true about the Capabilities object?

    A. It is a property of the System class.

    B. It is intended primarily for the development of content intended for persons with disabilities.

    C. It provides access to information about the user's machine.

    D. It doesn't have to be instantiated to be used.

    Answer: B – Although the Capabilities object does have a property related to those with disabilities (hasAccessibility), the object itself can be used for many other purposes, including determining the user's OS, device type, screen resolution, and media support.

4. What is the primary purpose of the Stage class?

    A. To size the Flash movie

    B. To layer objects on the Stage

    C. To position objects on the Stage

    D. To load objects on the Stage

    Answer: A – The Stage object provides very useful methods for controlling the size and alignment of the Flash movie in the Web browser.

5. What is the default maximum file size for locally persistent, shared objects?

    A. 50KB

    B. 100KB

    C. 1Mb

    D. Unlimited

    Answer: B.

Chapter 17

Sample Questions

1. Which of the following statements is true about ActionScript 2.0 in regard to the enforcement of private scope and public scope?

   A. It is weakly typed.

   B. You cannot manually set the scope of methods as either private or public.

   C. Methods of public scope are only accessible outside the object.

   D. There is strict enforcement of the private and public scope with ActionScript 2.0.

   Answer: D – ActionScript 2.0, being strongly typed, provides a means to set the scope of methods explicitly to either public or private.

2. Which of the following is *not* a good idea when working with methods?

   A. Try to minimize the number of tasks that an individual method provides.

   B. Use methods as an interface for use by other objects.

   C. Only write one method per object.

   D. Ensure your method names are descriptive.

   Answer: C – Your class can contain as many methods as necessary to handle all the tasks that will be asked of it. Each method should have a specific task and be as concise as possible.

3. Which of these statements best describes a method?

   A. A method is a function that is associated with a class.

   B. Methods are attributes of a class.

   C. A method is a variable assigned to a class instance.

   D. A method is a series of events contained within a function.

   Answer: B – A property is a variable that has been attached to an object instance and given a value.

4. How many parameters does a "get" method take/pass?

   A. 1

   B. 2

   C. Unlimited

   D. None

   Answer: D – A "get" method is a method with no parameters.

Chapter 18

Sample Questions

1. Which of the following is the key advantage of Flash's being a true client-side application?

   A. It uses a stateless protocol.

   B. It supports the use of ASP and JSP.

   C. It provides rich support of server-side session variables.

   D. It can maintain its state without help from the server.

   Answer: D – Since Flash is a true client-side application, it can function completely independently of the server. It can even maintain its state if the user is disconnected from the Internet.

2. When should you generally use the POST method instead of the GET method?

   A. When the query string contains periods (.)

   B. When the query string contains spaces ( )

   C. When the query string is particularly long

   D. When the query string has only one variable

   Answer: C – Since some servers have limitations on query string length, it's better to use the POST method for longer queries.

3. The data pulled by a loadVariables() function is stored where?

   A. The targeted array

   B. The targeted movie clip

   C. The main Timeline

   D. Any of the above

   Answer: B – Both the LoadVariables() function and the MovieClip.loadVariables method will return the data to the targeted movie clip.

4. Which of the following is the key advantage of using LoadVars instead of loadVariables?

   A. Data can be loaded into any object, other than the one making the LoadVars call.

   B. LoadVars can handle more variables.

   C. LoadVars is supported by Flash Players 4, through 7.

   D. LoadVars loads variables faster than loadVariables.

   Answer: A – The key advantage of using LoadVars is that any object can be targeted, not just the movie clip calling the method.

5. URL encoding requires that all nonalphanumeric characters are replaced with which character?

   A. &

   B. $

   C. %

   D. #

   Answer: C – URL encoding requires that all nonalphanumeric characters are replaced with a percent sign (%) followed by two ACSII-encoded hex digits.

Chapter 19

Sample Questions

1. Which of the following is *not* true about Document Type Definitions (DTDs)?

   A. They give you a means of testing your XML for valid output.

   B. They must be referenced when instantiating an XML object.

   C. They make your XML data sources more understandable.

   D. They let you create new markup languages.

   Answer: B – Flash does not require that you define or reference a DTD when instantiating an XML object. Although DTDs are not directly supported by Flash, their use will benefit your and other developers' work with your XML documents.

2. What does the `childNodes` property contain?

   A. The number of child nodes for the current node.

   B. The number of child nodes in the current document.

   C. An array of all the child nodes for the current node.

   D. A `true` or `false` value indicating whether the current node has child nodes.

   Answer: C – The `childNodes` property contains an array of all the child nodes contained within the current node.

3. What is the primary difference between the XML.sendAndLoad method and the XML.load method?

    A. The XML.sendAndLoad method has additional properties for checking load status.

    B. XML.load loads documents slightly faster because there is no error checking on the client side.

    C. XML.sendAndLoad allows you to send specific XML data to the server.

    D. An entire XML document can be sent to the server using XML.sendAndLoad.

    Answer: D – The XML.sendAndLoad method can send only entire XML documents, not their individual elements.

4. Which of the following is *not* true about the XML.ignoreWhite property?

    A. If the ignoreWhite property is true, all spaces in the XML document will be ignored.

    B. Carriage returns are treated as data if the ignoreWhite property is set to false.

    C. With the ignoreWhite property set to true, you can reduce the number of nodes that need to be created during parsing.

    D. The default value for the ignoreWhite property is true.

    Answer: D – The default setting for the ignoreWhite property is false. It's generally best to set the value to true unless you want spaces to be treated as data.

5. How does an XMLSocket server know when a received message is complete?

    A. The XMLSocket.onXMLLoad method is called by the client.

    B. The XMLSocket.onLoad method is called by the client.

    C. A zero byte is received.

    D. The XMLSocket server is unable to determine when a received message is complete.

    Answer: C – All messages sent either to or from the XMLSocket server must terminate with a zero byte to indicate the end of the message. The XMLSocket.onLoad method is called when an XML message has been downloaded *from* the server.

Chapter 20

Sample Questions

1. Which of the following steps is *not* required in order to test or deploy Flash Remoting?

   A. Install and configure a supported web server application environment.

   B. Download and install the server-side remoting components.

   C. Download and install the Flash MX 2004 Remoting components.

   D. Implement a Macromedia UI component

   Answer: D – Although there's a lot of benefit to using Macromedia's UIComponent class, these components are not necessary for remoting in Flash.

2. Which of the following external ActionScript files must you #include in your movie in order to use Flash Remoting?

   A. URLRemote.as

   B. Gateway.as

   C. NetServices.as

   D. GetRemote.as

   Answer: C – You need to #include the NetServices.as file (ideally in the first frame of your movie) in order to use Flash Remoting.

3. Flash Remoting *cannot* do which of the following?

   A. Access data directly from a remotely hosted web service

   B. Integrate seamlessly with existing Macromedia UI components

   C. Translate SOAP XML data into native Flash objects

   D. Marshal native Java objects into Flash objects

   Answer: A – Data cannot be directly accessed from a web service on another domain. Instead, the data must be accessed through a remoting gateway established on your local server.

4. Which Flash Remoting class binds RecordSet objects to Flash components?

   A. NetServices class

   B. DataGlue class

   C. NetConnection class

   D. DataBinding class

   Answer: B – The DataGlue class binds RecordSet objects to Flash components that have labels with associated data such as the ListBox or ComboBox.

5. Which panel monitors and displays any communications that pass through the Flash Remoting interface?

A. Services Browser

B. NetConnection Debugger

C. Gateway Connection

D. Marshaling Gateway

Answer: B – The NetConnection Debugger shows all calls and responses that pass through the Flash Remoting Interface, including those from; the Flash Player, Flash Remoting MX, Flash Communication Server and the Application server.

Chapter 21

Sample Questions

1. The World Wide Web Consortium (W3C) has begun describing and documenting a framework, which allows self-contained applications to communicate more consistently with one another. What is this capability otherwise known as?

A. Compatibility

B. Interoperability

C. Interconnectivity

D. Intercommunicabilty

Answer: B – *Interoperability* is the capability that allows self-contained applications to communicate more consistently with one another.

2. Simple Object Access Protocol (SOAP) is based on what protocol?

A. HTML

B. TEXT

C. XML

D. ColdFusion

Answer: C. – Simple Object Access Protocol (SOAP) is based on the XML protocol.

3. The Web Service classes of Flash MX Professional 2004 are located in which package?

A. `flash.webSevices`

B. `mx.services`

    C. `macromedia.eng.remoteServices\`

    D. HTML

    Answer: B – The WebServices classes of Flash MX Professional 2004 are located in the `mx.services` package.

4. How are WSDL files accessed?

    A. XML

    B. URL

    C. Flash Remoting

    D. `sockets`

    Answer: B – WSDL files are accessed via an ordinary URL.

5. Lazy decoding is a feature of the `WebServiceConnector` component. Why is it called "lazy"?

    A. It is more tolerant of "loosely typed" code and permits developers to be less strict with coding standards.

    B. It permits the `WebServiceConnector` to randomly (or "lazily") poll connections to a web service.

    C. Because you need to use a different instance of `WebServiceConnector` for each operation you want to call.

    D. It allows developers to defer the conversion of multiple records of data from XML/SOAP into ActionScript native data.

    Answer: D – Lazy decoding allows developers to defer the conversion of multiple records of data from XML/SOAP into ActionScript native data.

Chapter 22

Sample Questions

1. When Macromedia acquired the data binding components from CyberSage Software in 2003, what was their original name?

    A. FireStar

    B. Firefly

    C. FireStarter

    D. FireBug

    Answer: B – Macromedia acquired the Firefly Components from CyberSage Software in 2003, and then bundled them into the Flash MX Data Connection Kit.

2. What is data binding?

   A. The connection of SWF files

   B. The concept of component connection with data sharing and updating

   C. The linking of data to a single component instance

   D. The connection/association of dataSets

   Answer: B – Data binding relates to the concept of connecting components together and allowing them to share and update data.

3. What is represented within a `DeltaPacket`?

   A. Changes made within a dataset

   B. A list of connections to a relational database

   C. Definitions of an event, for which a Binding object listens

   D. Connections among other components and external XML data sources

   Answer: A – A `DeltaPacket` represents any changes that have been made between `dataSets`.

4. Which component acts as a data warehouse for storing data received from data sources?

   A. `List` component

   B. `DataSet` component

   C. `DataHolder` component

   D. `RDBMSResolver` component

   Answer: C – The `DataHolder` component acts as a warehouse for storing data received from data sources.

5. The `RDBMSResolver` component is used in association with which other data component?

   A. `DataSet` component

   B. `XUpdater` component

   C. `DataHolder` component

   D. `XMLConnector` component

   Answer: A – You use resolver components in combination with the `DataSet` component (part of the data-management functionality in the Macromedia Flash data architecture).

Chapter 23

Sample Questions

1. Which of the following cannot be automatically output by the `trace` action?

   A. String values

   B. Array values

   C. Object instance values

   D. Date and Time values

   Answer: C – Object instance values cannot be effectively traced in the Output window.

2. Which of the following is *not* a result of exporting a movie for a Debugger build?

   A. A normal SWF file is created.

   B. A SWD file is created in your working directory.

   C. The Debugger window appears.

   D. You can step through each breakpoint that you have set in the movie.

   Answer: A – The SWF file that is created by the Debug Movie command is actually larger than a normal SWF file and should not be used for deployment.

3. Which of the following is *not* an effective means of developing applications that are easy to debug?

   A. Separating and encapsulating each feature of your application

   B. Avoiding the use of external AS files

   C. Creating different classes for different tasks

   D. Making sure your methods and classes have descriptive names

   Answer: B – External AS files are actually a great way to organize your ActionScript into logical elements that can be easily identified for debugging.

4. When used within a `try..catch..finally` combination, when does the finally code block execute?

   A. Only when an error has been thrown

   B. When multiple `finally` blocks have been previously defined

   C. Only when control has passed to it from the `catch` code block

   D. Always

   Answer: D – A `finally` code block will always execute, regardless of whether an error has been thrown.

5. Which property of the Error class displays an `error` string to the Output panel?

    A. `error.message`

    B. `error.output`

    C. `error.throw`

    D. `error.show`

    Answer: A – When the `message` property of the Error class is used, a string that contains an error message associated with an error can be displayed in the Output panel.

Chapter 24

Sample Questions

1. Which of the following is *not* a key benefit of usability testing?

    A. To find out how potential customers will use your application

    B. For direct marketing exposure to test candidates

    C. To identify areas where the product is difficult to use

    D. To receive valuable comments from customers on how to improve the application

    Answer: B – Usability testing is an opportunity to learn how users will use and react to your application. It should not be considered as an opportunity to increase awareness of your application or try to make a sale.

2. At which point can you start usability testing?

    A. When some sketches of the product's interface are drawn

    B. When the application goes alpha

    C. When the application goes beta

    D. When the application code is complete

    Answer: A – As soon as you have something to show the user that is representative of the intended application, you can test its usability.

3. Which of the following is *not* a guideline for conducting effective usability testing?

    A. Avoid leading questions.

    B. Provide helpful, step-by-step instructions on how each task should be completed.

C. Ask users to think aloud.

D. Take lots of notes.

Answer: B – The tasks you assign users should be general in nature so that you can get an objective impression of how they will actually use the product. By providing them with specific instructions, you only determine their ability to follow directions.

4. What is generally considered the ideal group size for usability testing?

A. 1–2

B. 3–5

C. 6–11

D. 11–20

Answer: B – Five people are ideal for a single test group. If you've determined that you have more than one target group, three or four people in each group is generally considered ideal. Smaller groups don't provide enough of a sampling, and larger groups tend to provide redundant data.

5. Which of the following is *not* a recommended choice for a test group member?

A. Student

B. Co-worker

C. Homemaker

D. Engineer

Answer: B – Avoid recruiting fellow employees, since their experience with the application and company objectives will not be typical of your target audience.

Chapter 25

Sample Questions

1. Which of the following methods provides the most controlled printing of Flash content?

A. Printing from the Flash Player contextual menu

B. The `Print` action

C. The `ExportToPrinter` action

D. The browser's File menu

Answer: B – Although methods A and C will print the current view of your Flash movie, they are far less predictable and can lead to a very unpleasant printing experience for the user.

2. Which of the following is *not* a true statement about the `print` action?

    A. It provides quality vector-based prints.

    B. It prints all frames of the target Timeline unless otherwise specified.

    C. It is CPU-intensive.

    D. It doesn't print alpha channels.

    Answer: C – Far from being CPU-intensive, the `Print` action uses a minimum of CPU time as well as network bandwidth.

3. What will be the result of the following line of ActionScript?

    ```
    print(_root.myClip, "bmax");
    ```

    A. The `myClip` and `"bmax"` movie clips will be printed.

    B. A bounding box will be created by the location of the `myClip` and `"bmax"` movie clips, and this area will be printed.

    C. The `myClip` movie clip will be printed, and each frame will be scaled to fill the maximum space on the printed page.

    D. The largest printable frame in `myClip` will be used to determine the bounding box for all frames printed.

    Answer: D – All frames with a `#p` label will be evaluated and the one with the largest bounding box will be used to determine the size for all frames printed. If no frame has a `#p` label, all of the movie clip's frames will be printed.

4. Apart from being good coding practice, what is the benefit of deleting the `PrintJob` object after it has completed its life cycle?

    A. It removes excess byte code from the Flash Player.

    B. It clears the print spooler.

    C. It allows control to be passed to the printer.

    D. It resets the print bounding box.

    Answer: C – Deleting the `PrintJob` object clears the print spooler.

5. The PrintJob.`addPage()` method works in conjunction with which other two methods?

    A. `PrintJob.start()`

    B. `PrintJob.cancelPage()`

    C. `PrintJob.clearPage()`

    D. `PrintJob.send()`

    Answer: A and D – `PrintJob.addPage()`, `PrintJob.start()`, and `PrintJob.send()` work together. The other two methods don't exist.

INDEX

real world. real training. real results.

Get more done in less time with
Macromedia Training and Certification.

Two Types of Training

Roll up your sleeves and get right to work with authorized training
from Macromedia.

1. Classroom Training

   Learn from instructors thoroughly trained and certified by
   Macromedia. Courses are fast-paced and task-oriented to get
   you up and running quickly.

2. Online Training

   Get Macromedia training when you want with affordable, interactive online
   training from Macromedia University.

Stand Out from the Pack

Show your colleagues, employer, or prospective clients that you
have what it takes to effectively develop, deploy, and maintain dynamic
applications–become a Macromedia Certified Professional.

Learn More

For more information about authorized training or to find a class near you,
visit **www.macromedia.com/go/training1**

macromedia®
**TRAINING AND
CERTIFICATION**